TEIGNMOUTH

A View of Teignmouth by Thomas Luny (1833).

TEIGNMOUTH
A Maritime History

H. J. Trump

Phillimore

First published in 1976
under the title
WESTCOUNTRY HARBOUR
Second impression, 1978

Second edition, 1986
published by
PHILLIMORE & CO. LTD.
Shopwyke Hall, Chichester, Sussex

ISBN 0 85033 559 0

Printed and bound in Great Britain by
REDWOOD BURN LTD.,
Trowbridge, Wiltshire

To the shipmasters, pilots and boatmen
who by bringing their ships safely into Teignmouth harbour
have contributed to the livelihood of a maritime community

Contents

List of Plates

(between pages 96 and 97)

Frontispiece: *A View of Teignmouth* (1833) by Thomas Luny

The author and publisher would like to thank the following for permission to reproduce photographs: Bonham's Fine Art Valuers, London, Frontispiece; Teignmouth Quay Company, plates 12, 21, 22, 23, 24, 25, 26 and 27; G. C. Walker, plates 16, 17 and 20; Devon Library Services, Westcountry Studies Library, plates 1 and 4; Mr. G. W. Newkey-Burden, plates 9, 14 and 15; Exeter Reference Library, plate 5; Mr. A. D. Johnson, plate 10; Devon Record Office, plate 1; Mr. Reg Matthews, plate 6; A. P. & M. Jacobs, plate 7; Mr. H. Bucklow, plate 8. The original source of some photographs is not known and an acknowledgement may have been unwittingly omitted.

List of Text Illustrations

The author would like to thank R. E. J. Fry, University of Exeter Department of Geography, who drew figs. 1, 2, 4 and 7 (fig. 1 from Clifford and Courtenay estate maps, Devon Recrd Office; fig. 4 based on the Ordnance Survey Map with the sanction of the Controller of Her Majesty's Stationery Office, Crown Copyright reserved; figs. 2 and 7 copied from maps and plans in the custody of Teignmouth Harbour Commission); University of Exeter Library photographic service for permission to reproduce fig. 5; and the Devon Record Office for permission to reproduce figs. 3 and 6.

Foreword

Westcountry Harbour was published in 1976 and reprinted in 1978. This edition has been revised, rewritten in the middle section and brought up to date. Some topics, such as the Lifeboat Service, have been dealt with more fully and correspondence and conversations with readers of the first edition have made it possible to give more information about particular ships and particular families. Many of the illustrations are new.

The Notes in this edition have been abridged but it is hoped they will be of value to the general reader who may wish to follow up an interest as well as to the student who needs to pursue a documentary reference.

Acknowledgements

Any author who attempts to write the story of a Devon harbour must acknowledge a debt to two books which have become classics in their respective fields of local and maritime history: W. G. Hoskins' *Devon* and Basil Greenhill's *The Merchant Schooners*. I am also greatly indebted to my friends Jean and John Bromley who have given me invaluable guidance in writing the first edition of *Westcountry Harbour* and in revising this one.

The names of those who generously supplied information, often by detailed correspondence, which has been directly incorporated in the text are given in the Notes. Many others with Teignmouth associations readily answered my questions or told me where answers might be found; that I have not always found them is my fault, not theirs. In particular I am grateful to members of seagoing families and families involved in work around the Teign estuary who took the trouble to rack their memories and look up records, memoranda and photographs: Mrs. Nancy Brewer and Miss Jessie Drew, Mrs. Ellen Brook, Mr. J. A. Bulley, Mr. J. Dyer, Mr. J. C. C. Ellyatt, Mrs. Mary Freeman, Miss Mabel Heath, Mr. A. G. Lockyer, Mr. K. G. Sclater, Mr. F. Tibbs, Mr. G. Vallance and Mr. L. S. Waller. I have made substantial use of Mr. M. I. Osborn's scrap book of regional maritime history and Mr. Gordon Walker's valuable collection of historic and recent photographs of Teignmouth ships. Many local people have told me about their experiences in shipbuilding, not only Mr. Michael Morgan Giles who struggled to keep alive a fine tradition from the management side, but also those who played their part as craftsmen: Mr. G. K. Collyer, Mr. G. Cummins, Mr. W. Harvey, Mr. W. Lambert, Mr. W. D. Long and Mr. F. J. Westlake. Most Teignmouth seamen of the old school have, as a recent researcher in the new discipline of oral history put it, 'signed articles with the great Shipping Master in the sky'; I wish to record my appreciation of the late Sid Briggs and Fred Drew. Mr. Alf Broom and Mr. Sid Hook, with a lifetime of experience as pilots behind them, have enlightened me on matters of which I am ignorant. For information on the local fishing industry and many reminiscences I am indebted to. Mr. Ernie Chapman.

Amateur and professional historians (if historians can be so categorised) have generously shared with me the results of their research in aspects of family and maritime history. I am grateful in particular to members of the Hore, Mansfield, Mardon, Perryman and Warren families at home and overseas as well as to Mrs. Ann Primrose and Mrs. Beryl Varilone who have pursued their researches with great patience and determination. Correspondence and conversations with Michael Bouquet, Harold Bucklow, Robin Craig, Tony Ellis, Grahame Farr, David MacGregor, Tony Pawlyn and Christopher Schmitz have kept me, I hope, on the right track in fields of study where they have made significant contributions. My attempts to unravel the links between Teignmouth and Newfoundland have been greatly helped by the researches of members of the Memorial University of Newfoundland, St John's; Professor J. D. A. Widdowson has been especially helpful and encouraging.

Those whose job it is to look after archives and libraries have given me far more of their time and expertise than I am entitled to expect, especially the staff of Devon Record Office, the Exeter Westcountry Studies Library, the Library of the University of Exeter and the National Maritime Museum. I am indebted also to the librarians and curators of private libraries and museums, particularly Mrs. Sheila Stirling, librarian of the Devon and Exeter Institution, Mr. H. L. Douch, curator of the Royal Institution of Cornwall, Mr. David Goddard, director of the Exeter Maritime Museum, and Mr. Philip Burton and Mrs. Mollie Weare, respectively chairman and secretary of the Teignmouth Museum Society.

This book could not have been written without the co-operation of the Customs Officers attached to the port of Teignmouth and others concerned with the management and trade of the harbour: Mr. W. J. B. Watts and Mr. J. I. Mosley, chairman and clerk respectively of the Harbour Commission; Mr. C. A. Boyne and Mr. D. C. Copeland, partners in Pike Ward Ltd.; Mr. R. G. W. Matthews, Harbour Master, and especially Mr. Jeff Boyne and his colleagues in the Teignmouth Quay Company. The publication of this revised edition of *Westcountry Harbour* appropriately coincides with the centenary of the Teignmouth Quay Company whose fortunes have always been closely bound up with those of the harbour.

My wife has given me encouragement and advice and the Trustees of the Leverhulme Foundation gave practical help in the early stages by the award of an Emeritus Fellowship.

H. J. TRUMP
Exeter

January 1985

PUBLISHER'S NOTE

The Publisher regrets to announce the sudden death of Mr. Trump during the course of production of this new edition. In consequence of this sad event we are most grateful to The Teignmouth Quay Company; Devon Library Services; G. C. Walker; and R. E. J. Fry for their help with the illustrations, and to Mr. J. Boyne of The Teignmouth Quay Company for supplying information on the 1984-86 period in Chapter 9, indicated in the text by asterisks.

Introduction: The Teign Estuary

The Teign estuary has always offered a refuge to small ships. The entrance was difficult and sometimes dangerous for vessels without power because of a shifting bar at the river's mouth but, once inside the harbour, they could anchor safely in deep water or run themselves aground on sandy beaches for survey and repair; there was space for quays and shipyards on both sides of the estuary. Shallow-draught vessels could pass up river for six miles or so with a choice of convenient landing and loading places such as Coombe Cellars and Floor Point. The Teign was never as commercially active as the Exe or the Tamar but it was a natural home for a maritime community.

Natural advantages were supplemented by man-made improvements. The Courtenays, lords of the manor in East Teignmouth, developed the building potential of their lands and the Cliffords, lords of the manor in West Teignmouth, stimulated the exploitation of mineral resources; lesser landowners, notably the Templers, were pioneers of techniques which increased production and improved transport. These landed families were occasionally obstructive, but on the whole used their influence to their own and Teignmouth's advantage and the building of canals, trackways and steam railways, which were promoted largely by individual landowners, greatly contributed to the prosperity of the harbour. The initiative of proprietors was matched by that of 'merchants': as traders, speculators, agents and masters and part-owners of ships, 'merchants' played a major role in commercial development.

For centuries there was a convenient deep-water anchorage off Shaldon and Ringmore; this may be one reason why merchants lived in the parish of St Nicholas, which included both these villages, or further up the valley at Combeinteignhead and Stokeinteignhead. Other merchants lived in Wolborough or Newton Abbot, Highweek or Newton Bushel, parishes and settlements near the head of navigation for the main channel of the Teign and within easy reach of Dartmouth and the small ports of Torbay. On the Teignmouth side of the river most merchants and seafarers lived in West Teignmouth which, until the 19th century, was separated from East Teignmouth by the Tame brook. Bishopsteignton remained a traditional Devon village until very recently, but Kingsteignton expanded steadily because it was near high-quality clay deposits and close to the limit of navigation for the secondary channel of the Teign, the Hackney Channel, which later became the Hackney Canal. Partnerships in trading and ship-owning linked families together from all these communities and occasionally others in places slightly further away such as Abbotskerswell and Kenton. The extent of the Port of Teignmouth, like the spelling of the name, did not become fixed until around 1850. One material link between partners on either side of the river was the bridge, opened in 1827 and rebuilt after its collapse in 1838. Contemporary observers described sections on the Shaldon side which opened 'into two parts for the passage of vessels of from three hundred tons burthen';[1] when the bridge was rebuilt the opening span was transferred to the Teignmouth side.

Improved communications, of which the Shaldon Bridge was one example, brought tourists to Devonshire who commented favourably on the scenery of the Teignmouth neighbourhood. One as early as the 1790s wrote:

> ... the view up river is extremely beautiful, the ground gradually rising on each side into verdant hills, ornamented with wood and cheerful with cultivation. The cliffs over-hanging the sea have a singular, and, I think, very picturesque appearance.

A correspondent in *The Gentleman's Magazine* declared:

> The river Teign at high water ... is converted into a most noble expanse of water ... At this spot the bustle and importance of commerce attract the attention. Here stands the custom house, and here the axe of the shipwright and the mallet of the caulker are seen ... the view up the river is the most bewitching; it is one of those which the eye dwells on with delight and without wearisomeness ... the scenery on either side of its shores is of the most rural and pleasing kind, rich in wood, and interrupted with gentlemen's seats, villages and hamlets.[3]

These romantic perspectives brought fashionable visitors and, much later, holidaymakers and day trippers who contributed indirectly to the trade of the port but also created a tourist interest which from time to time appeared in conflict with a harbour interest.

Changes in the scale of the economy and in the location of industry meant that the shortcomings of the harbour threatened a loss of trade which caused some merchants to transfer their business to larger ports, especially Liverpool. Others, staying in Teignmouth, sought to develop local resources by making the port independent of Exeter and by taking advantage of a link with the new main line railway. These efforts met with some success in the 1850s and 1860s and again around 1900 when quay extensions were planned and executed. But the defects of the harbour for large ships remained and the First World War intensified local problems; by 1931 the port seemed on the brink of extinction. Commercial use survived because the clay industry has adapted itself to growing demand and the Quay Company has successfully met the changing needs of maritime traders. This recent enterprise is a quite different story from the varied small-scale adventure, the successes and disappointments, the initiatives and crises, all affecting a cross-section of local people, which are recounted in the chapters which follow.

Chapter One

An Outline to 1690

The earliest maps of the county of Devon, published on the continent between 1534 and 1575, do not show Teignmouth at all. Christopher Saxton's map of 1579 correctly indicates the position of 'Tyngmuth' as well as villages on or near the estuary: Newton Bushel, 'Bishopstaynton', 'Kingstaynton', 'Combe in Tine' and Stoke; the size of print implies that all these places were equally important and of much less significance than such places as Dartmouth or Lyme.[1]

This apparently inferior status of Teignmouth towards the end of the 16th century contrasts with evidence for its maritime importance in the Middle Ages. M. M. Oppenheim, in his *Maritime History of Devon*, gives examples of Teignmouth's contribution to naval expeditions which suggest that Teignmouth was one of the chief ports, after the Cinque Ports, on which the monarchs depended for their military policy against Scotland and France and for the defence of the realm. The account which follows is based on Oppenheim's study. Writs for the arrest of ships to provide transport for the Scottish Wars at the end of the 13th century and early in the 14th show that only Dartmouth, of all the Devon ports, consistently ranked above Teignmouth, although sometimes Teignmouth's contribution was less than that from Plymouth and Exeter with Exmouth. In the war with France, which immediately followed the truce with Scotland, Plymouth, Exeter and Teignmouth sent two ships each and Dartmouth four. In 1326, under threat of invasion, all ships over 50 tons were called up for service and the number of ships and men required under the writs suggests an order of importance at this time:

Dartmouth	10 ships	272 men
Teignmouth	8 ships	163 men
Exmouth	6 ships	144 men
Plymouth and Sutton	5 ships	152 men
Sidmouth	3 ships	75 men

The relative importance of Devon ports is also indicated by a general arrest of ships some time in the reign of Edward II (the exact date is uncertain) by which ships were prevented from sailing wherever they happened to be: 11 ships were stopped at Dartmouth, nine at Plymouth, seven at Teignmouth, two at Exmouth and one at Sidmouth. Teignmouth, like Plymouth a year earlier, was singled out for attack by a French invasion force in 1340; Dartmouth, which was a larger port than either, was known to be well defended. The demands on Devon ports diminished in the later 14th century and the early 15th, at first because of bad organisation and then because Henry V tried to build up a royal navy to reduce the state's dependence on merchant shipping. When demands were again made on Devon ports in 1439 Teignmouth's contribution was two ships, one of more than 100 tons, compared with three from Exeter, 10 from Plymouth and 20 from Dartmouth.[2]

1

Early Chancery proceedings show that Teignmouth seamen, like other West-countrymen, took full advantage of the opportunities for plunder offered by the wars with France and her allies and chose not to observe the short periods of truce. In 1432, for example, complaint was made to the Chancellor that a 'balinger' (a small sloop) of Teignmouth had seized a Breton vessel in time of peace and sold both ship and cargo. In the same year the representative of a Spanish merchant told what happened when he tried to press his legal claim for restitution: on his way to 'the baron de Carrewe's house', accompanied by the marshal of the Duke of Exeter,

> fifteen or sixteen people of Teignmouth had attacked them and thrown them from their horses and taken the merchant into a wood and intended to kill him by cutting off his head, and then came one and demanded that he should give an acquittance of his claim to save his life ... and in terror of his life he answered that he would do all they wished.[3]

By the Tudor period Teignmouth's relative importance appears to have diminished. In official returns of the number of ships of 100 tons and upwards for the years from 1560 to 1577 Teignmouth does not appear at all: of the 15 Devon ships in the 1577 return, for example, six belonged to Plymouth, four to Dartmouth, four to Exmouth and one to Barnstaple. Teignmouth does, however, figure in a list drawn up by Thomas Colshill for customs purposes in 1572 and which records vessels of 100 tons or less. For Devon it gives a total of 130:

	Number of Ships	Largest Ship (in tons)
Ilfracombe	3	30
Barnstaple	12	80
Bideford	6	80
Northam	3	35
Plymouth	26	100
Salcombe	5	40
Dartmouth	32	80
Kingswear	3	30
Torbay	5	45
Teignmouth	5	40
'Exwater'	1	20
Powderham	4	25
Kenton	6	30
Topsham	14	50
Exmouth	5	50

This decline in the relative importance of the port of Teignmouth in the 16th century may have been caused by the deterioration of the harbour as a result of tin mining on Dartmoor. A Stannary Court decree of 1532 ordained that all rubbish should be deposited in 'old Hatches, Tippits, mining Places or other convenient Places'[4] away from the main streams and an Act passed in the same year described the harm which had been done by the practice now prohibited:

> These portes for some time past the principall and most comodious havens and portes within the realm, shipes resorting from all places of the world as well in perrill and stormes as otherwise ... which said portes and havens ben at this tyme ... utterlye descried and distroied by mean of sertain Tynne works ... used (by) sertain personnes within the said counties (Devon and Cornwall), which personnes more regarding their own private luck than the common wealthe and suertie of this realm have by working ... so filled and choked the same that when before this tyme

a shippe of portage of 800 might easily have entered at low water ... now a shippe of a hundred can skantly entre at halfe fludde.[5]

It is unlikely that ships of 800 tons were able to enter Teignmouth, certainly not at low water, but the harbour may have been silted up by debris thrown into the river by tin miners in the same way as the larger estuaries in Devon and Cornwall about which the government was largely concerned. Queen Elizabeth caused further enquiries to be made about Westcountry ports, particularly Bristol, and the matter was debated in Parliament in 1601. On this occasion Sir Walter Raleigh spoke of the need to raise money for the improvement of south coast harbours and referred particularly to Teignmouth, of which he presumably had direct knowledge:

There be divers Havens which have been Famous, and are now gone to Decay, as Tynmouth ...[6]

All Westcountry ports suffered in the first half of the 17th century from 'Dunkirkers' which operated as privateers from Flemish harbours, and often included renegade Englishmen in their crews, as well as occasionally from Algerian and Sallee corsairs who found their way to the English Channel.[7] Operations of war added to the losses caused by piracy and, although Teignmouth did not play a key role in the Civil War, her inhabitants are unlikely to have escaped the exactions from both Royalists and Parliamentarians which were imposed throughout Devon. It is possible that for Teignmouth the most flourishing trade in the 17th century was smuggling, and William Culliford's Report of 1682-3 gives an insight into the evasion of the law which was encouraged by political disturbances and in which customs officers were themselves sometimes involved. Culliford wrote in April 1683:

I took the information of Wm Tapley and Ralph Monson in relation to Tho Drayton the Officer at Tingmouth who, when a Tobacco Shipp put into that harbour with the intent and on purpose to Smuggle good part of her Loading, tho he was the only Officer in the place, refused to Board the said Shipp ... whereon ... I suspended him and offer ... that he may be dismissed being an idle fellow ... keeping a Shoemakers shop and as I have been informed from some persons of Quality ... has consented to the running great quantities of Goods for several years past.[8]

Culliford appears to have been exceptionally conscientious in his office as 'Register of the Seizures' and was rewarded in 1684 with appointment as a commissioner of the Irish revenue so perhaps his strictures were exaggerated. Thomas Drayton maintained that he watched the ship concerned, the *Prudent Mary* which had called in from Virginia, diligently for a week.[9] Drayton also stated that no direct foreign imports were landed at Teignmouth although a variety of goods came coastwise, 'as Culm, Coal, Pitch, Tar, Deals etc.' These materials for estuary limeburners and shipbuilders, together with food for local consumption and exports from the saltpans which may have been in use until 1692, probably constituted the bulk of Teignmouth's small trade at this time. The one overseas activity of importance was that concerned with the Newfoundland fishery. Culliford himself remarked that Teignmouth was:

a place where many Shipps fit out every year for Newfoundland, Twelve at the least ...[10]

During the 17th century Teignmouth's economic welfare, like that of many other small Westcountry ports, came to depend on the cod fishery of Newfoundland, and

Westcountry merchants used political pressure to maintain their rights. The Western Charter of 1634 marked the success of their efforts: fishing regulations were to be enforced by the mayors of specified western ports and by fishing 'Admirals' on the spot; the master of the first fishing ship to arrive in a Newfoundland harbour at the beginning of the season in May was appointed admiral, had first choice of drying places ashore and was given absolute authority over British and foreign fishermen and any settlers who had the temerity to establish an agricultural holding. Captains like members of the Holdsworth family of Dartmouth and Christopher Martin of Cockington, who was 'Admiral' or 'Vice Admiral' for close on 20 years, exercised their authority with rough justice and kept the peace in a sometimes disorderly community. The role of 'Admiral' was eventually taken over by civil magistrates but the custom of arbitrary justice continued and much later the Chief Justice, Thomas Tremlett, himself a Westcountryman, answered accusations of unconstitutional behaviour in a letter addresssed to the Governor which has all the arrogant self-confidence of the Devon 'Admirals':

> To the first charge your Excellency I answer that it is a lie, to the second I say that it is a damned lie, and to the third charge that it is a damned infernal lie and, your Excellency, I have no more to say.[11]

At one stage Westcountry captains promised to train one 'green' man in five as a seaman and to purchase all their supplies, except salt, in a British port. Charles II, although he did not wish to take too harsh a line with French fishermen, protected Westcountry fishing interests against other competition. Restrictions were placed on 'byeboatkeepers', who kept small boats in Newfoundland and travelled out each season, and on settlers, who were forbidden to establish themselves within six miles of the coast. An Order in Council of 1671 probably marked the peak of Westcountry privilege. The authority of 'Admirals' and mayors was re-affirmed and extended and Commanders-in-Chief of the Newfoundland station, who were given supervisory powers, were ordered to encourage the settlers to emigrate so that they would not compete in the fishery. But Sir John Berry, the first commodore with the new powers and himself a Devon man who had risen from the lower deck, pointed out that the fishing crews needed help from the settlers when they arrived at the beginning of each season. Partly because of his advice, the threatened eviction never took place. The government continued to favour Westcountry interests, mainly because the Newfoundland fishery was deemed a nursery for the navy, but the Newfoundland Act of 1699 finally recognised the fishing rights of both byeboatkeepers and settlers. Ships based on English ports continued to fish inshore but increasingly turned their attention to the Banks, up to some 300 miles off the Newfoundland coast.

It seems likely that Teignmouth vessels sailing to Newfoundland were mostly small fishing ships of up to 100 tons or so with a crew of up to 50 men, bringing some of their catch home and bartering the supplies to 'sack' ships. The role of the two types of vessel is described by a contemporary writer who had spent some time in Newfoundland. The fishing ships:

> doe not onely catch as many fish as will lade their shippes but also as many as will lade vessels of greater burthens that in the summer come hither from England and other parts to buy up the same and purposely to transport it for Spain, Italy and other countries.[12]

The distinction between fishing ships and 'sack', or cargo, ships was not clear-cut because occasionally fishing ships took their catch direct to the Mediterranean and sometimes brought back to their home port cod oil and passengers as well as fish. Arrival and sailing lists suggest that towards the end of the 17th century, for Teignmouth, the proportion of fishing ships to 'sack' ships may have been of the order of six to one, but the evidence is incomplete.[13] In the next century the number of fishing vessels declined, but Teignmouth won a share of the important general trade with Newfoundland, a colony which came to be 'accompted the India to the West of England'.

In 1690 Teignmouth suffered a major disaster when, for the last time, foreign troops landed on English soil. After Admiral Tourville's victory over the combined English and Dutch fleets off Beachy Head on 11 July 1690, the French fleet anchored in Torbay and fine weather made possible a raid by some of the galley fleet which had been built up by Louis XIV.[14] Bishop Burnet, in his *History of his own Time*, describes the attack:

> ...they made a descent on a miserable village, called Tinmuth, that happened to belong to a papist (a reference presumably to the Clifford family); they burnt it, and a few fisher-boats that belonged to it; but the inhabitants got away; and, as a body of militia was marching thither, the French made great haste back to their ships: the French published this in their gazettes with much pomp, as if it had been a great trading town ...[15]

What happened is described in more detail, and with less bias, in a petition addressed by the inhabitants of East and West Teignmouth and St Nicholas to the Lord Lieutenant and the Justices of the Peace of the county:

> ... on the 26th day of this instant July 1690 by Foure of the clocke in the morning, your poor petitioners were invaded (by the French) to the number of 1,000 or thereabouts, who in the space of three hours tyme, burnt down to the ground the dwelling houses of 240 persons of our parish and upwards, plundered and carried away all our goods, defaced our churches, burnt ten of our ships in our harbour, besides fishing boats, netts and other fishing raft, to the utter ruin of your poor petitioners and their families, many of whom must starve for want and perish unless they are speedily relieved by your honours' charitable assistance in this their great extremity.[16]

The Justices examined on oath 'creditable persons' including William Rendle and Roger Rendle, carpenters, Richard Elliot and John Heston, masons, and Samuel Smith, shipwright, and then confirmed that:

> by the late horrid invasion there were within the space of 12 houres burnt downe and consumed 116 dwelling houses ... and also 172 dwelling houses were rifled and plundered and two parish churches much ruined, plundred and defaced, besides the burning of ten saile of shipps with the furniture thereof, and the goods and merchandise therein ...[17]

This account makes it clear that Teignmouth, if not 'a great trading town', was much more than 'a miserable village'.

As a result of the Justices' statement a Church Brief was issued by the Crown which authorised the collection of £11,000; vicars and curates were asked 'deliberately and affectionately' to publish the Brief and urge their congregations to contribute 'freely and chearfully'. The Brief itself added dramatic details to arouse the charitable and Protestant feelings of the congregations: the French, it was said, in a most Unchristian Manner tore the Bibles and Common Prayer Books in pieces scattering the leaves thereof about the Streets, broke down the Pulpits, overthrew the Communion Tables, together with many other Marks of a Barbarous and Enraged Cruelty.[18]

The congregation of Holy Trinity, Exeter, contributed £4 18s 6½d and that of Woodbury 15s 10d; outside Devon, contributions included 10s 10d from the parish of High Melton, Yorkshire and 2s 10d from Springthorpe, Lincolnshire.[19] Teignmouth clearly received substantial outside assistance and the rebuilding of the town, financed from these collections, made possible the further development of the port. Memories of the disaster remained, and when danger again threatened in 1744 the inhabitants built a battery on the Den at their own expense. Against a more serious threat, some 50 years later, from the armies of the French Republic, the battery was strengthened, fitted with six cannon and defended by a company of 65 volunteers who were dressed in a smart uniform of blue jackets and red trousers and, more to the point, trained 'in the use of great guns'.[20]

Chapter Two

Pattern of Trade in the 18th Century: 1690-1793

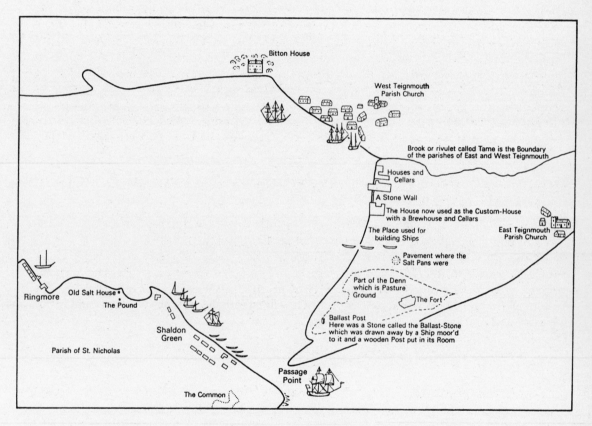

Fig. 1   An Impression of Teignmouth Harbour in the 18th century.

The French raid of 1690, destructive as it was, appears to have stimulated one new trade peculiar to Teignmouth. A witness before the Parliamentary Select Committee on the Teignmouth Harbour Bill in 1853 spoke of a custom which he implied was of very long standing and which may have originated with the extensive rebuilding programme some 150 years before. Red rock building stone, said John Hughes, was

> obtained about two or three miles outside the bar ... the men go there and take the stone from the rocks and bring it in for building purposes ... It comes very rough and they hammer it square ... I believe this local stone is imported by a class of poor men who make it their regular business.[1]

Since the trade which John Hughes described was carried on in open boats which paid no harbour dues, it was not recorded. Other forms of coastal trade are shown in the records of the port of Exeter and, after 1853, in those of the Teignmouth Harbour Commission.

Coastal trade was active throughout the 18th century because, despite interference by tolls and interruption by bad weather, transport of most goods by sea was much easier and cheaper than by road. Of all the cargoes carried, coal, primarily for domestic use, and culm, mainly for burning limestone, were the most important. In the fiscal year 1733-4 the port of Exeter imported approximately 4,000 tons of coal from Newcastle and 3,300 tons from Sunderland, with smaller quantities from elsewhere, as well as 6,000 tons of culm from South Wales.[2] It is not possible to determine in any one year what proportion of these cargoes was discharged in the Exe estuary, at Teignmouth or on the beaches of east Devon, but it is likely that a substantial proportion of both coal and culm came to Teignmouth because of the opportunity of picking up a return cargo of clay. In 1785, for example, the maiden voyage of the sloop *Unity* of Barmouth was to Milford where she loaded culm for Teignmouth, consigned to six importers, and then sailed for London with 80 tons of clay plus six hogsheads of cider and one ton of small parcels.[3] The traders of Teignmouth who petitioned for the status of an independent port in 1801 pointed out that the attraction of their harbour to ship-owners arose from two-way traffic; they declared there had been

> a great increase of Coals and Culm brought back by the ships carrying clay to the several Ports of Liverpool, Newcastle, Sunderland, Wales etc.[4]

It is possible that clay for the Potteries not only went via north-western ports such as Liverpool but also up the Severn as far as Bridgnorth.

Although clay was exported from Teignmouth at least as early as 1728, exports were not large until 1770 when they amounted to some 4,000 tons.[5] Polwhele, in his *History of Devonshire* published from 1793 onwards, stated that 'at least ten or twelve thousand tons' were currently exported, being carried on horseback to cellars at Hackney. He wrote that

> About sixty years ago a few teams of horses were employed to carry it to Exeter and Topsham (but now) it is taken ... to the navigable part of the Teign ... and employs a hundred horses a day.[6]

Polwhele explained that 'where Bovey coal [lignite] passes through it tinges it and forms what is called the black clay'. Lignite itself was a marketable product at times of scarcity of genuine coal and was exported from Teignmouth during and immediately after wars, but it produced much less heat than coal and gave off extremely unpleasant fumes. It was used locally for firing bricks and tiles but was not efficient for pottery manufacture. So Stoke-on-Trent and not Newton Abbot became the main centre of the pottery industry, a fact which greatly influenced the future of the port of Teignmouth.

Many other minerals apart from clay were exported from southern Dartmoor in the 18th century, but it is not possible to identify those which were sent from Teignmouth rather than Topsham or other Exe estuary ports. Records which have survived from the Pound Living Mine at Upton Pyne indicate the balance of exports towards the end of the 18th century. An account book details the cost of weighing manganese ore at Exeter Quay and sending it by lighter or barge to Topsham, Starcross and Teignmouth; in the five years from 1788 to 1792 the entries for 'lighterage' and 'bargage' show that eight consignments were sent to Topsham, three to Starcross and three to Teignmouth for transport to London, Bristol and Gainsborough. In 1791 a Teignmouth consignment came to grief:

| March 29 | Paid bargage to Teignmouth in order to ship it | £3 17 5 |
| | Paid Expenses attending the Barge Running aground | £1 6 0[7] |

The mines of the Bovey Tracey area and the Teign Valley were much nearer to Teignmouth than was the Pound Living Mine and it is likely that a higher proportion of their output was exported from Teignmouth than from Exeter, but the production of these mines was small until the 19th century.

Evidence on Teignmouth's general coasting trade in the 18th century is scanty. One Exeter Collector's Account Book for Teignmouth has survived which covers the period from October 1773 to June 1779 and shows the pattern of trade at that time.[8] Coastwise imports, apart from coal and culm, fell into three main categories: building supplies, particularly bricks; imported food such as sugar from Bristol and barrels of beef and pork from other Westcountry ports; and materials needed by local industry of which the most important appear to have been oak bark for tanning, staves and bottles probably for the small cider factories around the Teign estuary, and timber, sailcloth, rope, pitch, tar and oakum for shipbuilding and repair. This varied but small-scale trade was carried on by a fleet of vessels arriving fairly frequently from south coast and Westcountry ports such as Portsmouth, Lymington, Dartmouth and Plymouth, along with occasional arrivals from London and Liverpool.

It is not possible to determine how many of these coasters were locally owned; the following vessels which appear in the Collector's Account Book are classified as Teignmouth-owned in the first Exeter Register of British Ships which was compiled in 1786:*Greyhound*, a brig of 94 tons, the *Good Intent*, a brig of 79 tons, the *Betsy*, a brig of 56 tons, the *Joanna and Mary*, a brigantine of 82 tons and the *Hope*, a tiny schooner of 13 tons. Other locally-owned vessels engaged in coastwise trade may have gone out of commission between 1779 and 1786 and there is a further complication because two of these names were very common and a particular vessel cannot be identified with certainty. For the last two years of the period for which records are available, 1778 and 1779, Teignmouth's coastwise trade was distorted by the introduction of the convoy system to deal with French threats in the Channel during the War of American Independence; the warship *Beaver*, 16 guns, was a 'constant Convoy' from Starcross Bight to London or the Downs. But trade to places near at hand was not greatly affected by war until the end of the century and short voyages made up a high proportion of the total coastwise trade of Teignmouth as they did in most other small ports.

The Exeter Port Books show a very large trade between Exeter and the range of ports from Weymouth to Plymouth including Teignmouth; in 1788, for example, 85 bags of wool were sent in the *Delight* from Teignmouth to Exeter and 180 quarters of wheat in the *William and Nancy* from Topsham to Teignmouth.[9] The significance of local trade of this kind has been stressed by W. G. Hoskins in his pioneer study of Exeter trade and industry in the 18th century.

Teignmouth's varied coastal trade had no parallel in foreign trade. Indeed, with one exception, her overseas links in the 18th century were insignificant. The exception was the Newfoundland trade which was important in itself and for its stimulus to other trades; one example, the import of meat in barrels, has already been referred to, the other, which was much larger in volume, was salt, the local production of which had ceased by 1692. In the period from 1773 to 1779 26 vessels arrived at Teignmouth from Lymington with full or part cargoes of salt and other evidence on the extent of the salt trade comes from legal records. Since salt was subject to government duty, the owners of cargoes lost at sea were entitled to a refund and their formal statements at Quarter Sessions give facts which would not otherwise be known:

> At the Devon Epiphany Sessions in 1792 proof was made upon the oath of John Manley, Master, and Elias Davis, mate, of the ship called the *Maria* ... that Thomas Bulley and Son of Shaldown [Shaldon] ... shipped from the Harbour of Teignmouth ... six wheys of foreign Salt for which His Majesty's Duties had been paid ... to be conveyed to Newfoundland to be used in Salting and Curing Cod Fish there and that in her passage, to wit in going out of the Harbour of Teignmouth aforesaid on the Twenty first day of March 1790, the said Ship was drove on some Rocks in a Tempestuous Storm and stranded, by means whereof the whole of the Salt was entirely lost and Consumed.

A year or so later it was home-produced, not foreign, salt which was lost and its port of origin shows that a new source was being developed:

> Mr Nathaniel Beaman ... did purchase of Jonadab Mort Esquire of Northwich Eighty Bushells of Rock Salt ... together with five hundred and twenty bushels of refined Salt ... shipped on board the ... Brigantine *Tamazin* ... did proceed from Liverpool to Teignmouth ... but in the prosecution of the voyage through the violence of the weather she foundered about twelve miles off the Lizard.[11]

The British Newfoundland fishery, which, together with local demand, stimulated these imports of salt, was largely based on the Westcountry. The early history of this fishery is summarised in the previous chapter. In the 18th century trading arrangements were highly complex because of the mobility and changing functions of those who took part: the 'residents' were often temporary or seasonal and 'merchants' may have started, and sometimes continued, their Newfoundland interest as captains. A ship leaving a Devon port for Newfoundland might have an owner-captain, a crew of experienced seamen and green hands, and passengers. Some of the passengers would be owners of byeboats kept in Newfoundland for the summer inshore fishery, others would be going as employees in these boats and yet others might be vaguely hoping to win in the New World release from poverty in the Old. Some of those who worked or paid their passage may well have had visions of Eldorado; as late as 1798, a leading public figure in Teignmouth sent to an acquaintance in London 12 grains of Newfoundland wheat 'of a tolerable good quality' and a piece of metal, for analysis, which appeared 'fine and to contain some Silver'.[12]

Newfoundland voyages varied in length and pattern. A ship might sail direct to Newfoundland with stores, equipment and exports on speculation, possibly calling at a southern Irish port en route, or might sail to Brittany, Spain or Portugal and there load salt for the fishery if salt was not already included in her outward cargo. Having arrived in Newfoundland the ship would reload at St John's, or one or more of the outports, with dried codfish and other local products; the return voyage might be to a Mediterranean or British port and, if the latter, it is likely that her cargo would include, in addition to salt fish (for which there was only a small demand in England), cod oil for the soap and leather industries and spars for shipbuilding as well as other small consignments, such as furs and cranberries. Side by side with this highly complex organisation, the older and simpler trade, which has been described in the previous chapter, continued until the early 19th century. Small ships which were primarily fishing vessels brought back fish and cod oil and carried passengers in both directions, attracting large numbers because they often sailed earlier in the season than the general trading vessels.

Teignmouth had a large share of this extremely varied trade. Plymouth dropped out towards the end of the 17th century and Bideford's Newfoundland trade began to decline around 1750. The Exe ports kept their connections, but in the second half of the 18th century and the early 19th only Dartmouth, of all Devon ports, was more important than Teignmouth. Fanny Burney noted in her diary in 1773, with only slight exaggeration, that 'all the men (of Teignmouth and Shaldon) are at Newfoundland every summer, and all laborious work is done by the women'. What worried Miss Burney more than the strenuous net fishery in which the women were engaged was their working dress:

> Their dress is barbarous ... and their coat is pinned up in the shape of a pair of trousers, leaving them wholly naked to the knee. Mr Western declares he could not have imagined such a race of females existed in a civilised country; and, had he come hither by sea, he should almost have fancied he had been cast on a newly discovered coast.[13]

A list of 'Who was Who of Families engaged in the Fishery and Settlement of Newfoundland 1660-1840', compiled by Dr. Keith Matthews, traces some 5,000 surnames of British and Irish people and shows that roughly one-tenth (416) were associated by birth, death or livelihood with Teignmouth and nearby parishes. Some Teignmouth merchants made use of agents in Newfoundland to collect their debts and then re-invested the money for further development of the trade. Joseph Hall, for example, wrote on 14 March 1706 to his agent in Newfoundland, Philip Williams, asking him to collect debts and, at his discretion, spend the money to buy a ship of about 100 tons, well founded and 'fit for the Newfoundland trade'. If the agent were unable to collect enough money then he was authorised to draw a bill of exchange to be paid 'at my house in West Teignmouth or in Exon (Exeter) to the value of one hundred pounds which I doubt not but it will be sufficient for your occasion'.[14]

Two of the Teignmouth families most deeply involved were the Codners and the Warrens, both of whom appear to have been representative in that they engaged in the trade as owners or part-owners of ships rather than as charterers. In order to show the range of their activities and their family ramifications it is necessary to extend the story well beyond the 18th century.

William, John and Samuel Codner were three sons of Daniel Codner who had established a successful Newfoundland business. William Codner commanded successively the *Hebe*, a fishing vessel of 46 tons built in Teignmouth, the *Hawke*, a brigantine of 92 tons and the *Dove*, a brig of 118 tons; all these sailed from Teignmouth to Newfoundland between 1788 and 1790. From 1794 to 1798 William Codner commanded the brig *Apollo*, 130 tons, which had been built at Ringmore and was owned by his father. The *Apollo* made a voyage from Teignmouth to Spain and Newfoundland in 1794 and returned to Oporto and Teignmouth. Early in the next year she was reported as arriving at Exmouth from Teignmouth in ballast and then sailed for Cadiz, having probably loaded at Topsham, with 'bale goods'. In 1798, on the death of his father, William Codner obtained a share in the family firm and in 1830 he was said to own one-quarter of the manor of Abbotskerswell.

William's brother Samuel did equally well. He appears to have divided his time between his residence at Teignmouth and his business in St John's and was involved in the passenger trade from Waterford to Newfoundland. In 1817 he was registered as part-owner of the schooner *Mary*, with John Drew of St Nicholas and Robert Alsop the Younger of Highweek, and in 1824 as sole owner of the snow *Selina*; correspondence concerning the *Selina* suggests that Samuel Codner continued to take a personal interest in the family business and was not easily defeated by adverse circumstance. He wrote to his agents in Oporto on 29 May 1833 to express the hope that it would be possible to arrange a quick discharge if the port was closed, presumably owing to political disturbances.

> I have no objection to her discharging off the Bar at Oporto if you can get a good price for the Fish and the expense of landing and risk are the purchasers ...[15]

Samuel Codner was appointed to a committee to represent the Newfoundland trade in London and he took a broad interest in the affairs of the colony. His part in the foundation of the Society for the Teaching of Poor Children in Newfoundland, which later became the Colonial and Continental Church Society, is commemorated by a tablet to his memory in St Petrox church, Dartmouth, where he died in 1858 at the age of 82.

Less is known about the third brother, John. He commanded the *Joanna and Agnes* which sailed from Teignmouth to Newfoundland in 1777 and 1778, on both occasions with 80 passengers, and returned in the latter year with 70 passengers. The large number of passengers carried on some of these voyages suggests that conditions must have rivalled in misery the middle passage of a West African slave voyage. The masters of vessels from other ports appear to have exceeded even these high Teignmouth figures: James Lannon, master of a vessel of 101 tons which sailed from Waterford in 1811, was in that year fined £500 by a Newfoundland court for carrying 184 passengers, of whom five died on the voyage.[16]

The fortunes of the Warren family can also be traced over a long period. In 1758 'a Plantation in Greens Cove in Newfoundland' was leased to William Warren of East Teignmouth, husbandman, for 2,000 years and in 1789 Jane Warren petitioned for a pension because her husband had been drowned when serving as boatswain in the Newfoundland trader *Richard*. From these beginnings the links between Teignmouth and Newfoundland through the Warren family continued for at least four generations. Matthew Warren told the parliamentary committee investigating the Teignmouth Harbour Bill in 1853 that he had been in business for 35 years and his father before him. He was concerned with the welfare of the harbour and the region which it served as well as with his own business. He fought an unsuccessful case against the imposition of Town Dues by the Corporation of Exeter, and he succeeded two other Newfoundland merchants, Samuel Codner and William Wilking, as Lloyd's Agent in 1830, a post which he held until his death in 1857 at the age of 71 when he was replaced by his sons, first Henry and then George. As shipowners, the Warrens, like the Codners, supported local shipbuilders: the *Favourite*, 137 tons, was built in Teignmouth in 1804 and the *Reward*, 108 tons, in Shaldon in 1815, the *Hope* of 79 tons, a prize, was lengthened at Teignmouth in the same year, the *Sicilian* was built in Shaldon in 1824 and the *Rapid* in Teignmouth in 1825. After this date most replacements came from Prince Edward Island or St John's, as some earlier vessels had done. Heavy losses of ships and cargoes in a very demanding trade, together with increasing competition from foreign vessels and decreasing protection from the British government, apparently persuaded the Warren family to abandon the Teignmouth end of their business.

While merchant families like the Codners retired and others (as explained later) moved to Liverpool, some of the Warrens settled permanently in Newfoundland. An account of the activities of one of their members shows the vigorous participation of the family in colonial life. M. H. Warren gave a lecture in Quebec in 1857 before an audience of 400 people in which he complained of the surrender policy of the home government towards French fishermen and settlers who were abusing their treaty rights 'to the detriment of British subjects and the ruin of our fellow colonists' and declared:

> The homes of the Newfoundland fishermen are as dear to them as her palaces to the Queen ... if the Queen and her Ministers wish to be generous to France let them give the Emporor the Isle of Wight with Osborne House ...[17]

The fact that this report was printed prominently in the *Teignmouth Gazette* illustrates the continuing interest in Newfoundand affairs in the home base of Teignmouth.

It is difficult to determine how profitable to the Codners and the Warrens the Newfoundland trade was because none of their business records have survived. An account book kept by Captain Robert Wren of Bideford shows that profits were sometimes extremely small. In 1770-1 his ship *Sally* made a round voyage (Bideford – Cadiz – Newfoundland – Taranto – Marseilles – Cette – Rotterdam – Bideford) during which profit was £14 19s. 9¾d. on an expenditure of £1,356 1s. 3½d., and this did not apparently include any depreciation on the vessel. On a second, shorter voyage (Bideford – Newfoundland – Alicante – Bideford) the balance was only 4s 10d.[18] It is hardly surprising that Captain Wren switched to the culm trade where profits were appreciably higher and hardship and danger much less. Some Newfoundland merchants in Dartmouth and Poole amassed considerable fortunes but, although Newfoundland was 'accompted the India to the West of England', those who traded there did not attain the glamorous success of Indian 'Nabobs'.

Accounts for the Teignmouth brigs *Good Intent*, 79 tons, and *Endeavour*, 139 tons, suggest that, even in time of war and threatened war when some ship-owners made high profits, the return on capital in the Newfoundland trade was modest. These two ships undertook coastwise as well as ocean voyages and, like the *Sally*, they were primarily trading, not fishing, vessels although they combined a Newfoundland voyage with some fishing on their own account. In nine months from March 1803, shortly beyond the period under review, the *Good Intent* and *Endeavour* appear to have made together a gross profit of £255 8s. 1d. which was divided equally between the three partners, William Fox, Richard Ashford and Thomas Stigings, all of Shaldon. William Fox's account book shows that such profit was made only by strict economy. The *Good Intent*, on a typical voyage, sailed direct from St John's to Plymouth, where she discharged part of her cargo of codfish and oil, and disposed of the remainder at Teignmouth in very small quantities, for example, one quintal of fish to 'two men of Ipplepen' for 12s. and half a quintal to 'a man of Kingskerswell' for half the price. Cod tongues, broken fish and 'mundongo' (cod roes) were also sold and Captain Fox collected at Exeter a government bounty of three shillings per quintal of 120 fish.[19] Despite this subsidy, it is clear that every penny counted. Economies were made even on clothing essential for the harsh conditions off Newfoundland where, according to an early pioneer, there were 'great heapes and mountaines of yce' and 'at Sea ... perpetuall mists, and ... about the Banke ... no day without raine'. On one occasion Captain Fox purchased '6pr blanketting drawers' and '6 swanskin shirts', but for some other items cheap alternatives were substituted:

To 3 'blue' jackets at 11/6	£1 14 6
To 3 jackets at 6s	18 0
To 2 double brest skin coats	19 0
To 4 single brest skin coats	16 0

Most of the stores and equipment came from local people, apparently in competition with each other, and only occasionally were they bought from specialist firms elsewhere, fishing nets and lines, for example, from Messrs. Gundry of Bridport. Materials no longer useful, like old rope, were sold for the few shillings they would fetch, discount was deducted from the larger accounts, and a claim was pressed against a fellow shipowner:

To James and Kingdon, Lawyers, for writing letters respecting a dispute with Mr Warren ... 10s 6d.

Such careful husbandry was probably typical of the Newfoundland traders from the Teign estuary who, in this way, attained a modest comfort and respectability.

Many of them are buried in the churchyard of St Nicholas, within sight and sound of the building and fitting out of their ships, and their memorials are appropriately unpretentious. The measure of success which they achieved depended on their developing an efficient means of providing materials and men for a trade which was greedy of both.

One example of the efficient supply of materials was Holbeam Mill at Ogmore, almost exactly equidistant from the Newfoundland trading ports of Teignmouth and Dartmouth. In 1648 Thomas Reynell had sold to John Reynell and Richard Brooking 'the manors of East Ogwell and West Ogwell with ... the mills called Holbeam Mills'.[20] It seems that the Reynell family (if one can assume that the names 'Rendle' and 'Rendell' belong to the same family) retained their connection with the mill and its market continuously from the date of this sale. The Rendles were builders and owners of ships in the Newfoundland trade and built the quay at Teignmouth, on land leased from Lord Clifford, which later became known as the Old Quay. The mill itself manufactured large quantities of fish-hooks and fishermen's knives, and probably also many of the other needs of the Newfoundland trade: nails, anchors and the 'tinware' and 'ironmonger ware' which are recorded among the exports to Newfoundland from Westcountry ports in the 18th century. Situated on the banks of the river Lemon above its confluence with the Teign and using water power, Holbeam Mill kept alive a tradition of craftsmanship which owed little to the industrial revolution and made a useful contribution to the national and international economy for three centuries. Today the buildings are substantially unchanged although the machinery has been removed for preservation.

Some materials for ship repair and maintenance were purchased in Newfoundland rather than the home base. Captain Fox's account book, like Captain Wren's, enumerates such items as pitch, tar, oakum, 'new tarpaulin' and 'a spar for a topmast' which were supplied in the colony. But many of the products required by the fishery and the settlements went out from Westcountry ports. The following shipments, recorded for the port of Exeter in the spring of 1754, may be taken as typical:

Racehorse	100 bags bread
	2 quarters wheaten flour
	3 hogshead 'pease'
	5 hogshead English strong beer
	1 hogshead wearing apparel
John	602 ells British-made sailcloth
	209 pounds tanned leather
	1 box British-made tallow candles
	168 pounds British-made rope
Bedford	2 hogsheads English fishing nets, lines and twine
	? English twice laid cordage ('second-hand' rope made from old rope)
	2,000 English bricks
	2 hogsheads English 'lyme'

Other products sent out, such as Portuguese salt and 'narrow Germany linen', show the importance of Exeter's entrepot trade. The Port Books give a total of 16 ships leaving the port of Exeter for Newfoundland in February, March and April of 1754;[21] it is not possible to determine how many of these sailed from Teignmouth rather than Exeter or Topsham, but the nature of the cargoes, as well as somewhat later evidence on ship ownership and on sailings from Starcross Bight, suggest that about half may have loaded in Teignmouth.

Men were not as easy to supply as materials. As explained in the previous chapter, the British government gave relief and protection to the Newfoundland fishery and in return merchants and captains were obliged to employ a proportion of 'green' hands who would be trained as potential seamen for the Navy. These 'landmen' were recruited throughout the rural parishes of Devon and parts of Dorset; Oppenheim, in his *Maritime History of Devon*, describes, for example, how the *Dartmouth Inn* and the *Newfoundland Tavern* were 'famous centres for the recruitment of rustics who wished to seek their fortunes across the Atlantic'. During the Napoleonic War a visitor to Newton Abbot heard from his landlord how, in time of peace, as many as 16 captains of Newfoundland ships stayed in the town and upwards of 1200 men

at one time assembled ... to be hired, and those who had not made an engagement carried white rods in their hands to distinguish them from others who had made terms with the Captains.[22]

In 1779 John Foot, 'formerly of Newton Abbot but late of St John's Newfoundland', advertised for relief from debt and described himself as 'Mariner and Thatcher', an odd combination but not unusual for Devon in the 18th century. A seaman, Aaron Thomas, who kept a diary of his experiences on Newfoundland voyages late in the century, declared that 'the principal part' of the crew and passengers of a ship which was lost, the *Mary Ann* of Dartmouth, came from Newton Bushell and some of them 'from the Plow tail'. After living in Newfoundland for some time, Aaron Thomas gave his impression that

> The Countys of Devonshire and Dorsetshire supply the greatest number of hands for the Newfoundland Fisherys yearly than all the rest put together. Poole and Newton Bushell are the Emporiums for the Two Countys. Lads from the Plow, Men from the Threshing Floor and persons of all ... Trades and ages ... flock annually, in the Spring, to Newfoundland.[23]

The authors of a 'General View of the County of Devon', drawn up about 1790 for the consideration of the Board of Agriculture, commended the introduction of the drill plough by enlightened farmers in South Devon because it would save labour

> where the propensity of the young men to go to sea, in the Newfoundland and other branches of the fisheries and commerce of the kingdom, is so great as to render hands very scarce for the business of agriculture.

Some of those who went to Newfoundland were technically apprentices like John Samson. He was examined on 10 April 1781 by the churchwardens of Bovey Tracey who sought to establish whether he had acquired a legal settlement in the parish which would entitle him to poor relief. He declared that

> he was born in the parish of Bovey Tracey ... and at eight years of age he was bound by the Churchwardens and Overseers of the Poor to Philip Gillard of the Parish of Brixham ... till he was twenty-four years of age ... after which he went into the Borough of Dartmouth and bound himself an apprentice to John Newman and Company ... and soon after he went to Newfoundland and lived with the said John Newman and Co. during his stay in England that winter and then went to Newfoundland again ...[24]

Because ships faced the Atlantic with a partly 'green' crew and numerous passengers, experienced seamen were in a strong bargaining position. A formal complaint made in 1737 gives a hint of this:

> Whereas ... Nicholas Wills was master of a ship ... called the *Bee* laying at anchor at the Port of Teignmouth bound to Newfoundland in Parts beyond the Seas and from thence to some Port in Spain or Portugal ... (he) retained Thomas Barter (of Kenn) to serve him on board ... for Salary and Wages of £2.7.6 a month (and who) promised that he would well and faithfully serve the said Nicholas Wills ... as mate of the said Ship. (But Thomas Barter) fraudelently intending Craftilly and Subtilly to Deceive the said Nicholas Wills ... at diverse days and times ... wilfully neglected his duty of a Mariner ...[25]

How Thomas Barter answered this charge the document does not relate. In time of war, when impressment caused a shortage of crews for the merchant navy, the bargaining power of experienced seamen was even stronger. During the War of American Independence, in 1777, Christopher Hamlyn, a 'gentleman-adventurer' of Crediton who had contracted to supply the Navy with provisions, was told by his

London agent that his ship was short of a crew and that perhaps men might be recruited in Devonshire:

> If one or two of them are good stout lads that know not much of the sea they will do at 20s. a month but let them be those of the Neighbourhood you are acquainted with. Give able seamen £2.2s. per month or 45s. if you cannot get them under. Will Webb of Teignmouth will be glad to go I hear ...

The agent obtained a travelling protection from impressment for seven men to come up from Teignmouth and promised that

> they shall be conducted on board the ship immediately and sail forthwith ... without ever coming on shore; this is quite a different thing from lying amidst a Tier of Ships hearing new things about Wages.[26]

Manning problems, which were particularly acute during the second half of the 18th century, may partly explain the high rate of loss among British ships. In the gale of 25 February 1773 a Newfoundland trader, the *Phoenix*, inward bound from Alicante, got over Teignmouth bar safely but then drove ashore twice in coming up the harbour and received considerable damage; two other Newfoundland traders, both belonging to Dartmouth, were lost in Lyme Bay as a result of the same gale. The seasonal character of the Newfoundland trade meant that vessels frequently sailed westwards in March or April and eastwards in October, November or December when gales were to be expected and high standards of seamanship were essential. Two incidents within 10 days of each other in 1793 illustrate the hazards:

> On Monday the 16th inst. [December] was driven ashore and wrecked at Gunnel, near Padstow ... in a gale of wind the brigantine *Unity* of Dartmouth, Richard Bowden, master, laden with fish and oil from St John's Newfoundland bound to Teignmouth. The vessel immediately went to pieces, the master and seamen were drowned and two only, passengers, were saved.

> On the 26th December came in [to Starcross Bight] the *Two Brothers* ... from Renuse [Renewse] in Newfoundland laden with codfish bound to Spain; she was driven from the land (when anchored) by a gale of wind leaving behind the merchant and his son, also the boat, anchors and cables ...

Even heavier losses may have been prevented by the skill and long experience of masters and mates. John Lang of West Teignmouth, for example, was a master in the Newfoundland trade for nearly 30 years, successively in the *Samuel*, *Endeavour*, *Betsey* and *Enterprise* until, according to his widow's petition to the Corporation of Trinity House, he lost his life in the *Prosperous* in the autumn of 1788.[28]

Towards the close of the 18th century the difficulties facing Newfoundland merchants in manning their ships were overshadowed by political dangers at home. The response of the respectable classes in Teignmouth to the excesses of the French Revolution was no less emphatic than in other Devonshire towns, where effigies of Tom Paine were hanged and burnt. On 27 December 1792, according to an announcement in the *Exeter Flying Post*, 'at a numerous and representative meeting of Gentlemen, Clergy ... Freeholders ... and Merchants ... at the Globe Tavern' in Teignmouth it was resolved to 'spare no Expence in prosecuting and bringing to exemplary Punishment any Publishers or Distributors of Pamphlets or Hand-Bills which may ... poison the Minds of weak Men', and to request the merchants of

Teignmouth, Shaldon and Ringmore 'not to employ any Tradesmen who shall show the least inclination of Disaffection to the King or our present Happy Form of Government'. The committee of 12 which was elected to promote these and other resolutions included at least four Newfoundland merchants, 'Mr Thomas Row, Mr Thomas Bully, Mr Hingstone and Mr Wm Boden'. Representatives of the Codner family, who were keen promoters of schools in Newfoundland and of a generous policy towards Roman Catholics, and the Warren family, who were often critical of government policy, were conspicuously absent. The execution of Louis XVI early in 1793 hardened opinion in Teignmouth as it did elsewhere. Robert Jordan, who was a leading public figure in close touch with both merchants and landowners, founded a Loyal Association and stimulated his friends to patriotic duties. The Loyal Association, he argued, would confirm 'the unanimity of the higher and middle classes of people' and ensure that 'the lower and licentious part (were) kept in awe'.[28]

In Teignmouth, as elsewhere in Devon, companies of Volunteers were formed around 1790 to supplement the militia and to deal with internal and external threats to the government. The Teignmouth company, consisting of some 50 men, at first displayed 'an utter ignorance' of military duty and were insubordinate towards one of their officers, but then apparently settled down and gave useful service. Food prices rose alarmingly throughout Devon, partly as a consequence of the demands of the fleet based on Torbay and Plymouth which 'drained the coastal region of cattle, sheep, grain and potatoes'. Sporadic rioting broke out in market towns and in eight of the ten ports which were most active at this time, Barnstaple, Bideford, Brixham, Dartmouth, Exeter, Ilfracombe, Plymouth and Topsham. A recent study by J. H. Bohstedt suggests that Teignmouth and Kingsbridge were exceptions and that disturbances in these two ports were of a very minor character.[29]

Outbreaks of disorder in Devon coastal towns, provoked by high food prices and the infiltration of revolutionary ideas, may have been encouraged by the general mood of lawlessness generated from privateering. Privateering, an accepted concomitant of war at sea, was particularly rife during the most bitterly contested stages of the War of American Independence from about 1779 to 1782. Most of the prizes captured by Westcountry privateers during this period appear to have been auctioned at Plymouth, but the French ship *L'Emulation*, which had been captured by the *Prince of Wales*, was offered for sale, together with her cargo of sugar, coffee and cotton, at 'Rendle's Great Sale Room' in Teignmouth on 13 January 1779. Perhaps encouraged by this demonstration of success, Teignmouth people fitted out two other strongly-armed privateers, the *Dragon*, 16 guns and 70 men, and the *Bellona*, which was described as carrying '16 guns, 4 cohorns and 8 swivels'. The advertisement for the *Dragon* appealed to both patriotism and greed:

A new advantageous Plan of Privateering
For a Six Months Cruize
All Gentlemen Seamen and Able Landmen who delight in the
Music of Great Guns and distressing the Enemies of Great Britain
have now a fine opportunity of making their Fortunes by entering
on Board The *Dragon* Privateer ...
now ready to be launch'd in the Harbour of Teignmouth ...

Apply Capt Joseph Drew at Stokeintinhead; Mr Andrew Cause at the London inn, Newton Bushel, or Mr Manning, Sailmaker, Teignmouth. N.B. The Cutter will sail from Teignmouth by the last of March for Guernsey to take in her Stores and proceed on her Cruise against the Enemy

Any Person capable of beating a Drum, or blowing a French horn,
shall have great Encouragement.

The agents of the *Bellona* made a similar appeal, but without complete success and the captain, William Letton, was still advertising for 'two mates' a day or so before his ship was due to sail. This may be the reason why the *Bellona* was 'oversett in a violent Gust of Wind' off Dawlish when she set off on her first cruise on 5 September 1779; 25 of the crew of 63 were drowned as well as 'three women who were alongside in a boat'.[30] Other privateers were concurrently fitting out in the Exe, including the *Mary*, the *Swallow* and the *King George*, but neither the Teign nor the Exe was as large a centre of privateering as Dartmouth, where the Newman and Holdsworth families indulged in this legalised piracy on a big scale.[31] In the next period of war, from 1793 to 1815, Teignmouth merchants seem to have been less active in fitting out privateers of their own but they suffered heavy losses from those of the enemy.

Chapter Three

The French Wars: 1793-1815

During the French Wars, which lasted from 1793-1815, broken only by one short interval of peace, no fewer than 106 Exeter-registered ships were captured by enemy privateers or warships. Many of these belonged to Teignmouth and covered the spectrum of vessels owned by the port. The small coasting brig, *Rob and Mary*, owned by John Sharland, baker, and William Sharland, mariner, was captured by a French privateer; so was the full-rigged ship *Amphitrite*, one of the largest vessels owned in Teignmouth whose co-owner, Henry Penson, was described as a 'gentleman' although he was hanged for stealing. What was probably the smallest trading vessel belonging to the port was lost in an unusual way. The schooner *Griffeth*, so small that she was not registered when first built, was 'stolen from her moorings by six French prisoners' who, according to local tradition, broke out from a lockup near the quay, but may have escaped from the new prison on Dartmoor. Occasionally the *Register of British Ships for the Port of Exeter*, which records these casualties, gives the name of the enemy vessel concerned, as when the brigantine *The Hilton*, owned by Samuel Bulley the Elder, John Job and Samuel Bulley the Younger, all described as merchants of West Teignmouth, was captured and burnt by the French ship *Veteran*, commanded by Jerome Bonaparte. Jerome Bonaparte had been exiled to sea as a result of a quarrel with his more famous brother; his success against British shipping in the north Atlantic, of which the loss of *The Hilton* was one example, helped to persuade Napoleon to restore him to favour.

Losses were not all one way. Many French and other enemy vessels were captured by British warships or privateers, sold and given new names, like the small schooner *Le Pere de Famille Joseph* which was re-named *Squid* and registered in the port of Exeter for Teignmouth owners. The snow *Pomona* was recaptured and then restored to Elias Rendell of St Nicholas and James Hele of West Teignmouth. The brigantine *Ceres*, built at Ringmore in 1787 and owned by Abraham Hingston of St Nicholas and John Row of Stokeinteignhead, was taken by the French and

> since recaptured by a Squadron of His Majesty's of War under the command of Sir John Borlase Warren and restored to the Owners by a Decree of Restoration from the High Court of Admiralty of England ...

After this impressive statement, the clerk's note which follows is an anti-climax: 'This vessel is again taken by the French'.[1]

The record of losses in the Exeter Register of British Ships is supplemented by reports from Lloyd's correspondents. These show that coastal waters were sometimes as dangerous as the Atlantic. In 1797, the year of naval mutinies at Spithead and the Nore, British vessels were captured 'off Beachy Head', 'near Brighton', 'three leagues from Portsmouth', 'off the Isle of Wight', 'near Portland'

and 'off the Start'. Even when naval morale recovered, enemy privateers continued to attack close to land. On 15 January 1799, for example, Lloyd's correspondent reported:

> The *Susannah*, Williams, from Dartmouth to Torbay, has been taken near Dartmouth by a French privateer, retaken by a Brixham Armed Boat and brought back to Dartmouth.

The interruption to coastwise trade and the panic which enemy privateers caused is shown by a report of 8 January 1804, when war had broken out again after a short period of peace:

> The *Peggy*, from Cardigan to London, is carried into Plymouth by the *British Fair*, Cutter, having been deserted by the Crew, on supposition that the Cutter was a French privateer.

In this year French privateers captured three Teignmouth coasting vessels engaged in the coal and clay trades: the *Elizabeth* from Liverpool, the *Jane* from Newcastle and the *Ann* from Shields. In 1807 two Teignmouth-London traders were taken, the *Phoenix* and the *Owen*, one being carried into Calais and the other into Cherbourg. During the later stages of the war Westcountry shipping lanes were infested with enemy privateers close to ports. In 1812, for example, 'a French Lugger Privateer captured a Brig and a Schooner off Bolt Head' and three coasters, including one on passage from Teignmouth to Leith, were taken 'between St Alban's Head and Portland'.[2]

Newfoundland traders were protected by the convoy system but this did not prevent heavy losses when the fleet was scattered by fog or storms. On 4 December 1801, *Lloyd's* Casualty List included an unusually detailed entry:

> Last night arrived in the Sound (Plymouth) Twelve Sail of Vessels from Newfoundland. They sailed three weeks since under Convoy of the *Aurora* Frigate in company with 33 sail and parted company nine days ago.

When they reached the comparative safety of the Sound, four ships were wrecked by a gale and three of them can almost certainly be identified as Teignmouth vessels: the brig *Hero*, 49 tons, the brigantine *Argo*, 101 tons, and the snow *Mary and Betsey*, 102 tons. Losses by enemy action of Teignmouth-owned vessels trading to New-foundland up to the Truce of Amiens of 1801 included two which belonged to the Codner family, the *Dove* and the *Hebe*. Others were victims of the natural hazards of the sea: the *Industry* and the *Mary Ann*, wrecked on Oporto Bar, and the *Mercury* and *Jason*, both abandoned in the eastern Atlantic. When hostilities broke out afresh in 1803, British losses were again heavy and became particularly severe after the United States declared war in June 1812. Cancellations of registry in the Exeter Register of British Ships and casualties reported by Lloyd's correspondents, combined together, show that, within six months, 11 Teignmouth Newfoundlanders were captured by American privateers. Fishing vessels suffered as badly as trading vessels. The brigs *Henry* and *Fame* were both taken on the same day 'whilst fishing on the Banks of Newfoundland' and the *Alfred*, owned by Jacob Bartlett of Kenton, merchant, and John Lang of West Teignmouth, mariner, and probably a trading vessel, was captured on a voyage from Newfoundland by one of the most notorious of the American privateers, the *Yankee* of Rhode Island, 16 guns and 160 men, which took 40 British ships and confiscated property to the value of five million dollars.[3] Losses before and after the Americans declared war extended to another venture in which Teignmouth Newfoundland merchants sometimes engaged, the supply of salt fish to the negro plantations of the British West Indies. In October 1807, for example, the *Nancy*, in which the Warren family had an interest, was captured on a voyage from Newfoundland to Barbados and 'carried into Guadeloupe'. Poole Newfoundland merchants sought to escape the dangers in the Channel and off the west coast of France, if not in more distant waters, by bringing their cargoes to their home port first and then transhipping them to the Mediterranean in neutral vessels; but this practice seems not to have been followed, or not followed to any great extent, by Teignmouth merchants. Added to the destruction directly caused by privateers were the casualties through collision in convoy. At least two Teignmouth vessels were lost in this way: the brig *Success*, 'run down by a Man of War convoying her from Newfoundland to Spain', and the brig *Peace*, 'ran down and sank off Cape St Vincent by H.M.S. *Granicas*'.[4]

The voyages of a Teignmouth coasting vessel and an Atlantic trader and the experiences of their crews illustrate the effects of war and weather on a local maritime community. The sloop *Racehorse*, a recaptured prize, was purchased in Falmouth in 1798 by Robert Jordan of Teignmouth for £420 and his correspondence describes her fate.[5] Within a few months, according to a letter from Jordan to his insurers, she had the misfortune

> to meet with a most dreadful Gale of Wind ... She arrived at the Bar last evening at about eight o'clock and came to anchor, but this morning the wind blowing a strong Gale at S.S.W., Captain Briggs by order of the Pilot cut his cable and run over the Bar. She is an entire wreck.

This was clearly an exaggeration because Jordan was willing to accept £100 for the cost of repairs and by January 1799 the *Racehorse* was ready to proceed to Liverpool with her cargo of clay. She successfully completed this passage and was then chartered to Ipswich and Sunderland where she loaded for Teignmouth. On this voyage rough weather forced Captain Briggs to cut his cable while at anchor in the Downs and he accepted a pilot's offer to take his ship into Ramsgate for what Jordan described as 'a very extravagent charge' of £42. Shortly after leaving Ramsgate, the *Racehorse* was captured, 'along with 11 or 12 sail of coasters', by a group of French privateers operating off Dover. Jordan wrote to John Schank, one of the Commissioners for the Transport Service:

> I had the misfortune of having a fine Sloop belonging to me captured off Dover ... and carried into Boulogne in France, from whence the master, whose name is Wm. Briggs, writes me that he was soon, he apprehended, to be marched to Valenciennes. My request, therefore, is, Sir, that as this poor unfortunate man has a wife and very large family of children to provide for, you will do me the favour to get the poor fellow exchanged as soon as possible.

It is not clear whether Captain Briggs was exchanged or not, but the mate of the *Racehorse* escaped from prison, came safely back to Teignmouth and swore an affidavit in order to hasten payment of the insurance money. Jordan enquired about likely replacement vessels in Swansea and Guernsey and his agent offered a cut-price for an American-built brigantine at Weymouth. The last letter in the surviving correspondence implies that the *Racehorse* had been re-taken but that Jordan was not anxious to have her back; perhaps he found his other occupations of solicitor, house and insurance agent and moneylender more profitable and less worrying than ship-owning.

The *Friends* was an ocean-going brigantine which sailed from Teignmouth for Fayal in ballast on or about 10 January 1810, with John Whiteway as master. She struck heavy weather and took refuge in Torbay where, according to Lloyd's correspondent, 'it is feared (she) will go to pieces'. In fact she put into Brixham Pier 'with very little damage' and shortly resumed her voyage. On 23 January she was taken by the *Dame Ernouf*, a French privateer, but allowed to go free because her captor was trying to keep control of much more valuable prizes. The *Friends* returned to Plymouth and set out again on her Atlantic voyage with a new master, Hugh Merchant. Possibly because of the damage she had suffered, she was abandoned off the coast of Newfoundland 'in a sinking state'; her crew were eventually landed at Aberdeen by another Newfoundlander, the *Favourite*, almost a year after they had first started from Teignmouth, their ship having earned nothing for her owner, William Harvey of St Nicholas.[6]

Despite the loss of vessels like the *Racehorse* and the *Friends* and the interruption to coastwise and Atlantic commerce which has been described, Teignmouth's trade increased in some categories. In particular, the clay trade benefited from the opening of the Stover Canal. In 1790 James Templer, the owner of relatively infertile but rich clay-bearing lands around Teigngrace, started to build a canal to facilitate the transport of clay outwards and limestone and sea sand inwards. A Private Act of 1792 for the purpose of raising funds to complete the work emphasised the value of the canal for the development of the clay industry:

> ... the Black and White Clay might be sent from the Pits where the same is dug, and delivered on board Vessels in the Port of Teignmouth for Exportation at an easy Expence, which would greatly promote the Sale of such Clay ...[7]

Horse transport was still necessary from the pits to the canal, where cellars were built to store the clay, but the distance was less than to the existing loading points on the river. The river was dredged near the entrance to the canal and barges could load to a deeper draught than previously. One contemporary account, written in the 1790s, refers to the use of very small boats on the canal and transhipment to barges at the head of the river navigation. There is no other evidence of this practice but it may possibly have operated before work on the canal was complete.[8] From 1795, if not earlier, barges moved direct from loading points on the canal to Teignmouth harbour; a Register of that date, prepared for the recruitment of barge crews to the Navy, lists 17 barges regularly trading in the Teign estuary and 31 on the Exe. Of the Teign barges 10 worked between Teignbridge and Teignmouth and eight of these belonged to James Templer, all of approximately the same size and able to carry cargoes of about 30 tons: *George, James and Mary, Compton Castle, Tor Abbey, Lady Clifford, Lord Courtenay, Lovely Mary* and *Neighbour Hail*. In 1808 Templer added to his fleet the *Lady Duckworth*, described as 'a square-sterned smack with flush deck', built at Teigngrace, which may possibly have been able to venture to sea like the other vessel he owned, the sloop *Devonshire*, which had been built at Gravesend. The other two barges which worked between Teignbridge and Teignmouth were owned by James Hoccombe, whose place of residence is not given, and John Pidsley of Teignmouth. Apart from these 10 barges which used the Stover Canal, at least three others were concerned in the clay trade: the *Royal George*, owned by Parmenas Pearse of Kingsteignton, the *Friendship*, owned by Nicholas Watts also of Kingsteignton and the *Diana*, owned by Messrs. Watts and Mortimer. They brought clay from Hackney and Newton Marsh to Teignmouth harbour. Of the remaining four barges on the Register, three, owned in Teignmouth and Bovey, probably carried coal and bulky merchandise from Teignmouth to Newton Abbot; the other was owned in Ringmore and possibly brought timber to the shipyard there.[9]

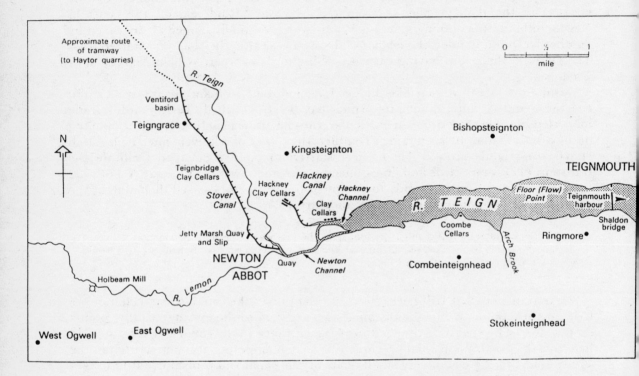

Fig. 2 The port of Teignmouth: river and canal communications.

The Stover Canal itself, although it was never extended to Chudleigh as the Act of 1792 allowed, did credit to Templer's foresight; it passed into railway ownership in 1862 and inward traffic dwindled, but a large export traffic through Teignmouth continued until the 1930s. This remarkably long commercial life made the Stover Canal, apart from the Exeter Ship Canal and one or two early experiments in Cornwall and Somerset, both the first and the last of all the Westcountry canals. A contemporary traveller, M. Dunsford, who declared that 'an active spirit of enquiry animated' his topographical researches, waxed eloquent about the immediate economic and social benefits:

> This little Canal, the first in Devonshire, and at the sole expence of Mr Templar ... is the means of great benefit to the inland country by the return of coal and other necessary and useful commodities

and the land around appears

> in consequence like a *new creation* from the wide chaos around it and, with the produce of the canal, afford(s) many increasing advantages to the inhabitants of the adjacent district as well as to the public spirited projector and cultivator.[10]

One agricultural improver, Robert Fraser, writing in 1794, appears to have been intoxicated by Templer's ideas and thought that further benefits would accrue if a series of canals were built into Dartmoor so that

> these wastes, which are at present a disgrace and reproach to the inhabitants of this county, would be speedily converted into arable lands and pastures and interspersed with cheerful villages ...

James Templer himself had more original plans for improving transport to and from his estates than the Stover Canal or an improved river navigation. He was particularly attracted by two inventions of Captain John Schank, ex-merchant seaman and later admiral, who conducted experiments with sliding keels and separate bulkheads.[11] Some of Captain Schank's ideas were incorporated in the small naval cutter *Trial*, which was launched in 1791, and Templer was invited on board for a voyage from Woolwich to Plymouth. Afterwards he wrote to Captain Schank expressing admiration for both inventions. Separate bulkheads would, he thought, prevent cargo from shifting and would also mean that 'mixed and separate commodities' could be carried in the same vessel. Sliding keels, which could easily be raised or lowered, would improve sailing qualities and would be of particular value to Teignmouth:

> Whenever my work is done I will immediately adopt it [the invention of the sliding keels] in the coasters from this harbour, as they will not only be able to get up quite to Newton, or even up the canal, with a cargo, but can get in and out of the harbour at any time in spite of the bar ... which will in season prove very advantageous to me, especially if I can carry stone from Barbicomb [Babbacombe] Bay up the canal, and Bovey coal in wartime ...[12]

Whether because Templer was preoccupied with other matters, whether, as he said, 'people are so unfortunately grounded in favour of old fashions', or whether, as seems most likely, the technical problems were not completely solved before the attention of marine architects was concentrated on steam propulsion, Captain Schank's invention of sliding keels failed to fulfil local expectations. It was used on the Tamar, but never on the Teign.

The natural resources of the hinterland of Teignmouth harbour were to be developed in less dramatic fashion. The production and export of clay at this time, apart from Templer's activities, was carried out by small family concerns which obtained leases from the lord of the manor or the ecclesiastical commissioners and then built up connections with consumers in the potteries and elsewhere. Between 1793 and 1815, despite the war, the export of clay became one of the staple trades of the port, and the character of the trading organisation which developed in this period vitally influenced the evolution of the harbour. A coherent account of the organisation can best be given by continuing its history well beyond the period immediately under review.

Among the families active in the earliest days of the clay industry were the Pikes, who moved to Dorset, the Watts and the Whiteways. The Clifford Estate Papers show that in 1794 a lease was granted to Nicholas Watts and in 1801 to John Whiteway. In 1802 Nicholas Watts paid royalties on 1,809 tons of clay cut and John Whiteway on 1,465 tons.[13] Whiteway, Watts & Co. was an amalgamation of the two family interests and the leading company in the first half of the 19th century. Around 1860 two separate organisations were formed from the previous partnership: Whiteway & Co., and Watts, Blake and Bearne. Throughout the century a number of smaller companies operated, of which the largest was the Devon and Courtenay. They competed for custom and in bad times accused each other of price-cutting but collaborated when it seemed necessary to reduce wages. Watts, Blake and Bearne had wider interests than the other companies and engaged in trade, such as the import of coal, which benefited themselves and the harbour. Perhaps mainly for this reason, they became the dominant, and eventually the only, Devon-based company in the Devon ball clay industry. Members and representatives of the clay companies greatly influenced decisions affecting the harbour and played an important part in the economic and social life of the region. William John Watts, son of Nicholas Watts and senior partner in Watts, Blake, Bearne & Co. who eventually became High Sheriff of Devon, established a banking business which helped other users of the harbour, especially shipowners, and John Hayman Whiteway, partner in Whiteway & Co., was Chairman of the Teignmouth Harbour Commission for 30 years until his death in 1887.

Valuable as their contribution to the well-being of the harbour was, the clay companies played virtually no part in ship-owning. Nicholas Watts was registered owner of the brig *Diana* in 1786 and 'James Hocombe' of Highweek (possibly the 'James Hoccombe' who was owner of one of the Teign barges) was part-owner of the sloop *Two Brothers*. At a later date Samuel Whiteway of Kingsteignton (son of the John Whiteway who was granted a lease in 1801) shared ownership of a number of vessels including the full-rigged ship *Agenoria* which was a family investment in which the partners, among others, were John Whiteway of Chudleigh, miller, and Philip Whiteway of Runcorn, described as a merchant, presumably a clay merchant. But these were exceptions to the rule that clay merchants were not ship-owners. In the period under review, and subsequently, they found that fluctuating total demand and wide variations in the size of consignments required by customers served from ports of differing capacities meant that chartering was more convenient and profitable than ship-owning. William Mortimer, who appears to have had clay interests in both Dorset and Devon, set the pattern as early as 1783 when he advertised in the *Exeter Flying Post* on 11 September for

A Few Hundred Tons of SHIPPING to load Potters Clay at Teignmouth for Liverpool at Twelve Shillings per Ton Freight. Speedy Application is to be made to Mr Wm Mortimer, near Teignmouth.

This advertisement appeared only once, which suggests that Mr Mortimer's requirements were met without difficulty. More than a century later, in 1914, Messrs. Watts, Blake and Bearne became ship-owners for a very special reason. They purchased the steam tug *Kestrel* to tow their barges and occasionally, in calm weather, to help a large steamer negotiate the sharp turn at the entrance to the harbour.

The fact that clay merchants were not purchasers of ships meant that the shipbuilding industry of the Teign estuary was dependent on the general trade of the harbour and the national economic climate. From 1793 to 1815 demand was keen and for most of this period the industry was probably more active than at any other time before or since. Some of the building places enumerated in the Exeter Register of Ships – Haven Banks and Parsonage Stile, Glass House and Franks Quarry – have a countryside air which suggests that wooden shipbuilding was a part of the rural as well as the maritime economy and sometimes took place inland. But in the Teign estuary, unlike the Exe, building was done at or very near the river mouth: at Teignmouth itself, Shaldon or Ringmore. The one exception, a small vessel built at Teigngrace, has been referred to earlier. In the whole wartime period of 22 years, 68 vessels were launched, varying in size from a small smack to a full-rigged ship, for owners within the port of Exeter.

These vessels were launched by six shipbuilders, three of whose yards were in Teignmouth and three in Shaldon and Ringmore. The Teignmouth shipbuilders were William Rendle, who was apparently continuing the family business which had long been closely associated with the life and work of the port, William Curtis (or Courtis), who was building ships at least as early as 1767 when he described himself as a shipwright and advertised for sale a sloop of 40 tons, and James Heath who built the warship *Talbot* of 18 guns, launched in 1807. William Rendle went bankrupt in 1816 but re-established himself and continued in business at least until 1834 when he did major repairs to two Teignmouth-registered vessels, the smack *Celerity* and the schooner *Feronia*.[14]

The shipbuilders on the other side of the river were John Stephens and Thomas Sutton, both of whom built ships at Ringmore, and Thomas Tucker, whose yard was described as 'Shaldon Green'. John Stephens' name appears in the Exeter Register of British Ships from its inception in 1786, when his yard already had a high reputation. A contemporary ship-owner described the launch of

a fine new ship belonging to Mr Rob. Stevenson of London, Turkey Merchant, ... perhaps as compleat a Vessel as ever launched from a private yard ... built by Mr John Stephens, whose great Ingenuity in Naval Architecture has gained him the greatest Reputation.[15]

Stephens retained part-ownership of some of the vessels he built, such as the snow *Minerva*, 148 tons, which was launched in 1791 and lost off Figuera five years later. Thomas Sutton built six naval vessels during the Napoleonic War, including two armed schooners, H.M.S. *Rook* and H.M.S. *Landrail*, and a much larger ship H.M.S. *Perseus*, which was fitted with 28 guns.[16] Thomas Tucker went bankrupt in or about 1831 but the business was apparently revived under the same name and transferred to the Teignmouth side of the river where ships were built for another ten years or so.

In the 1850s shipbuilding reached a peak of activity comparable to that from 1793 to 1815. At this time, Arthur Owen, who had earlier described himself as a shipwright, became owner of the Teignmouth yards (perhaps Tucker's) and supplied many local owners with ships adapted to their needs. John Stephens of Ringmore formed a partnership with William Follett and, after Stephens died in 1823, members of the Follett family built large ocean-going ships for owners in some of the major ports, probably achieving maximum production about 1855. The last of the long line of estuary merchant-shipbuilders was John Bartlett Mansfield who came to Teignmouth in 1849 and developed a varied business which prospered until his death 30 years later. The contribution which these 19th-century shipbuilders made to the local economy is described in the appropriate chronological place.

Towards the end of the Napoleonic War launchings for local owners tailed off: in the four years from 1811 to 1814 there were only five compared with 20 from 1804 to 1807. This decline is probably explained, not only by trade fluctuations as a result of the continental blockade, but by the increasingly ruthless character of the war itself. The condemnation of captured ships and their sale by the Admiralty meant that a wide choice of prizes was available to Westcountry owners at a much cheaper price than new ships; many of them were sold 'by the candle' at Plymouth. The other aspect of the growing intensity of the war was the impressment of men for the Navy and the Royal Shipyards without regard for customary exemptions. There is no direct evidence that shipyard workers in the Teign estuary were taken away for national service, but the frequent complaints in an otherwise extremely patriotic newspaper, the *Exeter Flying Post*, suggest that the press-gang was particularly hot in south Devon, which had long been regarded by Admiralty agents as good recruiting ground. Moreover, it is clear that the press-gang was supplemented by financial incentives and other methods of persuasion. For example, the First Lieutenant of the *Experiment*, anchored in Torbay, opened a 'rendezvous' in Teignmouth and 'a gentleman of the neighbourhood' offered each volunteer the sum of three guineas in addition to the King's Bounty. Under threat of an Act of Parliament, which required ship-owners to supply a proportion of men for the Navy with a sanction of embargo, the 'Commissioners for the Port of Exeter' invited 'all Young Men of Spirit to come forward immediately to serve their King and Country', offering as encouragement handsome bounties:

Able-bodied Seamen	25 Guineas
Ordinary Seamen	20 Guineas
Able-bodied Landmen	15 Guineas

One of the places of 'rendezvous' was the *Jolly Sailor Inn*, Teignmouth. Three weeks later the lugger *Alarm* arrived at Exmouth from Plymouth with '14 men returned, unfit for service', so it seems that the incentive had been over-generous.[17]

But, despite the harm done to commercial shipping by the demands of the Navy and the activities of privateers, Teignmouth suffered less severely from wartime policy as a whole than Exeter or Topsham. Exeter's trade dropped dramatically, largely because of the war. E. A. G. Clark's analysis of port records shows, for example, that the import of wine to Exeter fell from 1,086 pipes in 1792 to 235 in 1830 and the export of woollen goods, already affected by increased competition, from 11,331 bales in 1791 to 35 in 1820.[18] Supporting evidence of a less exact kind comes from reports in the *Exeter Flying Post* of shipping movements. In 1792 15 cargoes of fruit and wine and other products arrived at Exmouth, for estuary ports, from the Mediterranean and 36 vessels sailed with 'bale goods' for the continent. In 1816 there were only four arrivals from the Mediterranean and no direct sailings to the continent with cargo at all. On the other hand, the number of vessels sailing from Exmouth to Teignmouth, either light or with part-cargoes, rose from 11 in 1792 to 23 in 1816. These figures emphasise, and perhaps exaggerate, Teignmouth's good fortune in comparison with Exeter. Although Teignmouth suffered severely, like Exeter, from the demands of the Navy and from depredation to her coastwise and Newfoundland trade, clay exports expanded through innovation and Teign shipyards profited from war. Teignmouth had little direct trade with Europe and was therefore not greatly affected by Napoleon's blockade, and the counter-measures which it provoked, or by military operations on the continent. No Teignmouth vessel experienced the frustration of the *Flora* in January 1809, which returned to Exeter after 'beating off Oporto for five weeks' and then being 'ordered by a Frigate not to go in, as the French troops were in Portugal'.[19] The wartime years from 1793 to 1815 were a setback for the port of Teignmouth, but not a disaster.

Chapter Four

Post-war Problems and Initiatives: 1815-1840

The setback which Teignmouth suffered was emphasised by the general post-war slump in maritime trade. Difficulties are clearly illustrated from the letters of William Fox, a ship-owner of Shaldon, whose Newfoundland business has been described in Chapter Two and whose correspondence has survived for the year 1816.

William Fox by this time was part-owner of three vessels in which his nephew and two sons shared. William Fox Junior was master of the snow *Providence*, 130 tons; Thomas Fox, William Fox's second son, was master of the brig *Good Intent*, 79 tons; and Anthony Fox, his nephew, commanded the brig *Three Williams*, 95 tons. Correspondence concerning the *Three Williams* is sufficiently detailed to show the nature of the problems with which owners were confronted immediately after the French Wars. On 3 May 1816 William Fox Senior wrote to Captain Anthony Fox:

> The brig *Three Williams* now laying in this harbour of Teignmouth under your command being now laden with clay you are to proceed in her from here to Liverpool and then deliver your cargo with all possible despatch. At same time make every enquiry of every broker to obtain a freight for your vessel ... The present Clay freight and to return with Coals must leave a considerable loss to the owners of such a vessel as the Brig *Three Williams*.

William Fox followed up this letter three weeks later:

> ... I have some thought of sending her [from Liverpool] for Newf'd with salt and coals if she is tight in every respect.

He enquired from Richard Fogarty whether freight was on offer to Newfoundland from Waterford or Cork and, on the assumption that it would not be, wrote to his agents at Liverpool:

> ...please order 10 tons of coals & 100 tons of salt to be shipt on her [the *Three Williams*] for my acc't for St John's Newf'd. Unless you can get any goods that will pay about 20/- per ton freight you may lessen the quantity of salt accordingly, but if nothing offers at that rate ship 10 barrels of good pork & 20 bags of bread & a few small firkins of butter ... & when those are on board & the vessel is not deep & hath good room & your bread is of good quality you may add 10 or 20 bags more if the Master thinks proper, but if any charter can be obtained I should prefer it to this speculation.

It was important that Captain Anthony should take care of his vessel but practise strict economy:

> ... You'll get a painter to paint her stern I suppose for about 5 or 6 shillings. He will make it look well. Take a little paint with you to freshen the paintwork in Newf'd ... the miserable low freights will not bear out the expenses without the utmost frugality and attention ... You'll lessen your

expenses of your vessel if possible by hiring out one or more of your men or fitting out your longboat to catch some fish ... A great deal must be left to your discretion.

But William Fox could not resist the temptation to add 'Private Instructions':

... the times are difficult therefore we know not who to trust except our neighbours & a few others. If you can sell the pork & bread & butter yourself to safe men ... you will save me this commission (which would be charged by a wholesaler).

Shortly after leaving Liverpool the *Three Williams* sprang a leak and had to put back to Holyhead. William Fox gave his personal view in a note to Thomas Fox, 'I fear he was carrying sail without fear or wit', and wrote to Anthony:

I trust you were not pressing the vessel too much. No man ever gained a passage by carrying a press of sail against a head sea unless it was absolutely necessary to do it to weather a point of land or keep off a lee shore ... At Holyhead your charge for beer and spirits ... was extravagent ... I made no such charges in my time.

In the end all worked out reasonably well. Apparently the *Three Williams* sold her cargo in Newfoundland, loaded fish for Lisbon and then fruit for Bristol, crossed to Newport and brought back coal to her home port of Teignmouth. William Fox's statement in one of his letters, 'You will never find a better banker than your Old Father', has the ring of truth and one can only hope that his nephew and sons gave their mentor the confidence he seemed reluctant to place in them.[1]

At this time of depression other local ship-owners found different means of trying to make ends meet. One such means is clear from a report in the *Western Luminary* for 9 April 1822. The schooner *Olive Branch* of Teignmouth was bound from Liverpool to Bristol when she sent out distress signals off Lundy. 'By great exertions' from a pilot skiff she was brought into Ilfracombe harbour. It was then found that 'five holes had been bored from within through her bottom to sink her ... The vessel is insured at Lloyds'. The mate, who was the owner's son, absconded.

Most Teignmouth ship-owners, despite the bankruptcy of two individual merchants and one partnership, began to replace their wartime losses. In 1815 and 1816, 13 vessels were launched in Teignmouth, Shaldon and Ringmore and registered in the port of Exeter by local owners. In addition, two new vessels came from Prince Edward Island, an important source of Devon ships, and one was built on 'Monkwearmouth shore', County Durham. In 1817 and 1818 a further 23 vessels were newly registered of which five came from yards on the river. In 1820 John Hele came to work for Mr. Reed, tailor, of Fore Street, Teignmouth, and recorded in his diary various harbour events, including launching ceremonies for 'many brigs and schooners built by Mr Owen and Mr Randell'. His entry when the brig *Oscar* was launched fully-rigged and immediately capsized shows the industrious apprentice poking fun at a participator in aristocratic frippery. Three hundred guests were thrown into the water and

Mr Praed's servant was ejected through the stern window and ruined his brown frockcoat and scarlet plush breeches.[2]

More evidence of the revival of maritime activity comes from correspondence between the merchants and the Postmaster General. In 1822 William Codner,

William Fox, Gilbert Clapp and others complained that the post (by a postman on horseback) did not arrive until nearly ten o'clock and they were therefore not able 'to prosecute the necessary Avocations of their Business, and answer their letters by the Evening Post'. Insurance matters were particularly important

> as it often happens that very considerable Sums in Insurance are depending by Receipt of Letters from London on a Thursday; should your Memorialists lose the opportunity of answering by Return of Post they must wait until the Saturday following, Friday not being a London Port Day.[3]

The merchants did not, apparently, succeed in speeding up the morning delivery but they won a promise that the evening collection would be held back for half an hour.

A Guide to Teignmouth, undated but probably published in the 1820s, describes the trade of the harbour:

> The trade of Teignmouth consists chiefly in the export of pipe and potters clay from the pits of Kingsteignton; of granite from the rocks of Haytor and iron ore from the same neighbourhood ... which are conveyed in vessels from 80 to 400 tons burden ... the Newfoundland trade is also carried on in this place with great spirit.[4]

Most of the ships engaged in this coastal and overseas trade were owned and managed locally, either in Teignmouth itself or in the villages across the river which were within or just outside the parish of St Nicholas: Shaldon, Ringmore and Stokeinteignhead. Members of the Codner family, which has been referred to earlier, owned either separately or in partnership, seven vessels between 1817 and 1824: the *Apollo*, *Atalanta*, *Caroline*, *Commodore*, *Daniel*, *May* and *Selina*, all schooners or snows of between 50 and 100 tons, small vessels but quite capable of crossing the Atlantic. Three of them were built on the Teign estuary.

Other owners whose names appear frequently in the Register are Matthew Warren who was sometimes joint owner with Prudence Warren, William Boden and William Boden the Younger, William Blackaller, 'merchant', and Elias Blackaller, 'gentleman', Andrew and Nicholas Howard, 'merchant' and 'mariner' respectively, and the Clapps. The Clapps were an established sea-going family, who emphasised the wide range of their interests by registering one of their ships in grandiloquent fashion as owned by 'Robert Clapp of St Johns Newfoundland but at present residing in London, Kingdom of England' and 'John Squarey Clapp of St Johns Newfoundland but at present resident at Shaldon in the county of Devon also of the Kingdom of England'. Shaldon at this time, perhaps even more than West Teignmouth, was predominantly a maritime community. Of the 21 bridegrooms who recorded their occupations in the St Nicholas Marriage Register between 1813 and 1830 and who lived in the parish, 12 were mariners, two shipwrights, one a merchant, one a shipbuilder and one a 'master' in the Royal Navy.[5]

It was the Newfoundland trade which engaged the main attention of most of these partnerships. Thanks to the family links between Teignmouth and Newfoundland described in Chapter Two, this trade revived after the Napoleonic War, despite the weakening of Newfoundland's economy by disastrous fires in St John's and by political disputes. The Ropewalk in East Street, Newton Abbot, built in 1828 and with its name still clearly visible, is evidence of the last revival of this traditional trade. The records of ships inspected by Lloyd's surveyors in the port of Teignmouth in 1835 include the following vessels whose 'destined voyage' is given as Newfoundland or an intermediate port of call:

Vessel	Owner
? *Jane and Susan* 74 tons	Michael Rowell
Schooner *Rover* 57 tons	Michael Rowell
Schooner *Liberty* 84 tons	William Boden
Brig *Friendship* 75 tons	William Boden
Schooner *Theresa* 71 tons	Alan Goodridge
Brig *Miriam* 57 tons	Andrew Howard
Brigantine *Concord* 74 tons	Andrew Howard
Schooner *Phoenix* 89 tons	Andrew Howard
Brigantine *Nature* 129 tons	John Eales
Snow *Pillhead* 148 tons	John Clapp and Co.
Brig *Maria* 112 tons	Samual Bibbins
Schooner *Albion* 95 tons	John Rendle and Co.
Schooner *Lovely Sally* 66 tons	Mudge and Co.
Schooner *Two Brothers* 63 tons	Mudge and Co.

Apart from Mudge and Company, who were based on Torquay, all the recorded owners lived in Teignmouth, Newton Abbot or the nearby villages. It was not unusual for some merchants, like some shipbuilders, to have interests on both sides of the estuary. Rating assessments show, for example, that the Bodens had houses, lofts and cellars in Ringmore and in Teignmouth.[6] Communications were much improved by Shaldon toll-bridge, opened in 1827 and said at the time to be the longest wooden bridge in England, which supplemented the ancient ferry near the river mouth. For three of the largest ships on the surveyor's list, the *Pillhead*, *Maria* and *Albion*, the 'destined voyage' is shown as Cadiz or Figuera, which were loading ports for salt. There are no certificates for vessels belonging to the Warrens or the Blackallers presumably because they were not surveyed in this particular year or were surveyed elsewhere; no Codner vessels are included, probably because by 1835 the family had much reduced its local interests. A record of Teignmouth exports and imports to and from Newfoundland is not available before 1853 but the following consignments, shipped by Matthew Warren on the schooner *Haberdine* in April 1854, may be taken as typical for this earlier period:

> 8 bags nails
> 12 cwt iron
> 1 crate earthenware
> 5 wheelbarrows
> 14 casks tar
> 12 cwt leather
> 30 'feet' apparel
> 3 tons twine and nets
> 16 hampers plants[7]

The Memorandum Book of John Rendell of Aller shows that at least one hogshead of cider was also shipped on this voyage although it does not appear in the port records since it was presumably for the consumption of the crew.[8]

The passenger trade to Newfoundland was given a fillip from time to time by the opportunities offered in the rebuilding of St John's after frequent fires. As a consequence of one of the last and most disastrous of these fires, the brigantine *Nancy* carried 'upwards of 60 passengers – mostly masons, carpenters etc (to St John's) for rebuilding the town'. Passenger traffic from Teignmouth was with Newfoundland rather than the American or Canadian mainland and, apart from Devon people returning home, it was almost entirely one way. The few natives of Newfoundland, called 'Indians' by contemporaries, who were persuaded to leave their homeland did not long survive European civilisation. George Links who died in Teignmouth in January 1843 was an example of the very few immigrants who were tempted. He was a passenger on one of Matthew Warren's vessels and 'during his passage, by his gentle manners, greatly endeared himself to all the ship's crew'. Mr. Warren took him to Exeter which he thought was 'the city of wonders' but, while left alone, he was 'robbed of all his little earnings'. Shortly afterwards George Links succumbed to smallpox and was 'borne to the grave by his late shipmates who all evinced sincere sorrow at his untimely fate'.[9]

The import trade from Newfoundland and Labrador[10] picked up after wartime interruption and there was a little transhipment traffic in cod oil, but a full outward cargo for a direct sailing was hard to come by. Agents or owners advertised in the local press:

> Now lying in the Port and bound for St John's Newfoundland the fast-sailing brig *Ben and Susan*. Stands A1 at Lloyds, has room for Thirty or Forty Tons of Goods and will positively sail, wind and weather permitting, the last of this month. For freight and passage apply to Mr Benjamin Partridge, Regent Cottage, Teignmouth.

Teignmouth was not as well placed for exports as Bristol where local vessels were sometimes advertised to load, like 'the fine substantial British-built brig *Maria* ... now loading at Bristol (January 1823);apply to Samuel Wm. Bibbins, Teignmouth'.[11] The *Susan*, also owned by the Bibbins family, seems to have been substituted for the *Maria* and she loaded a cargo which included soap, starch, felt and 'plated' hats, leather caps, blanketing and '200 garments'. Another Teignmouth vessel, the snow *Hazard*, 114 tons, was taking on a general cargo at about the same time. Altogether, 19 vessels loaded in Bristol for Newfoundland between February and September, 1823, and many of the exports they carried were unlikely to be on hand in Teignmouth: gunpowder and leadshot, turpentine and linseed oil, paint and candles, hair brushes and umbrellas.[12] Liverpool was soon to become a much larger exporting centre than either Teignmouth or Bristol; at least as early as 1830 Benjamin Bowring, who built up from Exeter a far more prosperous business than any Teignmouth merchant, was touring northern industrial towns for manufactured goods to send direct from the Mersey to his warehouses in St John's. In the 19th century Devon was no longer a substantial manufacturing area and for the last 50 years of the Teignmouth-Newfoundland connection trade was almost entirely one way.

The constant feature of the Newfoundland trade throughout three centuries was its harsh and dangerous character.Two dramatic incidents, both involving Teignmouth families, are typical of many. A Teignmouth resident, Thomas Sclater, wrote a letter in the *Western Times* of 15 September 1863, describing a voyage which was vivid in his memory after some 40 years:

> Mr John Bond of Teignmouth, Mr Edward Drake of Teignmouth and an Oxfordshire butcher brought over from Newfoundland a small schooner, only 22 tons, laden with fish. They called at the Western Islands [Azores] and sold their fish and loaded the little craft with oranges, and they

sold them at Falmouth and brought the craft to Teignmouth. I saw her many times in the harbour before they sailed her back to Newfoundland. Mr Bond was ill all the voyage and Mr Drake navigated the little craft by Mr Bond's instructions.

Those concerned in the second adventure, reported in the *Exeter Flying Post* of 30 August 1838, appear to have broken the unwritten rules of the sea. The schooner *Sicilian*, belonging to Matthew Warren, struck an iceberg off the coast of Labrador and went down in less than ten minutes. Twelve men took possession of a boat and rowed for the land. Nine men, two women and two children were left on the iceberg where they were rescued the next day by the *Abeona* (another Teignmouth vessel), and Captain Williams, 'had the satisfaction of saving thirteen human beings from a watery grave for it was supposed the iceberg would not hold together an hour longer'. The experience of the Bulley family emphasises the loss of property, as well as of life, which seemed almost inevitable in the Newfoundland trade. During a period when the family was heavily engaged, from 1817 to 1830, they had part-ownership of seven vessels, the smallest 56 tons and the largest 137 tons. Records show that the *Shamrock* was 'lost on the coast of Newfoundland'; the *Favourite*, the *Pylades*, the *Cochran* and the *Elizabeth* were all 'lost'; and the official statement for the *Unity* is more detailed but equally a tale of disaster. 'The above Vessel sailed from Oporto on 11 September for St Johns, Newfoundland, since when no Account has been received of the Vessel or her crew.' Of all the Bulley vessels only one, the *John and James* survived and was sold, perhaps to pay off the mortgages still owing on the others since it is unlikely that they were fully insured.

The export trade in clay, like the import trade from Newfoundland, revived fairly quickly after the Peace. Croydon's *Guide to Teignmouth*, published in 1821, remarks particularly on shipment to Liverpool 'from where it is sent to the neighbouring potteries'. The clay was brought down the Stover Canal and the river by barges such as those described in the previous chapter. The navigation channel was circuitous and obstructed and groundings were frequent but, despite such problems, the clay trade steadily increased and in the 1820s the annual export amounted to some 20,000 tons.

The export trade in granite grew more rapidly in the 1820s than that in clay. George Templer, owner of the Haytor quarries, constructed a tramway linking them to the Stover Canal which had been built by his father. This tramway opened on 16 September 1820 with 'the greatest party Dartmoor had ever seen'. A procession '1½ miles long' was led by

one of the famous sailing barges, decked with flowers and streamers, with an admiral standing at the bow. There were acrobats and itinerant minstrels, bands and decorated wagons. At Hay Tor they danced, performed, ate well and drank heavily ... George (Templer) made a great speech.[14]

Haytor granite was used for many London buildings, including part of London Bridge (now in Arizona), the British Museum, the National Gallery and the hall of Christ's Hospital. Because it was 'found to excel in beauty of colour, texture and durability' it was also in demand for a variety of other purposes, obelisks, for example, to commemorate George IV's embarkation from Ramsgate and the achievements of a city of London worthy, Alderman Waithman. A seller's market brought profit to George Templer with which he indulged his expensive tastes; he hunted, entertained munificently and brought an All-England cricket team to play Teignbridge village team, the first permanent cricket club in Devon, at Stover Park.

Sales of Haytor granite brought trade and revenue to the port of Teignmouth. The *Exeter and Plymouth Gazette* reported that

> Four granite stones, weighing from 12 to 14 tons each, have ... been shipped on board the *Perseverance*, London barge, for conveyance to Woolwich.

In the same year, 1831, according to the *Western Luminary*:

> One of the Steam Navigation Boats of 100 horse power has been sent down to tow 14 large barges from this place to London, loaded with blocks of granite for the new London bridge. This steam vessel is the largest that has ever visited this place.

To make loading at Teignmouth more efficient Templer built the New Quay near the mouth of the river; although the quay now almost dries out at low water and has no fixed equipment, contemporary prints show deep draught vessels alongside, apparently loading by means of a large crane. According to the *Western Luminary*, a public dinner was given at Teignmouth on 10 October 1820 in honour of George Templer 'on the completion of the new Quay there, connected with the gentleman's canal and railroad'. The company consisted of 'about 100 individuals of the first respectability in the neighbourhood'. This celebration may have been slighty premature, but the New Quay was ready for use early in 1821 because in March of that year George Templer signed a Memorandum of Agreement with John MacCarthy of Teignmouth by which MacCarthy was allowed to store up to 200 tons of 'patent paving stones' on the quay for a maximum period of one month whilst awaiting shipment. MacCarthy promised to pay one shilling a ton for the use of the canal, wharves and cranes. The base of one of the cranes referred to in this agreement still stands alongside the overgrown Ventiford basin. George Templer was also responsible for the development of the iron ore trade through Teignmouth. He granted the use of the granite tramway and the Stover canal to 'a house in the iron trade' which planned to work the Dannamore iron mine near the granite quarries. The ore was said to be 'of superior quality' and by 1827 was 'an article of export from Teignmouth for Wales, for the purpose of being smelted'.[15]

Another flourishing trade at this time, a seasonal one, was the import of limestone for the numerous limekilns in the Teign estuary. A recent investigation has shown that 15 limekilns existed around the harbour and river and that most of them were probably working in the first half of the 19th century. Demand was high because by 1810 or so Devon farmers appreciated the value of lime in neutralising their generally acid soil and the majority generally considered it more effective for this purpose than the local sea sand. The limestone enterprise in south Devon is described by the Reverend Thomas Moore, whose *History of Devonshire* was published in 1829, in terms which have a period flavour. He writes that south-west Devon 'abounds with lime-works' and that the cliffs at Berry Head and Babbacombe supply the kilns on the Exe and Teign:

> The artist and the man of taste may possibly turn from works of this kind with something like disgust, lamenting that the ruthless hand of commerce is permitted, with provoking unconcern, to demolish by piecemeal the grand and magnificent ornaments of the coast, and that the owners of these splendid scenes, with sordid love of gain absorbing all other considerations, are literally

retailing the picturesque and beautiful by weight and measure; whilst the friends of industry and productive labour will observe only in such operations a rich increase of agricultural produce, and consequently of general benefit.[16]

'The friends of industry and productive labour' could fairly point out that this trade gave employment not only to those concerned with the delivery of the limestone, but also to those supplying the fuel for the kilns, culm from South Wales, the imports of which were at least equal to those of coal for domestic use. This very active culm trade from South Wales to south coast ports like Teignmouth encouraged a revival of the scheme, first proposed in 1810, to build a 'Grand Ship Canal' from Bridgwater to Seaton which would give 'a more certain, safe, quick and cheap conveyance to ... ports in the English Channel than the passage round Land's End'.[17] Although the canal was never built, the limestone and culm traffic continued until the kilns closed down as the demand for lime declined. Many of the small vessels which engaged in the stone trade, described in the Register as smacks, cutters, sloops or barges, were owned in Teignmouth. As late as 1869 the barge *Wonder*, owned by S. T. Bassett, brought in 1,292 tons of limestone in 43 trips during the year. From time to time, boats which ferried stone across the bay from Babbacombe to Teignmouth picked up a more profitable cargo, kegs of brandy which had been sunk by smugglers to await collection; on one occasion, according to the reminiscences of a local clergyman, coastguards intervened and the barge, valued at £700, was confiscated by the government.[18]

The export trade in clay and granite and the import trade in limestone, culm and coal was supplemented by general coastwise trade, particularly with London. For a short period in the 1820s the steam packet *Sir Francis Drake* called off Teignmouth on passage from Plymouth to Portsmouth, at which port goods were transhipped for London, 'the line of canal from the Metropolis to Portsmouth being completed', and passengers continued their journey by coach. More typical London trade at this time is illustrated by papers belonging to Captain William Chambers, R.N., who stayed in Dawlish. He received from Captain Beazley of Teignmouth '3 matted packages, 1 small case, 2 boxes with parcel tied on' for which freight was 19s. 9d., harbour dues 3s. and quay dues 1s. 6d. and dues 7d. The bills are headed 'United Shipping Co. of Teignmouth' and the list of vessels, sailing from Fenning's Wharf, London Bridge, includes the *Feronia*, *Ant* and *Triton*. These were probably sailing vessels, not steam packets, but a tradesman's note suggests that they sailed to fixed and regular schedules:

J. Ballantyne begs respectfully to acknowledge receipt of Captain Chambers' note and has this day sent his parcel to Fenning's Wharf from whence the vessel sails for Teignmouth on Friday next.[19]

When the war ended other naval officers made their homes in Teignmouth or nearby, attracted by the activities of the harbour in which many of them shared. Among them was Sir Edward Pellew whose expedition to suppress the corsairs of Algiers earned him the title of Lord Exmouth; Pellew was strongly attached to Teignmouth and apparently chose the title 'Exmouth' because 'Teignmouth' was already in use. Lady Exmouth bought West Cliff House (now Bitton House) on her husband's behalf and built the Orangery which was described by a knowledgeable contemporary as 'very handsome' and 'a very complete thing of its kind'; local people subscribed to its restoration when it had become derelict. Other naval officers who settled in or near Teignmouth around this time included Admirals Wight and Thornborough and Captains Brine and Tobin. It is possible that Thomas Luny, who leased a house in Market Street (now Teign Street) and was a prolific marine artist, had been a purser in one of Captain Tobin's ships. Many well-to-do families were attracted to Teignmouth by discreet advertising on behalf of speculators with land to sell, such as Robert Jordan. As early as the summer of 1789, when sea bathing was first becoming an aristocratic pastime, 'a correspondent' wrote in the *Exeter Flying Post*:

> Bathing in the sea, and drinking salt water, having been attended in many cases with great success, the following case is mentioned (among many others) for the benefit of the public. The Reverend Mr Partridge came to this place for the benefit of a complaint he had long laboured under, being deprived of the use of his legs and arms, and was obliged to be lifted into his whiskey ... By bathing a few weeks, and drinking the salt water every other morning, he recovered the use of his limbs ... and before he left Teignmouth was entirely restored.

Croydon's Guide to the Watering Places on the Coast between the Exe and the Dart, published in 1821 and one of the first of such publications to be widely circulated, drew attention to the varied facilities which Teignmouth offered its visitors: bathing machines, hot baths, sedan chairs, donkeys and pleasure boats. Mr. Croydon himself set up a Library and Reading Room in a building, now occupied by W. H. Smith, which stocked four London newspapers, as well as *Lloyd's List* for those who needed to be informed on the more commercial aspects of life by the sea. Croydon was also, together with other public figures such as Lord Exmouth and Serjeant Praed, a subscriber to the Assembly Rooms where 'one hundred couples may dance with ease'. Horse racing was introduced on the Den in 1823 and a few years later Mr. Kean, 'the celebrated tragedian', landed from his yacht at Teignmouth to perform in one of the two theatres, possibly the Athenaeum, now used by a Boxing Club and where the remains of an ornate portico are evidence of past glories. The Regatta held in August 1829 was claimed to be the first in England and followed the custom of the time by arranging rowing races in three classes: 'gentlemen amateurs', clerks and tradesmens' assistants, and 'professional boatmen'.

New houses were built and 'cottages' rented for the summer. 'Hermosa', for example, was a much admired mansion and was situated in 'a lawn studded with ornamental Trees and Shrubs ... Hot and Greenhouses with Orange and Lemon Trees in full bearing'. Bishop Phillpotts stayed in 'a pretty villa engaged for his reception' and made his home at Bishopstowe, near Torquay, which he preferred to his stately but decrepit palace in Exeter. John Keats, on the other hand, who came to Teignmouth in search of health, developed no love for the place and complained bitterly about 'the abominable Devonshire Weather ... splashy, rainy, misty, snowy, foggy, haily, floody; the flowers here wait as naturally for the Rain twice a day as the muscles (*sic*) do for the Tide'. He was also critical of the local libraries and theatre but wrote nostalgically to Teignmouth friends when he returned to Hampstead: 'you might praise it ... in the manner of a grammatical exercise – *The* trees *are* full – *the* den *is* crowded – *the* boats *are* sailing – *the* musick *is* playing'. The activities of the harbour did not greatly interest him but he made passing reference to the Newfoundland trade in his letters and in one of them included a few lines of verse which commemorated seamen safely home:

> A white sail shews above the green-head cliff
> Moves round the point, and throws her anchor stiff.
> The Mariners join hymn with those on land.[20]

The material needs of residents and visitors contributed to the trade of the port. Among the miscellaneous cargoes brought into Teignmouth were building materials, particularly Portland stone and Cornish slate, and luxuries such as wine and Mediterranean fruit as well as those items described collectively as 'groceries'. Coastal export trade was mainly in minerals, iron, lead and manganese ore in addition to clay and granite, but also included manufactured goods such as chimney-pieces, made of 'marble' from the Chudleigh and Harcombe rocks, the production of which was perhaps stimulated by local demand from the new stately homes. The population of East and West Teignmouth increased from 2,012 persons in 1801 to 5,149 in 1851 and that of the parish of St Nicholas from 585 to 1,297 in the same period, but these census figures are not wholly reliable because they may have included visitors and other temporary residents. Nor does the evidence for an increase of population, amenities and trade entirely obscure the harsher side of life in Teignmouth. While the correspondent of the leading Exeter newspaper learned 'with pleasure' that balls and parties were in contemplation which would 'promote social intercourse and rational gaiety', some townsfolk faced up to very different prospects. One illustration of the conflict between rich and poor was the long drawn-out dispute early in the century between the congregations of East and West Teignmouth churches. The churchwardens and some parishioners of East Teignmouth sought to exclude the people of West Teignmouth from the afternoon service in their fashionable church of St Michael's so that seats could be allotted to visitors; the argument was only settled when St James's, the parish church of West Teignmouth, was given its own vicar in 1862.

More direct evidence of contrasting circumstances comes, in the first half of the 19th century, from Petitions to the Corporation of Trinity House and from the Monthly Poor Book of West Teignmouth. These records raise the curtain slightly on the living conditions of those who shared neither in the rewards of maritime enterprise nor in the opportunities for 'rational gaiety'. John Willcocks of Shaldon, for example, in 1821 requested a pension from Trinity House for himself and his wife because, after having served for many years as boy and seaman on the brig *Fly*, he was shipwrecked off Newfoundland and 'after being in the Boat for seven days his legs were so frost burnt as to require amputation of both above the Ancles'; he had 'no Pension or Relief from any other Public Charity or Company'. William Williams was a seaman in the Teignmouth-Newfoundland trade for 30 years and then left the sea 'in consequence of his inability to go aloft'. He applied for a pension when he was 72 because, although he had his own 'cot-house' at Ipplepen, his 'savings were very nearly exhausted'. The lot of seamen's widows and families appears to have been at least as hard. The petition of Jane Wreyford of West Teignmouth, aged 61, stated that her husband went to sea at 13 and 'was employed in the Sea Service for fifty-five years' until he was drowned in 1847; she was left with 'no means of support 'except donations from her friends'. Mary Adams' husband, who lived at Bishopsteignton, had risen to be master of the *Mercury* but, even so, she had nothing to support herself and her two young children apart from 'what she earns by her hard and honest Industry by her little School and at her Needle'.

To the Honourable the Master, Wardens, *and* Assistants *of the* CORPORATION *of* TRINITY-HOUSE, *of* Deptford-Strond.

The Humble Petition of John Willcocks — Aged 54 years — residing with his wife at Shaldon near Teignmouth in the Port of Exeter —

Here put the Name, Age, and Habitation of the Petitioner, and, if a Widow, her Husband's Christian Name.

Sheweth,

THAT your Petitioner was bred to the Sea, and served there as a Boy and Seaman for many years — and more particularly on Board the Fly Brig — Robt. Selmon Master from Lisbon to Newfld. in which Vessell he was Shipwreck'd in the Ice on the Banks of Newfld. — & after being in the Boat for seven days his legs were so frost burnt as to require amputation of both above the Ancles —

Here put Qualifications and Circumstances, with the Number of Children, (if any) and their respective Ages; together with the Name of the Ship and Master he served on board, and what Voyage.

That your Petitioner is not now able to support himself & wife — without the Charity of this CORPORATION, having no Pension or Relief from any other Public Charity or Company, except Parochial Relief —

Add Family, if any.

To be particularly set forth.

Your Petitioner therefore most humbly prays that he — may be admitted a Pensioner of this CORPORATION, at the usual Allowance,

John Willcocks

Your Petitioner will ever pray, &c.

We whose Names are hereunto subscribed, know the Petitioner, and Circumstances, or have received such Information concerning him as may be fully relied on; so that believing the Contents of this Petition to be true, and that the Petitioner is a Person of good Character and Reputation, We recommend him as a proper Object of the CORPORATION's Charity.

As Witness our Hands, the 25 — Day of October 1821

This is to be signed by Younger Brethren, *or others well known to the* Corporation.

J. Wright
W. Ramsay
Richd. Wilkins

Sub Commissioners of Pilotage at the Port of Exeter

Fig. 3 Petition to Trinity House for a pension, 1820s.

Despite the charity dispensed by Trinity House and despite self-help by membership of sick clubs such as 'Babb's Club' and 'The Heart-in-Hand', some Teignmouth seamen became dependent on parish relief. The Monthly Poor Book of West Teignmouth, extant from 1825 to 1831, shows that Thomas Prowse, an 'old seaman, both him and his wife blind', was granted an allowance of 3s. 6d. a week, as was Thomas Long, an 'old seaman, rheumatic'. Some seafarers appear to have ended their days in the Poor House, like Philip Harris, aged 88, an 'old infirm seaman', who was perhaps more fortunate than his fellow inmate, David Davidson, who earned his keep by gathering rags and killing cats for their skins. Mothers and children were given help when their husbands and fathers had been drowned at sea or 'absconded' and a long family, such as 'Heath's Family', received a weekly supplement because the breadwinner was 'away at sea at 38/- per month'. Those in irregular work needed help in meeting family problems: a lumper had an allowance for a crippled child and a pilot for a daughter with 'the King's evil' who was unfit to be bound apprentice. Women received help for a variety of reasons: Mary Hunt, aged 21, because she was 'with child by Lord Carnarvon's coachman' and an older person of whom one of the overseers wrote feelingly, 'she is a horrible woman, never works'.[21]

One of the causes of unemployment and poverty among local seamen was thought to be the shortcomings of the harbour and river navigation. In 1824 a public meeting was called to solicit subscriptions for deepening the River Teign 'so that Barges and other Craft going to and from Newton and the Stover Canal may navigate the River at Neap as well as at Spring Tides'. At Neap tides, it was said

> the lighters are entirely prevented in their passage for several days, and for other days ... can only perform their trips with reduced freights or loadings.

Not only would merchants and ship-owners benefit from an effective dredging policy, but also

> great accommodation will be afforded to the public generally as the market boats will be enabled, by saving an hour up and an hour down, to remain ... two hours longer at Newton.

Whiteway, Watts & Co. headed the subscription list with a donation of £25. Proposals for deepening the river were closely linked with those for improving the harbour since

> the bar is extremely dangerous, affords only 10 feet 6 inches of water at neap tides, and is then impassable for vessels of upwards of 80 Tons burthen.[22]

Lloyd's Casualty Reports show that even local vessels like the *Three Williams* and the *Good Intent*, whose masters knew the harbour well, sometimes grounded.[23] Foreign vessels more frequently came to grief and the reputation of the harbour suffered. When a French vessel, *Le Bienheureux*, was wrecked on the bar in January 1826 a local character with an eye to the main chance took advantage of others' misfortunes: 'a fellow with mustachios' swore an affidavit that he was the unfortunate captain and collected £18 before he was apprehended.[24]

Threats from Exeter may have given urgency to the need for improvements to the harbour. The port of Exeter never fully recovered from the effects of the Napoleonic

War, but the deepening of the Ship Canal and the opening of a floating basin in 1830 led to a temporary revival of foreign and coastwise trade. On 4 August 1831 the *Exeter Flying Post* reported the arrival in the new basin of the *Packet*, 'a fine brig of 200 tons drawing twelve feet of water'; she arrived direct from Monte Video with hides and horns and, more threatening from Teignmouth's point of view, 'when discharged she will take a cargo of pipe clay from this port to Liverpool'. A final warning came when the French Vice-Consulate was transferred from Teignmouth to Exeter in 1835.

In 1836, Teignmouth merchants promoted a Bill for 'improving, maintaining and regulating the Port and Harbour of Teignmouth and the Navigation of the River Teign'; a body of Harbour Commissioners was given appropriate powers for this purpose, saving the rights of the lords of the manor of East and West Teignmouth and, a more significant proviso in the light of later controversy, the privileges of 'the Mayor Bailiffs and the Commonalty of the City of Exeter'.[25] The 21 Commissioners were representative of landed rather than maritime interests, but they set about improving the harbour and river with enthusiasm. They invited funds through deeds poll bearing interest at four per cent and, despite a slow response, they appointed a part-time Clerk, a Harbour Master, an Engineer and a Collector of Dues. When the master of the schooner *Byron* evaded the Collector he was pursued to Liverpool by one of the Commissioners. Members carefully considered whether their resources would enable them to hire a steam dredger from Dartmouth and they appointed a committee to recommend where moorings should be placed for the convenience of vessels loading in mid-stream. They also sought an opinion from Sir John Rennie on the most effective way to improve the harbour entrance; an agent was instructed to 'make him an offer of £150 but not to be particular as to £5.' Unfortunately these initiatives coincided with a period of depression which provoked a memorial 'praying for enquiry as to the propriety of expenditure in the harbour'.[26]

The depression in the late 1830s was caused by a variety of factors, some of them peculiar to Teignmouth. George Templer, architect of the tramway from Haytor quarries, while equally ready to apply new inventions, was not such a good business man as his father, James Templer. Largely as a result of his personal extravagance, the Stover estates, canal and tramway were sold in 1829 to the Duke of Somerset and Templer became the chief Devonshire agent for the company which had been set up, with a capital of £200,000, to work the quarries. As such he seems to have been incompetent for at least one contract delivery was delayed and blocks cut to wrong measurements.[27] These business shortcomings, combined with competition from Cornish and Scottish quarries adjacent to the sea, caused a drastic reduction of trade, and shipment from Teignmouth virtually ceased by 1840. When the agent for the Duke of Somerset, E. J. Bearne, was questioned by the Select Committee on the Teignmouth Harbour Bill in 1853 he said that no granite had been carried on the canal 'recently' and that the quarries ceased to work 'about ten years ago'. The closure he referred to may have been a temporary rather than a permanent shutdown and there is evidence that the quarries re-opened later, but shipment from Teignmouth did not revive.[28]

The Newfoundland trade also declined in the 1830s, but not as sharply. Many of the Teign estuary merchants transferred their business activities to Liverpool, although some retained their personal links with Teignmouth and Shaldon. The Bulley family, for example, were prosperous Newfoundland merchants and part-owners of the schooner *Shamrock*, the full-rigged ship *Favorite* and the brig *Unity*, their partner being John Job of Liverpool. After all three local vessels were lost, the last in 1830, the firm of Bulley & Job concentrated their business in Liverpool and Newfoundland. But Richard Bulley, who was master of the *Isabella Ridley*, landed his wife when his vessel was off Teignmouth on her way from Hamburg to Newfoundland in the summer of 1860 and had trouble with the Customs when she took ashore four bottles of spirits, four bottles of wine, an easy chair and a chiffonier which she had apparently purchased in Germany.

Other evidence for the transfer of business to Liverpool comes from the records of the brig *Heroine* jointly owned by 'William Tapley of Teignmouth, merchant, and William Tapley the Younger late of West Teignmouth, mariner, but now of Liverpool, merchant'. The full-rigged ship *John Blake* was registered in the port of Exeter as owned by John Blake (53 shares) and William Churchward (11 shares), 'mariners of St Nicholas': by 1843 the mariners were described as 'late of St Nicholas but last of Liverpool'. The brigantine *Margaret*, owned by William Vallance of Newton Abbot and trading to Newfoundland, was re-registered in Liverpool in 1840. Some years later William Wilking of Dawlish sold the schooner *Queen* to 'Wm. James Lamport and George Holt of Liverpool co-partners trading under the firm of Lamport and Holt'.[29] Other local merchants moved to Dartmouth or gave up altogether: the Codners, for example, transferred their activities to Dartmouth in the 1830s and the Blackallers stopped trading, perhaps because, as their memorials suggest, they had no heirs to succeed them.

One reason why the Teignmouth-Newfoundland trade declined at this time was probably the difficulty in raising capital. Teignmouth appears to have been an early centre of banking, but it was overshadowed by Exeter where five banks had been established by 1800, all closely associated with the woollen trade.[30] Benjamin Babbage, a banking pioneer and father of the mathematical genius Charles Babbage, was a Teignmouth man but there is no evidence that he did any business locally. Robert Jordan collaborated with his fellow solicitors in offering small loans on personal security and Langmead and Jordans Bank later issued banknotes which drew attention to the town's maritime importance by portraying the attractive, if unrealistic, scene of a brig under full sail passing the Ness headland. These are unlikely to have circulated far afield and the bank had failed by 1840. Advances for ship-owning in Teignmouth in the 1820s and 1830s were mostly made by a firm of bankers based on Newton Abbot, Messrs. Wise, Farwell, Baker and Bentall; this firm appears to have had close links with the clay trade and one of the partners, Ayshford Wise, had a life interest in five acres of clay-bearing land at Kingsteignton and rented a clay cellar at Hackney.

Particulars given in the Exeter Register of British Ships show how financing was done. The firm of Wise, Farwell, Baker and Bentall, or individual members of it, advanced money, for example, to Andrew Howard, 'merchant of St Nicholas', for the purchase of the schooner *Prince Regent* and the snow *Minerva*. The list of shareholders in the full-rigged ship *Orange Branch* in 1824 illustrates the combination of individual and collective investment:

> 8 shares Andrew Howard, Shaldon, merchant
> 4 shares Francis Hernaman, Woolborough, merchant
> 16 shares Ayshford Wise of Ford, Esquire
> 16 shares Nicholas Baker, Newton Abbot, banker

20 shares Wise, Baker, Bentall and Farwell all of Newton Abbot (trading) as Wise and Co., bankers

Between 1825 and 1837 this banking partnership financed 10 Teignmouth vessels by taking up shares or giving loans on mortgage. Apparently their last, and possibly biggest, loan was to William Row of St Nicholas for the barque *Speculator* in 1837; shortly afterwards they went bankrupt. A note in the Exeter Register explains that trustees took over on behalf of the creditors:

... Francis Hernaman of Newton Abbot and Torquay, banker, John Vicary of Newton Bushel, tanner, and William Creed the Younger of Abbotskerswell, gentleman, assignees of the Estate and Effects of Ayshford Wise of Ford House, Nicholas Baker of Newton Bushel and William Searle Bentall of Totnes, bankrupts who carried on business at Newton Abbot under the firm of Wise, Farwell, Baker and Bentall ...

The public examination of Wise, Baker and Bentall at Exeter did not suggest any corrupt behaviour and the assignees were able to do reasonably well for the 650 creditors; they made a satisfactory deal with the family of Ayshford Wise and arranged for the *Speculator* to be sold by auction at Gloucester. It seems probable that the failure of Wise & Co., like that of Langmead and Jordan, came about as a result of the national and international economic situation. The harmful effects on trade of speculation and unsophisticated credit management were aggravated by disorders in Canada and Chartist riots at home. According to the *Exeter Flying Post*, which quoted reports from London, the year 1837 was marked by 'great vicissitudes in foreign commerce', the forced sale of vessels and 'an almost complete extinction of confidence'. Laurence Maxton, who was appointed Customs Officer at Teignmouth after having been attached to Exeter and also acted as honorary agent of the Shipwrecked Fishermen and Mariners' Benevolent Society, was in a good position to assess the state of maritime trade and he declared in his evidence to the Select Committee on the Teignmouth Harbour Bill that 'in 1837, 1838 and 1839 there was a great depression all over the country' which had adversely affected local trade.[31]

Within a few years Teignmouth's trade had picked up dramatically and the decade from the early 1840s to the early 1850s was probably the most prosperous in the port's history. This prosperity was the work of the new Harbour Commission and of two outstanding national figures who arrived in Teignmouth at this time, one on visits and the other to settle permanently: Isambard Brunel and J. B. Mansfield.

Chapter Five

A Peak of Prosperity: 1840-1854

By 1842 the Harbour Commissioners felt confident enough to reduce their rates and advertised the new ones in the *Shipping and Mercantile Gazette*. In 1844 they congratulated themselves that both trade and revenue had increased and granted the Collector a gratuity for his diligence. Work on the construction of a second canal, the Hackney 'cut', had been held up by legal as well as financial difficulties but appears to have been completed by 1843: it enabled barges to get within a short distance of the mines around Kingsteignton and eventually 16 cellars, with a capacity of some 7,000 tons, were built to store the clay. Lightermens' cottages, the foundations of which may still be seen, were built at the entrance to the canal close to the *Passage House Inn*.[1] In Teignmouth harbour the Commissioners laid down four 'patent screw moorings' and removed silt from the New Quay. They also resolved to erect a lighthouse and the work was completed in 1845 at a cost of £196 7s., the surveyor's fee being met by the Earl of Devon, himself a Commissioner. This initiative did not receive a unanimous welcome and one local critic declared that 'the feeble glare emitted from the lantern is of no service by night, except it be to light the fishes to their sandy beds'. But the equipment and structure of the lighthouse apparently satisfied an Admiralty investigation and the original building, now supplemented by other aids to mariners, still stands as a monument to the Commissioners' zeal.

Commercial traffic on the river benefited from the Commissioners' dredging policy. A list of 'goods at present conveyed on the Teign', prepared as supporting evidence for the 1844 prospectus of the Torquay and Newton Abbot Railway, shows a varied and considerable riverborne trade. Apart from clay, commodities carried in one year amounted to almost 10,000 tons:

Iron	250 tons
Salt	200 tons
General groceries	1,000 tons
Bark	250 tons
Hides	200 tons
Ironmongery	50 tons
Coals and culm	6,000 tons
Timber and Corn	2,000 tons[2]

This growing traffic on the river was threatened by the advance of the railway from Exeter and the Harbour Commissioners asked the Earl of Devon to watch their interests in the House of Lords.

Whatever the likely effect of rail competition on the Commissioners' revenue, the coming of the railway was welcomed by most local people. Brunel himself, the driving force behind the South Devon Railway, took trouble to woo public opinion. At 'a very numerous and highly respectable meeting' in Teignmouth on 31 January

1844 he argued that the coastal route was preferable to the direct inland one from Exeter to Newton Abbot because 'experience had shown him that it was necessary to carry a line through populous towns'. Brunel may have had his tongue in his cheek when he said that the deep cut through the heart of Teignmouth would remove densely-packed houses and so create 'a healthiness to the inhabitants otherwise unobtainable by the free circulation of air which this occasions'. Brunel's proposal was carried with acclamation; only Mr. Praed, who lived close by what is now Bitton Park, objected because his house and grounds would be cut off from the river.[3] In a little over two years, on 21 May 1846, the first train arrived at Teignmouth.

Having won the argument, Brunel took a special interest in Teignmouth, rented a house near the beach 'to sojourn awhile in this salubrious place' and negotiated with local solicitors, Tozers, to buy land for a permanent residence at Watcombe. Because he was known to be well disposed the Harbour Commissioners asked Brunel for advice and he replied in a very friendly way:

I should be delighted (to give advice) for the sake of benefiting a port of great value to the South Devon Railway, and without involving the parties in any expence which would be inconvenient to their limited means.

Brunel modestly added that 'I have always known Sir John Rennie as the advising Engineer (of the Harbour Commission) and I would not interfere in any way with his position'.[4]

One of Brunel's main contractors was George Hennet and the two men worked closely together on engineering works for the Bristol-Gloucester Railway, the Bristol dock gates and the atmospheric experiment for the railway from Exeter to Totnes for which Hennet supplied the cast-iron tubes. George Hennet's association with Teignmouth was even closer than Brunel's and when he died a correspondent commented in the *Exeter Flying Post* on 30 April 1857 that 'Teignmouth has lost one of her warmest and best friends'. The service which local people particularly appreciated was his leadership in the fight to win independence from the port of Exeter.

Agitation for independence was nothing new but all previous campaigns had failed. The Teignmouth case rested on two separate but related issues: the collection of customs duties and imposition of town dues. Teignmouth merchants complained about the need to travel to Exeter to deal with customs formalities and, more emphatically, of the injustice of the right claimed by Exeter Corporation to collect dues on imports without accepting any responsibility for the maintenance or improvement of the harbour.

On a number of occasions groups of local merchants and ship-owners petitioned the Lords Commissioners of the Treasury for the provision of separate customs facilities. As early as 1799 the indefatigable Robert Jordan, who was constantly seeking advantage for the townsfolk and for himself, told his patron, Sir James Wright, that 'several merchants of this Town and Shaldon have lately spoken to me on the practicality of establishing a Customhouse in this place'. He explained to Sir James

the great inconveniences and hardships the merchants now labour under by being obliged to travel so far as Exeter to transact their concerns of entering and clearing out their Ships and

Goods ... It has often happened that, while the master of a vessel has been waiting to clear out, an easterly wind has sprung up and prevented him from sailing for more than a fortnight.

It was typical of Robert Jordan that he offered himself for the post of officer-in-charge at a salary of £100 a year, instead of the usual one of £200, 'the merchants in general wishing that I should fill this important Place'.[5]

Jordan's London contacts appear to have been remiss on this occasion and it was not until the 1840s that the agitation effectively revived. Supporting the petition presented in February 1849 were no less than 15 persons who described themselves as ship-owners as well as a cross-section of local inhabitants which included solicitors and surgeons, a schoolmaster, a bookseller, an innkeeper and a relieving officer.[6] The petition presented on 5 July 1852 was even more impressive in its apparent strength of support:

Noblemen, Magistrates, Gentlemen, Proprietors of Land, Merchants, Shipowners, Traders and other Inhabitants of the towns of Teignmouth and Shaldon, Newton Abbot, Newton Bushel, Ashburton, Chudleigh ... and their Vicinities

The 'memorialists' pointed out the natural advantages of the port of Teignmouth and emphasised its efficiency achieved by the building of canals and harbour works, as well as by the provision of a steam-tug, the only one between Plymouth and Portsmouth. They referred to the locally-owned fleet of roughly 100 vessels, many of them engaged in colonial and foreign trade, and they described the growing commerce of the port – foreign imports of timber, oil, fish, salt, hides, bark, corn, apples, wine, spirits and fruits; coastwise imports of coal and culm; exports of clay, granite, iron ore, lead ore, manganese, leather and wool to Ireland, London and other ports of the United Kingdom. With expansionist optimism, they drew attention to the developing connections with towns in the hinterland and to recent examples of industrial enterprise: the Dartmoor railway, the main line connection with the quay and the establishment of a large company in the parish of Hennock which had imported three steam engines for working the mines.

As on previous occasions, the Exeter Collector was asked to comment on the petition and he wrote rather testily:

This is not the first, second or third time ... upon which we have been called upon to report ...

He criticised the exaggerations and inaccuracies in the petitioners' case: only 37 vessels were owned in Teignmouth, not 100 as claimed (a discrepancy perhaps explained by his very narrow definition of Teignmouth to exclude the surrounding villages); the Dartmoor 'railway' was drawn by horses, not by locomotives; and some of the towns and villages said to have a trading connection with Teignmouth were extremely small, like Bovey Tracey, 'a very small village ... of not the smallest consideration'. Altogether, he maintained, Teignmouth could not bear comparison with Exeter, 'Exeter being we may say the Emporium of the West'.[7]

The dispute appears to have been settled by considerations of economy. The petitioners had wisely offered to guarantee 'the Honourable Board' against additional expense and one of their number, George Hennet, had started to build warehouses with cellars underneath which could be taken over as bonded stores without cost to the revenue. Within two months, and despite the Exeter Collector's objections, the Clerk to the Teignmouth Harbour Commission, who had worked hard to co-ordinate joint action, received the letter he had been hoping for:

> I am directed by their Lordships (the Lords Commissioners of the Treasury) to acquaint you that my Lords have signified their approval of Teignmouth being constituted an independent Port ... upon warehouses and vaults being fitted up.[8]

This grant of independence was an occasion for much local rejoicing and people crowded into Teignmouth from neighbouring towns and villages for the celebrations on Tuesday 14 September 1852. Stations on the Exeter line were besieged by intending passengers and at Dawlish 'a stone truck was hooked on behind' one of the midday trains in which second-class passengers were glad to travel. The procession comes to life in an account in the *Illustrated London News* which carries a picture with a banner in the foreground, inscríbed 'Industry, Perseverance and Independence':

> A Royal Salute was fired from the Den and a procession was formed headed by a herald on a white horse ... then followed sailors, the masters of various vessels; fishermen, gardeners, bands of music, harbour and river masters ... deputations of sail and rope makers; smiths at work with anvil and forge; coach builders; maltsters with barley; plasterers with models of villas; builders and sawyers at work ... a cider merchant and barrel; model railway and engine; shipbuilders, each man carrying a tool or symbol of his department ...

The procession extended the circumference of the Den and was 'the most gorgeous display witnessed in South Devon since the passing of the Reform Bill'. Newspaper correspondents commented on the attractive decorations throughout the town, especially on the front of Croydon's Library, and the magnificence of the dinner, for 300 guests, in the Assembly Rooms. Speeches included one by J. H. Mackenzie, Clerk to the Harbour Commissioners, who pointed out that Teignmouth was 'the first port touched by the broad gauge on its road from London to Land's End' and, once the bar was removed, the harbour 'would be open to all nations and warehouses would be filled with goods'. George Hennet, in an equally optimistic speech, said that, if Teignmouth people 'would but unanimously put their shoulders to the wheel', 'their exports and imports ... should not be in tens of thousands of tons, nor in forty thousands of tons, but in four hundred thousand tons a year', a forecast achieved more than a century later.

The contribution of the Harbour Commissioners to these jollifications appears to have been a modest £50, an expenditure which was agreed to without dissent.[9] One immediate result of independence was the compilation of a Register of British Ships, meticulously kept until the present day. The first entry, appropriately enough, was the full-rigged ship *Harriet* of 925 tons, recently built at Quebec, classified A1 at Lloyd's and owned by George Hennet; although too large ever to enter the harbour, she was a symbol of success.

The struggle for exemption from Exeter town dues was more bitter than the campaign for local customs facilities and the outcome much less satisfactory. The Corporation of Exeter claimed that the town dues were collected in an arbitrary and irregular way, and one of the lessees, a Mr. Pollard, instructed his collector to make the best bargain he could. Slates, for example, were charged at ½d. a dozen although some were 'as large as a hat and some as large as a table'. There was confusion about dues on coal because apparently it was sometimes measured in

Newcastle chaldrons and sometimes in Winchester chaldrons and 'one is nearly double the other'. A leading Teignmouth importer, T. W. B. Hutchings, who was a coal and salt merchant as well as a ship-owner, complained feelingly about the whole system:

> 'I told him [Mr. Pollard] how really trying it was, how very trying it was ... I asked Mr. Gidley [Town Clerk of Exeter] very civilly if he would be kind enough to furnish me with a legal schedule'. Mr. Gidley consented if Mr. Hutchings would display it on a board in the town. 'I said No I will not. I wrote a Letter to the Corporation but I never received an answer to this day.'

John Vicary of Newton Abbot, who described himself as a tanner and woolstapler and was an importer of hides on a large scale, declared that if Exeter Corporation continued these unjust impositions then, as far as he was concerned, 'Teignmouth might as well be in Van Diemen's Land'.[10] Matthew Warren, one of the family of Newfoundland merchants whose activities have been recounted earlier, had already refused to pay and had been prosecuted by the corporation; he lost both his original case and his appeal to the Queen's Bench.

Some of the Teignmouth ship-owners and merchants tried other methods and at one stage presented Exeter Corporation with a silver salver for the use of the Mayor during his year of office.[11] The Harbour Commissioners, under the guidance of their Clerk, tried patiently to work out a compromise and the Clerk reported that he had 'accidently' met in Fore Street, Exeter, a representative of the Corporation who assured him that the members wished to behave reasonably. So, after some delay, it was resolved, on the casting vote of the chairman, to offer the Corporation £2,000 for the relinquishment of all rights. The offer was refused. For the Teignmouth Harbour Commissioners and the traders they represented there was now no alternative but to go ahead with their private bill and run the risk of Exeter's opposition.

The Commission mustered before the parliamentary committee an impressive array of witnesses which included landowners and the chairman of the South Devon Railway as well as merchants and ship-owners, but they seem to have been unlucky in their senior counsel who was not well briefed and was outmanoeuvred by his opponents. The Town Clerk, for example, quoted effectively the judgment of Lord Denman in the Warren Case that 'evidence (in favour of Exeter) was clear, unambiguous and uninterrupted'. In an ingenious but somewhat questionable final move he asked leave to call upon a Mr. John Daw, who was said to be present by chance and gave his opinion, based on wide experience as a surveyor, that the Devonshire mining industry would not be adversely affected by the town dues. Teignmouth counsel admitted defeat and compensation was agreed at £3,000, whereupon the Teignmouth Harbour Bill received the royal assent in June 1853. The Harbour Commission raised a loan to meet this payment and added it to their existing debt of £5,600. Interest charges, as well as occasional demands from bondholders for repayment, were a constant source of worry to the Commission for the next 60 years. These worries were in the future; for the present those associated with the port were encouraged by the mood of confidence which had been inspired by the patronage of Brunel and the enterprise of George Hennet.

Teignmouth also greatly benefited from the arrival in 1849 of a shipbuilder who had already begun to win a national reputation, J. B. Mansfield. Mansfield, after working with his father at Lyme Regis and at the Government Yard in Portsmouth, was attracted to Teignmouth because of 'the facilities for shipbuilding, proximity of the best timber and the existence of a steady and orderly working class'. This last advantage was proved almost as soon as Mansfield arrived when some of the workmen asked for an advance of wages:

> The men agreed to take the sum which Mr. Mansfield said was the utmost he could give. The Foreman thanked Mr. Mansfield and the interview ended very satisfactorily to all parties.[12]

In May 1853 a correspondent wrote in the *Western Times* that Mansfield's yard was well worth a visit because there were 'five vessels on the stocks, among them two very beautiful yachts'. Among the vessels built by Mansfield in these early years were a 'clipper schooner', the *Bonita*, for Azores fruit imports, 'the splendid full-rigged ship *Golden Cross*' for world-wide trading and the schooner *Witch of the Wave* for one of the most active local ship-owners, T. W. B. Hutchings. The yard also won orders from local yacht-owners. In 1853 Mansfield launched the cruising yacht *Lancashire Witch* for Sir Lawrence Palk of Haldon and the cutter *Ladybird* for Robert Cary of Tor Abbey; in the same year the yacht *Beatrice*, belonging to Sir Walter Carew, was lengthened by several feet to improve her sailing qualities, her owner's competitive spirit perhaps having been aroused by his defeat, along with 13 other British owners, in the first America's Cup. By this time it is likely that Mansfield's Strand Yard employed considerably more men than the 42 recorded in the Census of 1851.

Probably the most famous vessel built by Mansfield in this period was the full-rigged ship *Crystal Palace* of 700 tons; at her launch Miss Lidgett, daughter of the owner, explained that the name had been chosen because of 'the interest and pleasure its owner took in the Great Exhibition (of 1851)'. Two thousand spectators watched her 'glide to her future home amid deafening cheers and loud strains of music'; a few weeks later Mansfield's workmen sat down to 'a good substantial supper' at the *New Quay Inn*. The *Crystal Palace* scraped the bar as she left for London to be coppered but no harm was done and the captain was said to have commented favourably on his ship's sailing qualities when she called off Teignmouth on her maiden voyage to Shanghai.[13]

Shipbuilding on the estuary, where Mansfield's yard set an example of efficiency, was generally flourishing in the early 1850s and made a significant contribution to coastwise and foreign trade. In 1854, for instance, Mansfield himself imported 288 loads of round timber from Exeter, Topsham, Lyme and Plymouth as well as smaller quantities of planks and spars. Messrs. Follet's imports in this particular year were small but they and the other major shipbuilder, Arthur Owen, brought in from nearby ports most of the materials needed for wooden shipbuilding: resin, oakum, pitch, paint, white lead, varnish, iron and nails. Full cargoes of deals and spars arrived more erratically from Canada and the Baltic. Square timber from places as far away as Plymouth normally arrived as a raft and thus avoided tonnage dues.

One of the facilities which had attracted Mansfield to Teignmouth was the new main line railway. Some Westcountry Port Authorities were reluctant to give a rail connection to their harbours: Exeter Basin, for example, was not provided with a rail link until 1867 and Totnes Quay not until 1873. Those in charge of the harbour at Teignmouth were more enterprising. The Harbour Commissioners readily agreed to sidings being constructed to the Old Quay and the work was finished by 1851. Coal imports increased from 10,790 tons in 1851 to 20,099 a year later, truck-loads being carried as far as South Brent in one direction and Cullompton in the other.[14] The Old Quay, previously known as Rendle's Quay and named Old Quay to distinguish it from Templer's New Quay, was strengthened and improved so that other traffic as well as coal benefited. A correspondent in the *Exeter Flying Post* on 2 October 1851 reported that:

> Already large vessels ... are to be seen discharging there. (Their cargoes) are speedily, with little trouble and expense, carried off on trucks to supply all parts of the county.

The most striking effect of the rail connection was the establishment of a steamer service from London which offered through-transit to nearby towns. An advertisement in the local press in October 1853 drew attention to the new facility:

> The first-class and powerful screw steamships ... *Ranger* and *Dublin*, one of which will leave London every Thursday morning for Teignmouth ... with goods for Exeter, Crediton, Honiton, Tiverton, Taunton, Cullompton, Ottery, Sidmouth, Topsham, Exmouth, Starcross, Dawlish, Newton, Ashburton, Torquay, Paignton, Brixham, Totnes, Dartmouth and all places adjacent. This will be found the most economical and expeditious mode of conveyance for merchandize between London and the West of England, it being loaded into Railway trucks direct out of the steamers at the Old Quay, Teignmouth, and forwarded without delay.

The cargo brought by the *Ranger* on one of her first voyages suggests that maritime trade was serving both everyday needs and the more exotic requirements of aristocratic visitors:

4 puncheons, 2 hogsheads and 11 casks spirits	5 cwt cocoa
3 x 4 cases wine	18 cwt coffee
7 chests tea	9 cwt fruit
5 half-hogsheads vinegar	14 cwt ginger
9 bags nuts	3 cwt pepper
44 loaves sugar	1 cwt tobacco
3 chests lemons	9 cwt blacking
6 cwt rice	8 sacks seeds
18 cwt bacon	9 bags nails
10 cwt candles	6 cwt lead
2 cwt cheese	24 cwt iron
30 cwt oil	70 cwt non-enumerated goods and 26 tons tallow

With such mixed cargo needing quick discharge to catch a tide and keep a schedule one can well imagine that, as a local reporter put it, 'the plying of the steamer causes much bustle and animation'. On subsequent voyages from London the *Ranger* or her sister ship carried other miscellaneous cargoes which included consignments of beer, hops, mustard, starch, cement, marble and floorcloth.[15]

The coming of the railway brought exciting prospects for the port in ocean, as well as coastwise, trade. In the autumn of 1851 the *Comet* arrived off the port, landed mails and passengers from Madeira and then proceeded to London. A few months later the *Hannah* put in 'from contrary winds' so that her passengers from Port Natal and Cape Town could complete their journeys by train; the *Hannah* 'was visited by great numbers of the inhabitants and two Bush children excited a great deal of interest'.[16]

Amidst all these exciting developments of the post-railway decade there was one serious loss to Teignmouth's maritime trade as a result of rail competition. Four

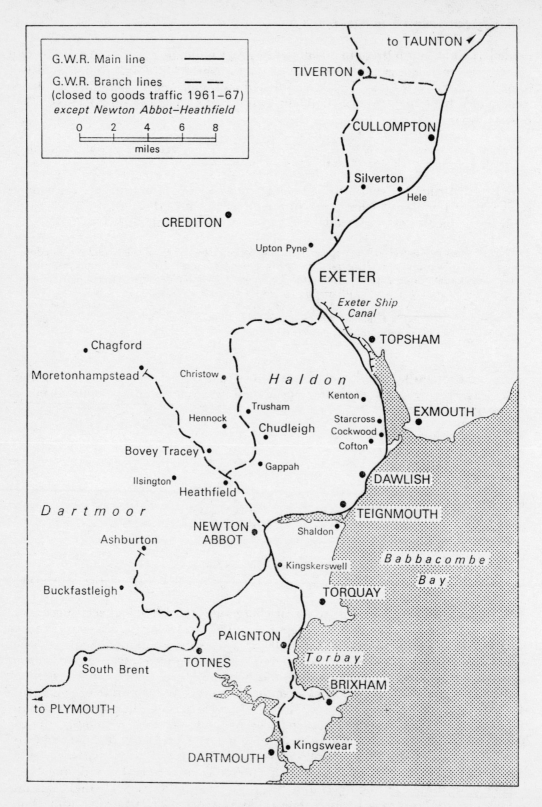

Fig. 4 The port of Teignmouth: communications by rail.

small vessels, the *Hope*, *Ann*, *William Whitty* and *Bristol Packet*, which sailed regularly from Bristol to Dartmouth, Torquay, Teignmouth and Exeter were unable to compete effectively on their roundabout route, despite the high charges of the Bristol and Exeter Railway, and the service stopped in 1846. The *Bristol Packet* kept trading a little longer by substituting Salcombe for Exeter and the *Ann* continued to carry cargo to Dartmouth which never had a rail connection.[17]

The great majority of ships which used the port of Teignmouth were still sailing vessels and not steamers. For their benefit the tug *Industry* was permanently based in the harbour, at the time the only steam tug between Plymouth and Portsmouth. Described as 'a sloop propelled by paddle wheels', the *Industry* had been purchased by George Hennet and ownership then passed to a local partnership which illustrates the way in which the profits of maritime trade were widely spread; the range of occupations of the partners was typical:

Name	Occupation	Place of residence	Number of shares (sixty-fourths)
S. W. Hutchings	Merchant	Teignmouth	8
H. Hallett	Master mariner	Teignmouth	8
J. Heyman Whiteway	Gentleman	Kingsteignton	8
T. Babbage	Accountant	Teignmouth	8
T. W. B. Hutchings	Merchant	Teignmouth	4
J. B. Mansfield	Shipbuilder	Teignmouth	4
G. Carlile	Ship-owner	Teignmouth	4
J. Holman	Ship-owner	Topsham	4
J. Vicary	Merchant	Newton Bushel	4
E. Hawkins	Merchant	Exeter	4
J. Beater	Ropemaker	Teignmouth	4
J. Greenslade	Innkeeper	Teignmouth	4[18]

From time to time the *Industry* was employed on pleasure trips: one of her excursions attracted about 40 persons 'availed themselves of an opportunity to view the delightful grounds of T. L. Fish, Esquire, of Knowle Cottage', Sidmouth, 'its rooms stocked with curios and its gardens with peacocks and parrots'.[19]

Despite all these examples of successful enterprise, some local ship-owners were worried by the opening of coastal trade to foreign vessels. On 1 January 1850, the date when the Navigation Acts were repealed, many ships in Teignmouth harbour 'hoisted their flags half-mast high, the Union downwards, mourning the repeal of the late British Navigation Laws'. But at a meeting in the *Devon Arms*, called by local ship-owners and merchants, it was decided on the casting vote of the chairman not to present a petition of protest to the government. Within a year or so the principle and practice of Free Trade was widely if not universally accepted. On 18 May 1854 the Teignmouth correspondent of the *Exeter Flying Post* reported in a matter-of-fact way, without any hint of complaint:

> The *E. and P. Schelbeck*, 158 tons, belonging to Denmark ... has cleared for Liverpool with a cargo of potters clay, being the first foreign vessel cleared from this port coastwise with a cargo under the new law for the admission of Foreigners into our Coasting Trade.

The mood of local and national self-confidence which had led to an independent port and to Free Trade seemed also to have brought local and national prosperity.

Chapter Six

Fluctuating Fortunes: 1854-1886

Within a few years this mood of optimism was destroyed by a recession in international trade and by problems peculiar to Teignmouth. These factors acting together brought about a minor disaster to the port when Follett's Shipyard at Ringmore ran into difficulties and closed. Follett built the *Magna Bona* for Messrs. Redway of Exmouth in 1856, said to be 'the longest and largest (vessel) ever built in the West of England', but another large vessel, the *Avery*, proved troublesome to launch because of the silting of the berth as well as the width of the opening span of Shaldon Bridge. Mansfield's men had to be summoned to help, an example of the traditional co-operation between the estuary shipyards. This local problem was exacerbated by the outbreak of the American Civil War which destroyed the cotton trade, one of the major markets for the Ringmore Yard. Perhaps the temperament of Charles Follett himself had something to do with the final closure. A Lloyd's Surveyor who inspected the *Avery* on the stocks reported back:

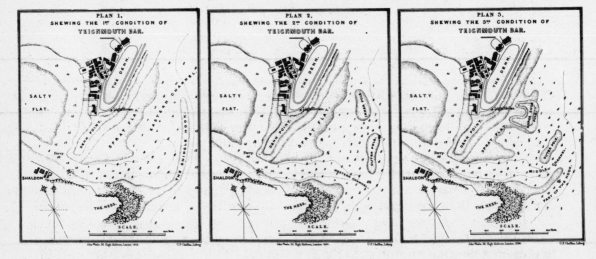

Fig. 5 Captain Spratt's charts of the Bar, 1856: the Eastern Channel, the Western Channel and the Middle Channel.

In my examination ... I found the lower deck shelf foxy and requested it might be cut into to ascertain the extent, to which he (Follett) positively refused. I then said if that is the case, I have no further business here and therefore wish you good morning and left. But having to wait a short time for the train at Teignmouth I received a note from his Foreman who is his nephew, and who said, we should do better if my uncle would keep away, he is so passionate.[1]

The Harbour Commissioners had brought about the improvements to the harbour which have been described, but they were unable to deal effectively with the natural drawbacks which had always plagued local mariners: the silting of the river and the unpredictability of the bar. In 1857 the Commissioners were greatly impressed by the imaginative proposals of Captain Thomas Spratt which also won the support of Brunel. Captain Spratt had gained wide experience as a marine surveyor in the Far East and when he visited his parents in Teignmouth used the opportunity to put forward a plan to benefit his native town. He explained that he had been 'greatly struck, in the spring of 1850, with the exact re-appearance of the Bar and banks forming it, to what had existed in the summer of 1836 ...'. As a result of a detailed survey, Spratt published *An Investigation into the Movements of Teignmouth Bar* showing how what he called 'cycloidal movement' could be controlled, and other benefits accrue, from a relatively modest expenditure

which, setting aside all considerations of the benefit to result to the Harbour and Bar, would in time amply be repaid by the value of the land reclaimed from the sea and added to one of the most beautiful promenades on the south coast of England.[2]

The Harbour Commissioners, greatly impressed by Captain Spratt's imaginative proposals, resolved immediately to spend up to £3,000 on carrying out the essential part of his plan. But it was easier to vote the money than to find it. A year or so later one of the ship-owners drew the Commissioners' attention to 'the state of the bar which from its height and extent was very dangerous'. On this occasion the Harbour sub-committee was asked to do what was necessary at an expense not exceeding £25.[3]

The timidity of the Commissioners was understandable because of the debts they had incurred as a result of the harsh settlement with Exeter Corporation. It may be also that some of the Commissioners whose income came partly from visitors were disappointed that the arrival of Louis Philippe's widow, Marie Amélie, in 1852 had not given the expected boost to aristocratic tourism; although the Queen expressed herself 'much delighted with the charming scenery and the arrangements at the Royal Hotel' she left after about a month. Day trippers were beginning to arrive by train at the expense of enlightened factory-owners, like the Heathcotes of Tiverton, but these visitors were unlikely to contribute to the local economy in a way which would encourage investment in the harbour.

So, few improvements were made. The restrictions which nature had imposed on the harbour were particularly frustrating to a steam packet service timed to a tight schedule. The *Ranger* and *Dublin* ceased to call at Teignmouth partly for this reason and partly because Teignmouth's leading merchant, George Hennet, over-reached himself and went bankrupt despite Brunel's efforts to save him. A court action was brought by Symons and Gillett, cut nail manufacturers of Bristol, and in August 1857 most of Hennet's property was sold by auction at the *Royal Hotel*; it included the Old Quay, the bonded stores and railway trucks as well as 'his late residence at Shaldon' and '18 dwellings for the working classes'.

After Hennet's failure his agent, F. Shaw, tried to develop a direct London service under the name of the London and Teignmouth Steamship Company with a vessel specially designed at Jarrow to meet the limitation of the harbour, the *City of Exeter*, described as a 'steamer, schooner-rigged' and registered in the port. The service was inaugurated on 2 August 1859 and the fares reduced in September, but sailings ceased in April 1860. The new company's plans were brought to naught by the competition of more favoured harbours, especially Torbay, where Elizabeth Barrett Browning complained of regular interruptions and wrote that 'whenever the steam packet leaves the harbour or enters it, my bed [where she stayed in Beacon Terrace] is shaken with the vibrations'.[4] The *City of Exeter* sailed for London every Saturday morning but the company was obliged to announce that 'on certain sailings the steamer will wait over Teignmouth Bar for Passengers arriving by the down train at 7.30 a.m.'.[5] Return cargo did not compensate for the hardly surprising shortage of passengers. Between 50 and 150 tons of clay was carried on each voyage but less than 20 tons of general cargo on each of the last ten passages. What finally killed the service was an office fire which destroyed the company's books and papers, 'said to be the work of an incendiary'. Arson, although suspected, was never proved but it is possible that this destruction was the work of 'Luddites' who saw employment prospects threatened. Shaw himself apparently lost heart and emigrated to Australia where he built up a prosperous transport business free from traditional restraints. So Teignmouth, after a short period of outstanding enterprise, relapsed into traditional habits. In the second half of the 19th century it is possible to illustrate in Teignmouth a typical Devon maritime community of the traditional kind.

During this period probably a higher proportion of local people drew their livelihood from the port than at any other time. Relevant Directories show up to 45 master mariners (including those living across the river at Shaldon or Ringmore) and 13 shipbuilders, ship-owners and shipping agents, as well as sail-makers and block and spar makers. Some of these descriptions are vague and there seems little correlation between one year and another. More reliable evidence on the life of the maritime community may be found in the records of the ships themselves. A representative cross-section of Crew Agreements and Log Books has been preserved and from these a fairly complete picture is given of Teignmouth ships in three categories: those which were owned in Teignmouth but did not regularly trade there, those which engaged in foreign and coastal trade with Teignmouth, and those which were limited to the 'Home Trade' only. To give a more complete picture a further category needs to be added: those vessels which contributed to the local economy when they had major repairs at one of the estuary shipyards. The four ships which may be taken as typical are the *Rifleman*, the *S.R. and H.*, the *Fiona* and the *Caroline*, re-named *Superb*.

The brigantine *Rifleman* was owned in Teignmouth but did not regularly trade there. Of 132 tons, built by J. B. Mansfield in 1858, her master, John Small, was part-owner. In 1868, a year for which papers have survived, five of the crew were Devon men, including John Beater of Teignmouth, aged 15, who signed on as cook's mate at a wage of 1s. a month. When opportunity served, the *Rifleman* called at Teignmouth; in 1874 for example, she carried 148 crates of earthenware to Malta for the Bovey Pottery Company and in 1881 unloaded pipes for sewerage works at Combeinteignhead. But, unlike most Teignmouth-registered vessels at this time, she was frequently chartered for ocean voyages away from her home port. Among voyages for which papers have survived are ones from Cardiff to Naples and Liverpool to Jamaica. The Crew Agreement for 3 June 1867 reads:

Hull to Sete and any ports or places in the Mediterranean Black Sea, Sea of Azov and Rivers and Seas adjacent and any ports or places in British North America, the United States, West Indies, South America or Newfoundland ...

An Agreement signed in Teignmouth for one of the Malta voyages was even more encompassing:

Teignmouth to Malta and from thence to any port or ports in the known world ...

Crew Agreements are notoriously vague and in fact on this occasion the *Rifleman* came back from Malta to Southampton. This was perhaps just as well because the crew included William Beater, aged 14, on his first ship (possibly brother of John Beater who had signed on as cook's mate) and an indentured apprentice. Towards the end of the *Rifleman's* working life John Small became sole owner and the ship herself was relegated to coastal trade; she made fairly frequent visits to Teignmouth to discharge coal and load clay. Captain Small was clearly a competent and resourceful master but he lacked the business acumen of those Teignmouth owners who earned extra freight by topping up their coal cargoes with such things as glass bottles, grindstones and pipes for cider. His widow sold the *Rifleman* away from the port and the vessel was lost on passage from London to Plymouth. A note from the new owner to the Teignmouth Registrar states that:

The Certificate of Registry was lost with the vessel (on 26 July, 1891) as the crew had barely time to get out of the vessel to save themselves.[6]

The *S.R. and H.*, unlike the *Rifleman*, traded regularly to Teignmouth all her life. 'A beautifully-modelled schooner' of 121 tons, she was locally built for G. P. Ward in 1872; the name was said to be the initials of his relatives, Selina, Richard and Harriet. On her first voyage, from Teignmouth to Glasgow, the master, mate and two of the crew came from Teignmouth or Shaldon; there were four others, of whom one deserted in Glasgow. In July 1878 a new crew was signed on under Foreign Articles, the master remaining:

Teignmouth to Swansea, thence to Cadiz, thence to St John's Newfoundland or any port in North America where freight may offer, then to any Final Port of Discharge in the U.K. ...

From this time onwards, the pattern of trading was a combination of coastal and Newfoundland voyages based on Teignmouth. The demanding and dangerous character of the Newfoundland trade is illustrated by some of the official papers. On 17 February 1881, for example, the Mercantile Marine Superintendent at St John's certified: 'Thomas Lytton fell from the topsail yard and was drowned'. There is a more elaborate certificate from the master, William Hore, written in a mood of shock which perhaps explains the repetition:

7 a.m. (13 February 1883) Lat.46.30N. Long.42.10W. Henry Northway was washed off the deck whilst in the act of knocking out the bulwarks to save ship and all hands. The ship was laying too at the time when a terrific gust of wind struck the vessel and laid her port side under the water, the sea running over the vessel fore and abaft. There was no possibility of saving him at the time all hands was on deck at the time expecting the vessel to founder with all hands.

The need, or perhaps the habit, to economise even from disaster is shown by the fact that Henry Northway was replaced as mate by Edwin Neiass who was paid £1 a month less, £3 10s. instead of £4 10s. The condition in the Articles that the voyage back from Newfoundland should be to any port in the United Kingdom continued;

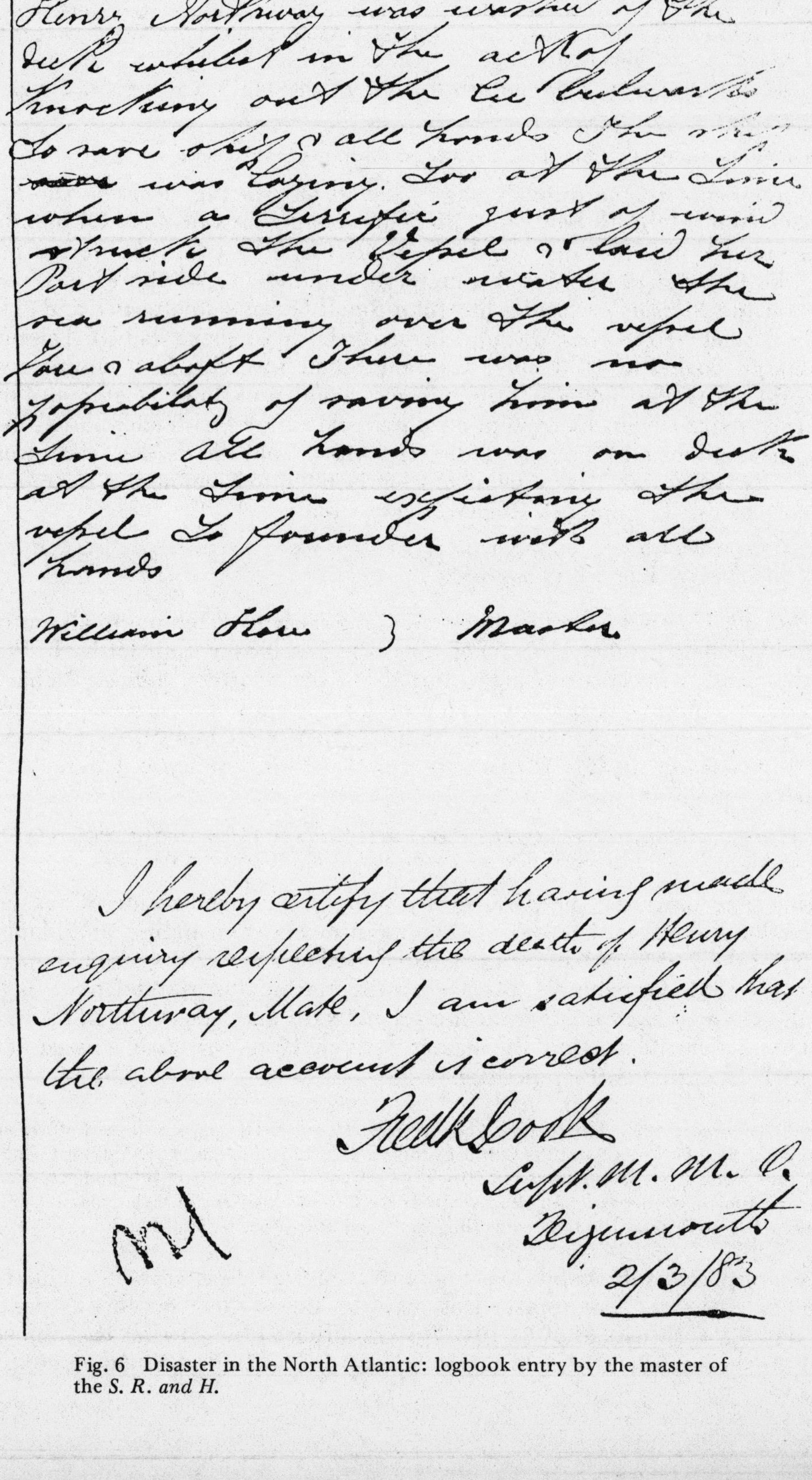

Henry Northway was washed off the
deck whilst in the act of
knocking out the lee Rolum
to save ship & all hands The ship
was laying. To at the time
when a Terrifice gust of wind
struck the Vessel & laid her
Port side under water the
sea running over the vessel
fore & abaft There was no
posibility of saving him at the
time all hands was on deck
at the time expecting the
vessel to founder with all
hands

William Howe   } Master

I hereby certify that having made
enquiry respecting the death of Henry
Northway, Mate, I am satisfied that
the above account is correct.
                    FdK Cook
                    Supt. M. M. O.
                    Teignmouth
                    2/3/83

Fig. 6 Disaster in the North Atlantic: logbook entry by the master of
the *S. R. and H.*

the final destination was usually Teignmouth but occasionally another Westcountry port such as Bristol. William Hore, a local man, experienced and certificated, was master continuously from the time the *S.R. and H.* was launched until 1884 and possibly later; he owned eight shares. The *S.R. and H.* continued trading, coastwise and to Newfoundland and Iceland until she was sunk by collision off Port Lynas, Anglesey, on 14 July 1899. In 1884 she carried the last recorded export cargo from Teignmouth to Newfoundland, 153 tons of limestone.[7] The *S.R. and H.* was one of more than 30 vessels owned by the Ward family and their partners in the second half of the 19th century, some of them purchased second-hand and some built in Teignmouth or, probably more cheaply, in Prince Edward Island. The family fortunes were founded by George Perkins Ward, one of whose partners had been Thomas Pike, a local butcher, and whose contribution towards the success of the joint enterprises apparently persuaded G. P. Ward to christen his son 'Pike Ward'. This became the business name of the firm which is still active and locally owned and managed. G. P. Ward himself appears to have been a forceful character who on occasion championed popular rights, as when he supported public use of the Den, but was a demanding employer. When the crew of his schooner *Heroine* brought an action for arrears of wages he retaliated by prosecuting them for disobedience. It may be that the prosecution was justified because Teignmouth crews, having been largely brought up in the Newfoundland trade, had a reputation similar to that of Peterhead crews accustomed to Arctic whaling; thoroughly dependable in a crisis but obstreperous in periods of calm weather. One of the Ward partners in the 1860s was Alonzo Ward who had an unconventional view of his duties as ship-owner and was charged with 'keeping a disorderly house (*The Foresters' Arms*) and causing persons of both sexes to frequent the said house, and there to be drinking, tippling, whoring and misbehaving themselves'. The prosecution was instigated by the incumbent of West Teignmouth and a Methodist ship-owner, T. W. B. Hutchings.[8]

The ketch *Fiona*, 66 tons, had been built at Dartmouth and was registered at Teignmouth in 1874 as owned by John and William Vicary. She was restricted to voyages within Home Trade limits, defined by the Board of Trade as British ports or ports between Brest and the Elbe. Her Voyage Accounts have been preserved for 1876, 1879, 1881 and the first half of 1883; during these three and a half years the majority of the *Fiona's* voyages were round trips between Liverpool and Teignmouth, with a small number of voyages to and from London and occasional deviations to Antwerp. Cargoes carried were mainly raw materials for Messrs. Vicary's tannery and associated fellmongering business to supplement direct foreign imports. In 1876, for example, one of the cargoes discharged at Teignmouth from Liverpool by the *Fiona* was:

> 36 bales of sheepskins
> 15 tons of coal
> 10 tons of pelts
> 3 tons of bark
> 17 tons of gambia [a plant extract used in tanning]
> 12 tons of myrobalan [a fruit, also used in tanning]

At other times during the year her cargo included salt, valonia and hides, and occasionally rice, bread and biscuits, which may mean that Messrs. Vicary supplied their work-people as well as their customers. On her return voyages the *Fiona* carried clay and sometimes additional consignments such as dressed pelts and scrap iron. The *Fiona* was manned by a local crew and based on Teignmouth. Charles Seagell was master for most of the period; George Seagell was one of the seamen for a year or so and John Seagell became mate. The other members of the crew were at all times local men or joined from Teignmouth-registered ships.[9] In 1883, at a time of slack trade, the *Fiona* was sold. Messrs. Vicary continued to bring in many of their raw materials by sea for another 70 years but by regular steamer services from Liverpool to Teignmouth or from London to Torquay and not in their own vessels.

The connection of the *Caroline* with Teignmouth was more fortuitous than that of the *Fiona*, the *S.R. and H.* or the *Rifleman*, but her short-lived association with the port influenced the lives of a much wider spectrum of the local community.

The American ship *Caroline*, 776 tons, recently built in Boston, ran ashore on Watcombe beach, four miles from Teignmouth, on 12 May 1869. She was on passage from Havre to Newport to load railway iron and her captain explained that he mistook Portland lights for those of the Lizard and found himself in Lyme Bay instead of the Bristol Channel, an odd mistake or, as G. P. Ward put it, 'a Kentucky tale'. As soon as the ship touched ground, or possibly just before, local boatmen offered help which the captain firmly rejected. Whatever one may think of his navigation, there was some justification for his apparent ingratitude because he declared that, after the *Caroline* struck:

> a number of small open boats came off ... and from their behaviour and actions, I saw plainly all they wanted was the liberty to plunder ... I asked them who are you? I then told them such boats as you have got are of no use to me and asked one of them to go immediately for a steamer ... when the coastguard officers came on board I found *them* to be gentlemen.

John Stigings, a local fisherman and pilot and one of the prospective plunderers referred to, felt himself grossly insulted and said that the captain's remarks showed that 'his vision was as obscured in this respect as his calculations were as to where he was'.[10]

Lloyd's casualty report stated that the *Caroline* 'will probably become a total wreck' and Mansfield bought a share of the hull, which was auctioned for £250. What happened next is vividly, if not objectively, described by a *Teignmouth Gazette* reporter:

> To show what English pluck and energy can do Mr. Mansfield and his men went to work again, night and day continually and ... just six days after commencing, the inhabitants of Teignmouth were gladdened with the sight of this splendid wreck off the bar.

But the *Caroline* grounded, a gale sprang up and

> the chances were a thousand to one she would now be entirely lost, but ... pumps of every size and shape were procured from the shore and ... finally ... hundreds of spectators cheered heartily as this persevering man and his trusty fellows brought the wreck of this once splendid vessel safely in Teignmouth harbour.[11]

Mansfield renamed his ship the *Superb* and fitted her for the East India trade. She was exhibited to the public for the benefit of the Infirmary; there was dancing on board 'to the merry strains of the Teignmouth Subscription Band', and a 'Grand Ball' was advertised on behalf of the Lifeboat Institution under the sponsorship of a distinguished committee headed by Sir Warwick Tonkin, a local public figure who lived in Teignmouth House in Teign Street.[12]

Those who went to sea in ships like the *Rifleman, S.R. and H.* and *Fiona* followed a profession which offered a better chance of advancement than most land-based occupations at that time. It was at least theoretically possible to move from seaman to mate and to master and then to become a partner or to share the profits at the end of the voyage or the year. The master of the Teignmouth brig *Nymph* was 'for his exemplary conduct put in possession of a quarter part of the ship' and was 'in a fair way to get forward in life' when his ship was lost. George Heath, master of the *Polly* owned by George Taverner, coal merchant of Chudleigh, was rewarded for his diligence by being given 2½ per cent of the vessel's gross earnings in addition to his wages.[13]

Advancement was often more a matter of chance than application because there was no formal system of education or training and indentured apprentices picked up what information they could at the whim of the master. An investigation conducted for the *Morning Chronicle* in London would have been true for many ships at the time:

Did my master teach me navigation, do you say, when I first went to sea? He did not, sir, for he didn't know it himself.[14]

When Emmanuel Perryman of Teignmouth was in charge of the *Witch o' the Wave* on a voyage from Glasgow to the West Indies in the spring of 1863 he suffered from the incompetence of those who called themselves seamen but had no proper training. The ship's log recorded that John Mitchell was incapable of steering and 'I was obliged to order him from the helm'. He was replaced by Samuel McClure who was equally 'incapable of steering the vessel ... knowing very little about seamanship. James Burns was not much better and he was 'incapable of splicing the foretopgallant stay'. His resistance perhaps lowered by these worries, Emmanuel Perryman died from yellow fever contracted in Demerara. With an experienced crew the *Witch o' the Wave* was brought safely home to London by the mate who was reprimanded by the Shipping Master, unfairly one would think, for not having made the necessary attestations.[15]

Mr. Hatch of Teignmouth offered a more thorough training and a start higher up the ladder. In 1858 he advertised his 'Nautical, Mathematical and Commercial Academy' in Clampit House, within sight of the harbour, which would give 'superior advantage to Young Gentlemen intended for the Sea'. They would be able to take their own observations 'for which the Den at Teignmouth is well adapted'. Apart from this institution, which appears not to have prospered, Teignmouth provided educational opportunities only of a very limited kind. The town had one of the earliest Mechanics' Institutes, started in 1834 on the initiative of John Sweetland; in 1848 it appears to have merged with the Useful Knowledge Society and in 1857 the committee purchased the Athenaeum with the idea of establishing a reading room and 'classes for writing, arithmetic, navigation and drawing, as well as French and German'. Lectures were regularly given and papers taken in the reading room included the *Shipping Gazette* and *Mitchell's Maritime Register*; J.B. Mansfield promised to pass on *The Engineer* and he gave a lecture on 'the origin and beneficial results of the screw propeller'. Not for the last time a society set up to help manual workers was taken over by the middle classes and by moralists. The President of the Society urged that popular illustrated lectures should be arranged 'to keep up the public interest' and the Society's correspondent thought that members had greatly benefited, 'in the truest sense of the word', from an exposition of *Pilgrim's Progress*.[16]

Those seamen who, like the master of the *Nymph*, 'got forward in life' did so through their own unaided efforts. From records and memories it is possible to trace the life stories of two of them which may be taken as typical of many others.

John Whitear was a member of a Teignmouth seafaring family which stayed in their home port and did not seek a fortune in Liverpool or one of the other deep-water harbours. John's father, Samuel, was master of three Teignmouth vessels in turn and John himself followed a career which was typical for an intelligent, conscientious and lucky seaman: Boy Seaman in the *Conquest* from March, 1863; Ordinary Seaman in the *Elizabeth*; Able Seaman in the *Schyrd*; Mate in the *Vectis*. All these were Teignmouth vessels (despite one of their names) engaged in coastwise trade. John Whitear then signed for foreign service in a much larger Teignmouth ship, *Witch of the Teign*, which made passages from Liverpool to South America. After this wider experience he became master successively of the *Prothesa* and the *Jehu*; these were Teignmouth-owned vessels trading to British ports and the near continent. The *Prothesa* was a brigantine owned by T. W. B. Hutchings and much of her working life was spent in a regular Teignmouth trade: round voyages between Teignmouth and Glasgow, clay outwards and coal inwards. She normally carried 250 tons, slighty less in the winter months.

The diary which John Whitear kept gives much more detail than the official documents: it shows that the coal came in for the Gas Works of Teignmouth and Newton Abbot and that the clay was delivered to the Barrowfield Works of Kennedy & Co., a leading firm in the British pottery industry which exported to North and South America. Sometimes the pattern varied and the *Prothesa* made her round voyages to Newcastle instead of Glasgow but with the same cargoes. In Newcastle the clay was consigned to Maling & Co., a good customer for Devon clay throughout its history because, according to an investigator on behalf of the firm, it was found there 'in great perfection and well adapted for working'. Maling's trade catalogue of the time advertised jugs marked 'Devonshire Clotted Cream' but there is no evidence that they came back to Devon in the holds of the *Prothesa*. When the *Prothesa* was dismasted on one of her voyages in December 1875 17 miles north-east of the Wolf Rock, Whitear brought her into Plymouth under tow although, contrary to orders, the mate and three crew members had abandoned ship. On another occasion Whitear may have saved his ship more by luck than judgment: when the *Prothesa* was loaded at Teignmouth in January 1881 the brig *Willie*, apparently unmanned, broke away from her buoy in a strong wind, tore out the iron railings of Shaldon Bridge and caused general havoc.

After a long and moderately profitable life the *Prothesa* was dismantled and turned into a hulk. Whitear then transferred to the schooner *Jehu* which was owned by another member of the Hutchings family, T. W. Hutchings. The sailing qualities of the *Jehu* justified her name because she created a record by sailing from Glasgow to Dartmouth in 60 hours. A story of the *Jehu* is written up, with some embellishment, in *Round the Galley Fire*, a collection of sketches which became a best-seller among those seamen who could read. The *Jehu* was run down and slighty damaged by a much larger vessel sailing at night without lights. John Whitear gave chase.

We'll stick to her skirts and have her name, though she should go all on sailing till we comes to Australey.

The *Jehu* caught up with 'the cowardly runaway' the next night and she turned out to be the barque *Juno* of Nova Scotia. The family tradition was broken when John Whitear's son, John Carlile Whitear, became a schoolmaster but the younger John retained his father's love and respect for the sea and regularly competed at Teignmouth Regattas in his sloop *Snail*. He also treasured his father's papers, including his Discharge Certificates on which 'Ability' and 'Character' were always assessed in the highest category, 'Very Good'.[17]

Fred Drew, like John Whitear, came from an established maritime family. His career belongs to the 20th century rather than the 19th but is equally representative of the earlier period because the lives of Teignmouth seamen did not change in any fundamental way until the 1930s. His father owned the brigantine *Clarissa* jointly with his son-in-law B. J. Cox, described as 'master mariner' and recorded as owning 16 of the 64 shares. When the partners bought the *Transit*, also a brigantine, a year or so later Cox had six more shares. The *Transit* was lost in the gales of November 1893 but the crew was saved by a Dutch lifeboat whose coxswain earned a gold medal from the Board of Trade. Cox then moved on to steam and became master of the *Cairnglen*; his daughter remembered sailing round the world with him three times. The Drews stayed on in Teignmouth and Fred's first voyage was a coastal one in which his ship put in at Falmouth, Fishguard and Dublin from stress of weather. Fred Drew joined the Navy at the outbreak of war and took part in the Dardanelles and other actions. When he returned to Teignmouth jobs were hard to come by and he did not, like John Whitear, move steadily up the ladder. He took whatever opportunities were available to someone with a seaman's skills: fishing for salmon in the river or sprats at sea; working the Shaldon ferry; dredging sand from the estuary channel; taking summer visitors for boat excursions. His was a very active life and as open to danger as John Whitear's; he had little patience with his brother who chose a soft option as one of the 50-man crew of the Duke of Bedford's steam yacht *Sapphire*. Fred Drew retained his links with the Navy and was disappointed when the Admiralty turned down his offer to take his launch *Taurus* to Dunkirk in 1940. When he became immobile in his eighties Fred Drew used his traditional seaman's skills to make shopping bags and maps for his friends.[18]

Teignmouth maritime families like the Whitears and the Drews had little in common with the lightermen who worked the estuary and who lived in Newton Abbot and the riverside villages rather than in Teignmouth. The work on the estuary was probably more strenuous and at least as dangerous as work at sea. Barges, like sea-going vessels, ideally carried cargo both ways and the barges which brought clay to the harbour sometimes carried coal back, but because of the risk of pollution the carriage of coal ceased and the barges moved up river empty. Two lightermen worked each barge, loading from a wharf on the Stover or Hackney Canal or by the railway bridge at Newton Abbot, where the jetty is still usable. They helped to load a vessel at the buoys in Teignmouth harbour and then returned. This was normally a day's work and hours were irregular, depending on the tide; evidence for the very irregular hours comes from a complaint by the Managers of Kingsteignton National School that children's progress was being hindered because they were employed in carrying breakfasts to their fathers on the barges or in the pits.[19]

The journey up and downstream was accomplished by means of a square sail, aided by the tide and the long poles of the lightermen. Each barge carried up to 35 tons of clay and when fully loaded there was a risk of sinking either on the voyage down or in the choppy waters of the harbour. On the night that Samuel Sercomb was swept overboard his mate said that it 'was very dark and half a gale of wind was blowing'. When his body was found it was seen that he had managed to struggle out of his sea boots and get one arm out of his jersey. In another tragedy, when Alfred Ellis was drowned, the Coroner elicited the fact that the rule that a small boat should always be towed astern was sometimes broken and that only one of the clay companies provided lifebuoys.[20] When a barge owned by the Devon & Courtenay Co. sank just below Shaldon Bridge there were no casualties but subsequently a barge belonging to the Frank Mills Mining Co. stranded on the wreck and her cargo of lead ore, worth £200, was salvaged only with great difficulty. Occasionally a barge ranged against the vessel she was alongside and the master of the regular trader *Bessie Stephens* was paid £1 by the owner of No. 1 barge; this was a Hackney Canal barge and the money was paid by Lord Clifford's agent.[21] The Stover Canal barges continued to carry names, as they had done in the early days, and not numbers. From 1904 onwards the lightermen's task was made easier because most barges were towed by the steam tug *Kestrel*; they were brought down in long strings two abreast and sometimes as many as six dropped off at one vessel although usually fewer.

The clay barges comprised the bulk of estuary traffic in the 19th century but mineral ores also passed down the river, more erratically, and a variety of goods moved upstream, especially culm for the limekilns. A few cargoes were carried to and from the beaches and to the quays at Newton Abbot in very small sea-going ships. At Floor (now Flow) Point there is a record of 'a quantity of rare stocks for gun carriages' being shipped to Woolwich[22] and large amounts of culm were unloaded there and taken to kilns at Lindridge; the remains of a stone jetty are clearly visible at Flow Point as they are at Archbrook and other beaches on both sides of the river. Regular 'market boats' added to estuary traffic. Local Directories advertised services to Newton Abbot run by Mr. Perryman, Mrs. Davis and Mrs. Heath and, although Mrs. Davis's service stopped because 'the evil eye of Brunel crossed her path' (when the railway came), the others appear to have been well patronised. It was said that Mary Heath always tried to oblige her passengers and sometimes ran her boat aground as a result; she was given at least one 'benefit' at *Coombe Cellars Inn*. In this category of river traffic women played an important part and Teignmouth has a claim to be a pioneer in recognising women's right to follow a maritime occupation from the time that Fanny Burney's party was shocked by the working dress of fisherwomen near the Ness. Pike Ward's mother was the only woman shipbroker in the United Kingdom and said to be a formidable character; she did the job very efficiently while her son was away for long spells in Iceland.

The lightermen were a community quite separate from the men and women who ran the market service to Newton Abbot. Most of their lives were spent on the barges which were generally well looked after. The barges which worked the Stover Canal were built by a family firm at Teigngrace and those which used the Hackney Canal were latterly built at the successor yard to Mansfield's at Teignmouth. Both sets of barges were normally surveyed, caulked and painted during one week each year; the painting included touching up the gunwales in the colours distinctive of the various clay companies, red, green and white. When the jobs were done the workers dressed themselves up as 'water rats' and invited their friends to an excursion down the river and out to sea. Some of the lightermen's recreations were less innocent than this because their hard life led to hard drinking: the landlord of the *Coombe Cellars Inn*, despite the value of the custom he received, brought a court action when he was knocked up for cider at four o'clock in the morning and the lightermen refused to take 'No' for an answer.[23]

It was this unruly behaviour, combined with similar lawlessness among seamen in the numerous waterside inns at Teignmouth, which offended Victorian morality and called for prohibitions. Action was taken primarily from religious beliefs at a time when personal religion was a strong motive force. In Teignmouth religious life, as well as religious controversy, was stimulated by the arrival of Queen Marie Amélie and her suite and, not long afterwards, by a community of French Benedictine nuns who had escaped at the Revolution and came to Teignmouth after a sojourn in Hammersmith. The advance party of nuns caused consternation as they walked up the hill towards St Scholastica's Abbey which had been made ready for them by the generosity of Lord Clifford and a leading Teignmouth solicitor, Mr. Tozer, who was a member of another old Catholic family.[24] The 'invasion' added fuel to the controversy between High Church St Michael's and Low Church St James's. Much of the consequent passion spent itself in theological argument but some, especially on the Evangelical side, was directed towards the spiritual and social welfare of those who were thought to be backsliders among the maritime community.

Miss Agnes Weston, who had already been successful in naval ports, exhorted the ladies who managed the Globe Coffee Tavern:

> Now what they wanted to do in Teignmouth was to get the sailors in – no matter if they were ever so drunk – so much the better, and the easier to get them in, and the easier to get them to take the pledge.[25]

The Ladies' Committee set up shop close to the waterfront in premises now occupied by the Conservative Club but they had a lot of competition, particularly from the *Jolly Sailor* nearby.

Other voluntary organisations joined in this moral crusade and the one which made the most dramatic, although not the most lasting, impression in Teignmouth was the Salvation Navy. In the Spring of 1886 the Salvation Navy steamer *Iole* came into the harbour and the captain and crew conducted three services in the Athaenaeum, one of which was 'rather noisy'. A Salvation Army Captain who inspected the *Iole* explained the kind of crew the ship needed:

> The Captain should have ... a proper man that has a heart as large as a cork fender, cook, play a piece of music, sing, take the lead at meetings ...; also an engineer, he must play some musical instrument; mate, he must play some instrument also; man, he must beat the drum; boy, he must play some instrument likewise.[26]

With this emphasis on the musical rather than nautical skills of the crew it is hardly surprising that the *Iole* sank in the Humber a few months later; but her loss is likely to have been primarily a consequence of the unsuitability of the ship herself for missionary work in all weathers. She had been a pleasure yacht, donated by 'Mr Cory of Cardiff', and was described by a Teignmouth correspondent as 'a very smart craft' but 'exceedingly narrow'. The Salvation Navy did not recover from this setback and failed to make the impact on social history, either locally or nationally, which was achieved by the Salvation Army.

Enterprise in Teignmouth by the Anglican Missions to Seamen had much more lasting influence. As a result of local effort, a lay reader was attached to the port of Teignmouth in 1877; he was withdrawn after about two years, but in 1881 J. F. Dunning was appointed on a permanent basis. Dunning was a man of great determination who made a significant contribution to the life of the harbour in that sphere of combined spiritual and social welfare which the Victorians made peculiarly their own. An illustration in the Missions to Seamen annual reports around 1890 shows Dunning rowing out in his boat, the *Vanguard*, to a tier of sailing ships in Teignmouth harbour, the Flying Angel, which was the crest of the Society, clearly visible on the bow. Dunning meticulously performed his duties in the *Christopher*, the *Vanguard* and two other boats named *Love* and *Quiver VIII* for half a century; when he 'felt compelled to resign owing to advancing years' in 1934, his period of service was almost identical with that of W. J. Newkey Burden who ceased to be honorary secretary of the Lifeboat Committee a year later. The careers of both men were typical of the continuity in Teignmouth's maritime affairs.

In addition to his missionary work as a distributor of bibles and scriptural texts, Dunning arranged evening classes in basic subjects for young seamen and fishermen. He extended his 'parish' to Exeter and Dartmouth but always paid special attention to Teignmouth. His very broad interest in maritime affairs is clear from one of his annual reports to the Society:

> ... in recent years by some strange mistake a vessel came chartered to discharge in Cofton Harbour to find that such a place was only known by tradition and that for a hundred years or more green fields and waving corn had covered the spot ...

The Seamen's Institute which Dunning served moved to larger premises in Teignmouth House as the work expanded; the Institute provided 'books, papers, games and musical instruments' and one of the managers had a skittle alley made 'as there were no places of amusement for the sailors in the town, only streets and pubs'. In later days the notice, 'Lloyds List kept here', possibly attracted the attention of seamen away from the *Teign Brewery Inn* and the *Blue Anchor* opposite. Dunning was an officer of the Missions to Seamen for 53 years, a record. When he first arrived in Teignmouth the nickname 'Holy Joe' may have been derisory: long before he left it had become a token of respect and affection.[27]

There were many other individuals who helped seafarers in Teignmouth apart from 'Holy Joe' Dunning. When Mr. Arnold of Rowdens (now The Beacon School) died in November 1881, for example, all the ships in the harbour lowered their flags to half-mast; but what form his generosity took, apart from opening his gardens for the benefit of the Lifeboat, was not generally known. Other charitable efforts on behalf of the maritime community were perhaps trumpeted too much. In the autumn of 1879 a public meeting was widely advertised at the Temperance Hall, Teignmouth, 'to consider the expediency of establishing a local Society for organising Charitable Relief and Repressing Mendicity'. The dual purpose of the projected Society was significant and the Reverend James Metcalfe was reported to have said:

> The fundamental object of the Society was to strengthen the power of self-help, to encourage in the minds of the poor the conviction that they should and ought to help themselves, and so to teach them self-reliance.[28]

Some of the poor may have thought that self-help was not enough to save them from the profiteering of local tradesmen. In the winter of 1867, when trade in the harbour was very slack for a short period, 'a procession of nearly 2,000 persons marched through the streets demanding "Drop the bread, Drop the beef!" '. It was said that they chanted their protest to the tune of Puseyite hymns being sung in Father Simpson's St Michael's church, thus neatly combining two protests in one.[29]

Partly as a result of the charitable activities which have been described, such protests were unusual. One of the factors which had brought Mansfield to Teignmouth in 1849, 'the existence of a steady and orderly working class', appears to have operated throughout the 19th century. A court action illustrates this.

> The Teignmouth magistrates sent Wm Hutchings to gaol for seven days for neglecting to go on board his ship ... It appears that all hands had agreed to miss the tide but Hutchings alone kept his word.[30]

Combined action by seamen was more effective in the larger ports. When some unemployed Teignmouth seamen were recruited to take the places of striking crews of Atlantic liners at Liverpool they arrived back disconsolate. They told a reporter that 'the unionists had played practical tricks on them, purloining their money and throwing their clothes overboard'.[31]

The depression of the 1880s also caused disputes in the clay industry which supplied much of the trade of the port. Watts, Blake, Bearne, the largest employers, showed the authoritarian paternalism common to many Victorian industrialists. In 1876 they set up the Kingsteignton Sick Club which provided sick pay for a subscription of 3d. per week. Interest was paid on the subscriptions and workers' representatives served on the Management Committee, but conditions were strict:

> No Member shall receive any pay from the Club if disabled by Fighting, Wrestling, Cudgel playing, or from any result of his own intemperance, or whilst suffering from venereal disease, or in respect of any accident received whilst working for other employers.

Hard working conditions and low wages provoked protests which came to a head when Samuel Whitear and W. J. Dobbs presented a petition signed by a large number of workers. Watts, Blake, Bearne considered the requests and promised that each workman would receive a weekly pay slip showing how his wages had been calculated. But the Board added an ominous final paragraph to their formal reply:

> And now we will say a few words as to Samuel Whitear. We think that as for a long time he has been dissatisfied with his work and with his masters, he had better find work and masters more agreeable to him.

'We have no doubt', said the Board, 'that the usual pleasant relations between employers and employed will be re-established'. Samuel Whitear, an unsung hero of the early Trade Union movement, appears to have lost his job in the spring of 1891.[32]

There is more general evidence that by the 1880s the affairs of the port and the industries on which it depended were approaching a crisis.

Chapter Seven

Attempts at Modernisation: 1886-1904

After the setback which Teignmouth suffered as a result of George Hennet's bankruptcy and the failure of two attempts to establish a packet service to London, trade recovered and the port prospered, in a traditional way, until the late 1870s.

The staple trade was the export of ball clay for which there was a steadily increasing demand. Most cargoes went coastwise to large ports, such as Glasgow and Newcastle, and to small inland ports such as Gainsborough; but the potteries of Staffordshire were by far the largest customers, particularly Wedgwoods who used increasing quantities of Devon clay for their prestigious Queen's ware. For these Midland markets the clay went to Runcorn or Westonpoint and then by barge to its destination. Runcorn Docks were greatly extended between 1850 and 1870 to cope with the growing imports of ball clay from Teignmouth and china clay from the Cornish ports of Par and Charlestown. A few pages of the account books for Runcorn Docks have survived; they show the gratuities paid to the ships' masters and tabulate the types of clay: potters clay, blue clay and black clay which was so called because of the streaks of lignite which ran through it. The names of the vessels, which are also recorded, suggest the affection which owner-masters and partners had for their ships: *Fairy Flower, June Rose, Island Maid.*[1]

All the companies working around Newton Abbot shared in this coastwise trade. Foreign trade was almost entirely in the hands of two firms, Whiteways and the composite firm of Watts, Blake, Bearne. Most consignments to foreign ports were appreciably larger than to coastwise destinations; in 1874, for example, they included one of 320 tons to Seville and one of 400 tons (the largest in the year) to Genoa. There was a fairly regular trade between Quebec and Teignmouth inwards with timber and outwards with clay. The locally-owned barque *Galatea* was in trouble with the Customs when pirated editions of English copyright books were found among her inward cargo.[2] This clay trade was promoted by leases of up to 14 years granted by Lord Clifford. In 1861, for example, he granted a 12-year lease to John Hayman Whiteway and William Rogers Mortimer 'to open, dig, search for gain, raise and get up and take and carry away all pipe, potters and other merchantable clays' on condition that they were shipped by barge on the Kingsteignton (Hackney) Canal to Teignmouth. A few years later Lord Clifford negotiated a lease with William Browne of St Austell which introduced a Cornish link perpetuated by the shipments routed through Teignmouth by the English China Clays Company. In a lease granted to Edwin Goddard in 1890 Lord Clifford imposed, apparently for the first time, a condition of full restoration of the land.[3]

Apart from clay, there were many other mineral and mineral-related exports from Teignmouth during this period. The granite trade had stopped by 1850 partly because of George Templer's extravagant habits which had caused the sale of the Haytor quarries. Other mineral exports fluctuated widely. Since the market price of minerals varied according to booms and slumps, mining in Devon, as in Cornwall, attracted bubble companies and individual speculators. Charles Wescomb, who was a major exporter through Teignmouth, rose from rags to riches to become Sheriff of Exeter but when he died suddenly in 1869 it was found that he owed vast sums to his friends, including £9,000 to the rector of St Sidwell's.[4] Exports through Teignmouth from 1853, when separate port records begin, included lead, iron, zinc and copper as well as small quantities of other minerals which were mined or were by-products of the mining process: umber, ochre, arsenic and 'shining ore', which was micaceous haemitite used at first as an ink-drier and later in paint manufacture.

One of the first large-scale enterprises which sent ores through Teignmouth was the Hennock Mining Company to which the petitioners for Independence in 1852 drew attention. The Company tackled the problem of drainage by replacing a water-wheel with a steam engine from a Tavistock foundry and brought to Morwellham by canal, by sea to Teignmouth, up the estuary to Newton Abbot and by wagon to the mine.[5] The mineral trade through Teignmouth was largely a trade of small cargoes in small ships to small ports. Consignments went from Teignmouth to harbours in South Wales, like Pembry and Penclawdd, which have long since disappeared together with the blast furnaces they served. Other cargoes went to smelters such as Michell and Sons whose works were on the creek of the Fal at Penpol.[6] The most important mine in terms of Teignmouth trade was the Frank Mills Mine at Christow, named after one of the 'Adventurers'. Since one of the shafts was sunk near Lord Exmouth's new Canonteign House the engine house was embellished with castellated battlements not unlike Brunel's engine house at Starcross. The Company won the favour of Lord Exmouth who allowed water from his ornamental waterfall to be used for dressing the ore and the mine continued in production until 1880.[7] It is not possible to determine the origin of all lead ore exports from Teignmouth but it is likely that some of the exceptionally large cargoes, such as the consignments of between 150 and 200 tons which went fairly frequently to Llanelli, came from the Frank Mills Mine. The Firestone Hill Quarry at Newton Abbot, which produced iron ore, was more typical. It functioned only during the mining boom period around 1872; between August 1872 and April 1874 it sent 1,134 tons of iron ore through Teignmouth in the names of W. Harrison and W. Hosking, consignees. Then export stopped apart from one or two isolated consignments. The largest cargo was the first one, 236 tons to Hull in the schooner *Victoria*.[8]

Other exports sent coastwise were not significant in relation to clay and minerals: small quantities of bricks, round timber, old rails and leather shreds, for example. Probably the largest single item in this general category was cider, sent mainly to London. A local historian of the early 19th century contended that it was not consumed as cider but was 'sold to wine merchants who best know to what purpose it may be applied'.[9]

Imports, like exports, were well maintained up to the late 1870s and most items steadily increased but without any spectacular advance. The import of culm dropped sharply with the closure of many estuary limekilns but coal, the other very large import, kept pace with expanding industrial and domestic demand. The Brixham market was lost to Torquay but Exeter was not a serious rival owing to the heavy canal charges and Exmouth floating dock, another potential competitor, was not fully operational until 1886. Devon farmers, not yet bankrupted by cheap American wheat and meat, brought increasing quantities of fertiliser and oilcake through

Teignmouth. In a bad season for the local crop, cider apples came from Brittany. During the minor building boom when Powderham Terrace and Orchard Gardens were built, substantial tonnages of Cornish and Welsh slates and Medway cement came by sea. Foreign, as distinct from coastwise, imports were mainly raw materials for local industry such as rags from Memel for the Hele Paper Mill and flints from Dieppe for Bovey Pottery Works. The largest importer in this category was Vicarys of Newton Abbot who, in addition to transhipment cargo in their own vessel which has already been described, brought some raw materials for their tannery direct from overseas. One of the largest cargoes to come into Teignmouth during this period was a mixed consignment of 295 tons of hides, 92 tons of tallow, 11 tons of bones and 9 tons of hooves from Paysandu, Uruguay. Vicarys also shipped valonia direct from Smyrna and tanning bark from both British and continental ports.[10]

This pattern of trade up to the late 1870s shows that the port prospered in a modest and traditional way without any example of an exciting new venture. The spirit of outstanding enterprise which had been demonstrated in the fight for Independence was continued in just one facet of the maritime scene, Mansfield's Strand Shipyard. After the combination of luck and sound judgment which transformed the wreck of the *Caroline* into the fine full-rigged ship *Superb*, Mansfield went on to further success. The range of launchings from 1860 to 1879 covered almost every type of craft except the merchant steamer to which Mansfield never transferred his faith. With this exception Mansfield applied power in a highly imaginative way: 'a beautifully modelled saloon steamer' for a river service based on Plymouth; a combined gunboat and yacht supplied to 'the Rajah of Laroot'; the yacht *Vanda* rigged as a schooner and equipped with two compound engines for a Dawlish owner who was wealthy enough to afford an after cabin of teak, a main cabin of polished oak and a leading cabin painted in white and gold. To celebrate the launch of this luxurious craft a workmen's supper was held in the *London Hotel* presided over by Mansfield and at which the special guests were the foreman of the yard and the prospective captain of the *Vanda*.

Mansfield continued to build more ordinary vessels for those local owners who still put their trust in sail. One of the yard's best customers in the 1870s was Pinkhams of Plymouth and for them Mansfield maintained his very high standards. When a Lloyd's Surveyor dared to give the *Kitty Pinkham* classification for eight years rather than nine William Pinkham wrote indignantly to Lloyd's Committee in London:

> I have myself inspected this vessel ... and I with confidence say that a more faithful vessel cannot be built.[11]

Despite his authoritarian attitude towards his workmen Mansfield was public spirited and always took a keen interest in local affairs as is shown by his educational activities which have already been described. It was said that the figure-head of one of the first ships he built, the *Witch of the Teign*, was modelled on a celebrated local beauty. In a matter of greater practical importance Mansfield in 1871 formally recognised the public right of way, to be challenged many times in the future, across his Patent Slip. As a working Committee member for the Lifeboat Institution Mansfield exhibited a model of the Rajah's gunboat for their Fete at Rowdens, and he lent his name to many other organisations, such as the Teignmouth Botanical and Horticultural Society which showed among other novelties 'Miss Bellairs' display of 70 varieties of ferns'.[12]

Mansfield was a zealous Churchman of Evangelical persuasion and he accepted the office of Vicar's warden after being given an assurance that 'those ritualistic practices introduced by the late incumbent would be discontinued'. He was a sponsor of the appeal to build a chapel of ease to St James's in the growing parish of West Teignmouth and may have helped to bring a redundant iron church from the Isle of Wight to Teignmouth where it arrived, appropriately enough, in the locally-owned ketch *Reformation*. The church served its purpose for many years although no trace of it now remains. Mansfield was also deeply concerned with life saving in a more material sense; his 'extempore or rough raft' was one of the pieces of life-saving apparatus tested at the Grand Nautical Fete held at Teignmouth in August 1857. It is hardly surprising that such a remarkable career encouraged journalistic exaggeration; an item in the *Western Times* of 5 April 1878 announced that the novelty of 'Mr Mansfield's screw boat *Playmate*' was that she had an engine 'capable of instantaneous reversal whilst running at high speed'.

By the late 1870s most of the estuary shipyards had closed although there were some flourishing boat builders on the Shaldon side of the river such as Bulley and, rather later, Pengelly and Matthews. The 1870s were a difficult time for shipbuilders because ship design was changing very rapidly and the market for new ships was unpredictable. It was Mansfield's experience and his readiness to experiment, combined with his sound practical judgment and concern for economy, which kept the Strand Yard prosperous. He was by far the largest employer in Teignmouth and his death in 1879 was one of the first signs of approaching crisis.

There was other more general evidence for difficulties ahead. Teignmouth ship-owners, like those in other small ports, were suffering from what would nowadays be called shortage of cash flow at a time when traditional partnerships in sixty-fourths were being replaced by single or joint ownership and when the growth of the national economy was slowing down. In December 1878 the West of England Bank in Exeter stopped payment and, although in Teignmouth the successor to Jordan's Bank which had William John Watts and Samuel Whiteway among its partners appears to have got through the crisis largely unscathed, the shock to the regional economy is likely to have made some holders of loans and mortgages anxious to foreclose. Some Teignmouth ship-owners, like the Wards and the Hutchings, were protected by a wide family base and also managed to pick up paid jobs related to their ship-owning. Others who had no such secure base came to grief. John Temple is typical of this less fortunate class.

Temple set up business in 1861 as a partner of J. Coysh, master mariner of Shaldon, and soon became sole owner of six vessels, all of them purchased second-hand. The records illustrate his problems. The brigantine *Alma* 'foundered at sea through springing a leak' (presumably through poor maintenance), the smack *Vectis* was detained by a Board of Trade Inspector because she was loaded below the recently-imposed Plimsoll Line and the brigantine *Fanny* was also reported by a Board of Trade Inspector, on this occasion for 'defective hull and equipments'. The new regulations were not always enforced by a central government preoccupied with Irish and Colonial affairs and the papers of Temple's ships give a hint of the abuses which continued. Across the columns which tabulate the items of food issued to the crew, the master has written the prevarication which seemed a habit among masters at the time: 'Sufficient without waste'. The crew of the brigantine *Aratus* provides further evidence of the economies which Temple felt obliged to make. Early in 1876 the *Aratus* carried a master, a mate, four able seamen, one ordinary seaman and an indentured apprentice. By the end of 1878 she carried a master (the same one), a mate, three able seamen and three apprentices, Isaac Sanders, Lewis Bending and John Chanter, all of Teignmouth. In view of the fact that these apprentices were clearly expected to do the work of experienced seamen it is not surprising that two of them deserted, even if they only exchanged one hell for another by escaping into the dockside slums of Glasgow. Despite these economies Temple went bankrupt and at the bankruptcy proceedings in 1886 it appeared that none of his ships was insured.[13]

Teignmouth ship-owners' difficulties were increased by the short-comings of the harbour which caused delay, and occasionally damage, to their ships. The Harbour Commissioners, burdened with debt, were unable to give effect to Captain Spratt's imaginative scheme for removing the bar or to carry out any other major improvements. The Local Board, predecessor of the Urban District Council, complained that the Commissioners did nothing except 'just to coal tar the buoys'.[14] Mansfield, himself a Commissioner, warned his colleagues of the threat to the future of the port as early as 1864 when, at a meeting of the Commission he

> called attention to ... scheme for the improvement of the harbours in the neighbourhood such as Torquay and Exmouth ... which must all seriously affect the Port of Teignmouth unless this Commission took steps to keep pace with the times by improving the harbour.

Eventually the Commissioners acted; a new patent steam dredger was ordered from Messrs. Priestman 'complete including all recent improvements which experience has suggested for the sum of £500'. Some of the Commissioners appear to have been horrified when the total cost, including a barge, doubled to slightly over £1,000. A steam dredger was something beyond the Harbour Master's comprehension and he plaintively reported a month or so later that 10 pieces of the dredger had arrived – what should he do with them? An engineer came down from Messrs. Priestman and, after he had stayed in Teignmouth for five weeks, received a telegram to return. He was thanked by the Chairman of the Commission and given 'a douceur of £2'; the Clerk seemed surprised and hurt when the firm sent a bill for £12, their engineer 'having been detained longer than expected'. Throughout these discussions the Commissioners, who met sometimes in Teignmouth and sometimes in Newton Abbot at the Town Hall or the *Passage House Inn*, showed themselves deeply concerned with the welfare of the harbour but constantly hampered by their lack of resources.[15]

The lack of resources became even more acute because there was inadequate financial supervision. The entries for 1884 are clearly incomplete and partly incomprehensible. The auditor drew attention to this at the first meeting in 1885, and a special committee of inquiry was appointed which reported that the Collector of Dues (John Beater, perhaps the same John Beater who first went to sea in the *Rifleman*) 'was constantly in a state unfit to attend to business'. At the next meeting he was 'absolutely dismissed'. Presumably John Beater's habits had escaped earlier reprimand because drunkenness must have been common in a seafaring community which, according to a Directory of the time, had 29 inns, as well as seven people who described themselves as brewers or retailers of beer. John Beater also lost his job as Lloyd's Agent and the Committee of Lloyd's decided not to replace him but to add Teignmouth to Lloyd's Agency at Brixham. Clearly the relegation of Teignmouth to a subagency was partly accidental, but it also indicated a loss of both trade and status.

At this time of depression and crisis there were few additional opportunities for those who depended on the port for their livelihood. Smuggling, a source of income for Devon seamen from time immemorial, was a dying trade. Measures to stop smuggling had been intensified after the Napoleonic War and a series of government regulations from 1822 onwards made the smuggler's work more difficult. In 1831 the haphazard organisation of revenue cutters, waterguard and riding officers was consolidated into a Coastguard service under Admiralty supervision. In South Devon, as elsewhere, officers and men of the Coastguard operated under a senior naval officer, with the title of 'Inspecting Commander', who was expected to outwit the smuggler and counter any local sympathy he may still have enjoyed.

It took a generation for the new system to become fully effective and as late as 1857 the Inspecting Commander for the Exmouth district complained that smuggling persisted in some of the creeks in and around the port of Teignmouth:

> Coombe Cellars had always offered a safe and easy means of Transit for Tobacco and Tubs landed anywhere west, the Smugglers passing over Lower Haldon ... and from thence by bye roads to Powderham, where Boats have been in readiness to tow the Goods ... to Lympstone on the River Exe at any time after dusk, tide permitting. Lympstone is as free and open from Contrabandists as any Smuggler could wish ... consequently a notorious haunt of Smugglers who are in constant communication with groups at ... Teignmouth, Coombe Cellars, Bishopsteignton and even the Bristol Channel.[16]

But the officer at Teignmouth declared that 'constant supervision' had been 'strictly observed' at Coombe Cellars 'both by night and day on land and water'. As late as 1877, a case was investigated in which a French vessel was suspected of passing cases of tobacco to Teignmouth fishing boats in the bay, but such incidents were increasingly rare and local families named by the Teignmouth Controller, such as the Bassetts and the Martins, appear to have withdrawn from an increasingly risky and unrewarding occupation.

Fishing was another ancillary occupation which suffered from legal prohibitions, in this case the law of privilege rather than of public goods. When the lord of the manor of Bishopsteignton, the Reverend Comyns, granted a shellfish monopoly to a Mr. Baxter of Billingsgate local people organised a petition in 1885 'to uphold their ancient rights of the fisheries of the Port of Teignmouth'. Their petition was not successful and a fisherman was sent to prison in 1886 for refusing to give an undertaking not to trespass. The argument was settled to no-one's advantage when the Medical Officer of Health decreed that the shellfish was poisonous and that remedial measures would be too expensive. The local seafishermen suffered from the Morton's Fork of all commercial fishermen: either fish were plentiful and therefore virtually unsaleable or else there were no fish to sell. In the 1885 sprat season it was said that the price was very low and in 1886 there were no sprats.[17]

The growing tourist industry, which provided some irregular employment for seamen, was changing in character. Aristocratic visitors were being attracted elsewhere and a correspondent in the *Teignmouth Journal* in 1875 complained, for example, that the owners of large yachts were moving away and Teignmouth was being overtaken by 'places of much greater pretension' elsewhere in the Channel.[18] The day trippers who were arriving in place of more select visitors may have taken a sea excursion to a new attraction like Labrador Tea Gardens, 'amidst flowers, strawberries and cream', but it is more likely that they were ensnared by the amusement machines on the Pier or by the brash entertainments which upset some of the residents, such as 'Cheap Jack's Mart' where those so inclined were invited to 'dip their heads for sixpenny pieces into tubs of flour mixed with ginger'. The one aspect of the tourist industry which directly benefited the maritime community was the steady influx of middle-class visitors who took apartments; in the cottages around the harbour beach, for example, which are now mostly taken over as holiday flats, it was quite usual for a wife and family to live in the basement boathouse while her husband was away on a yacht or engaged in other seasonal employment outside the town. The custom was a sign of very hard times.

The extent of the depression which had settled over the town as well as the port was demonstrated when the Local Board made fools of themselves by resolving that, since the public gas lamps cost ten shillings an hour, they should not be lit for three days before and three days after a full moon. At this stage, when the port seemed on the brink of extinction, local opinion at last asserted itself in a characteristically English way: a public meeting was called, to which a number of eminent persons of impeccable respectability had accepted advance invitations. Also in a characteristic way, the meeting elected a committee to do something. This committee, chosen on 9 September 1886, became the nucleus of the Teignmouth Quay Company which, through many vicissitudes, restored the port to prosperity.

At the public meeting the chairman, C. R. Collins, J.P., drew attention to the shortcomings of the harbour and declared that 'owners of foreign vessels are averse to sending them' because of delays through lack of adequate berths, a deficiency which was emphasised by the fact that, despite improvements to the Old Quay as a result of the railway connection, some vessels still followed the practice of discharging their cargoes into lighters in mid-stream. The meeting gave full support to the outline proposals for quay extensions and E. T. Scammell, who was one of the prime movers, followed up this success with a letter to the *Exeter Evening Post*:

> Let the disappointment and delay of the past move to fresh energy for the present ... the Teignmouth of the future will become a still more prosperous and attractive town than the Teignmouth of the past.[19]

Scammell pointed out that the Harbour Commissioners and the members of the Local Board cordially and unanimously approved of the scheme. He suggested that shopkeepers would benefit from increased custom and private residents from a reduction in the share of rates borne by house property. Finally, in an attempt to turn economic ills to advantage, he argued that the present time was propitious because 'labour is cheap'.

It was announced that a limited liability company had been formed under the sponsorship of Seale Hayne, M.P., the Reverend Anson Cartwright and Messrs. E. Goddard and R. Vicary of Newton, H. B. Varwell of Exeter and P. Ward and E. T. Scammell of Teignmouth. Two of these sponsors were important public figures: Seale Hayne was Liberal M.P. for the mid-Devon division and Anson Cartwright, also a Liberal, was chairman of the Teignmouth Local Board and had accumulated a large number of minor offices in local government which had made him a popular and respected local leader; he had headed the poll at the Local Board elections in

April 1884. The others named in the announcement were merchants who contributed to the trade of the harbour: R. Vicary, who soon dropped out, cannot be identified with certainty but he was probably a member of the tanning firm of that name, Goddard represented one of the large clay companies, and Varwell was an Exeter coal merchant who imported via Teignmouth. Pike Ward, shipbroker and appointed Lloyd's subagent at about this time, was probably the one most closely involved in the day-to-day work of the port. The absence of any representative of Devon landowners, who had played such an important part in earlier harbour development, was one aspect of the shift in the balance of power locally as well as nationally.

E. T. Scammell, whose actions suggest that he was the most optimistic member of the new committee, was a partner in the business of William Scammell and Sons, builders' merchants, with interests in Exeter, Ipplepen and Newton Abbot as well as Teignmouth. He was also, with his father William Scammell, part-owner of the schooner *Elizabeth* which was registered in Teignmouth in 1885 and made regular voyages from London, and occasional voyages from Rochester, with cement and 'general goods'. The younger Scammell lived in Luny House, Teignmouth, was President of the Teignmouth Building Society and played a very prominent part in public affairs and in the religious life of the town. He was described in the local press as 'a gentleman of excellent business pursuits' and many of his activities were reported at length. At a social gathering in January 1891 he

> wished the men to understand that the firm would not throw them over after their years of labour but would recognise their earnest endeavours by rendering them aid in case of accident or illness and by letting them share a portion of the business which they had helped to bring together.

On another occasion he delivered 'an excellent discourse on You cannot serve God *and* Mammon'.[20]

Despite the reputations and connections of the sponsors and directors, the new company soon ran into difficulties. Work began in January 1888, when 'a gang of men were employed in removing the decayed timbers for the purpose of reconstructing and strengthening the wharf so as to make it safe for trucks to be run out to the extreme end'. A few months later 'a portion of the new wharf ... fell in, the dredging ... having undermined the piles'. When contracts were invited for further work the contractor whose estimate had been accepted, John Hayman of Teignmouth, refused to honour it.[21] Scammell had written in his first letter to the press that 'a work of this nature must necessarily be a work of time' and he then tried to encourage and reassure shareholders by stating:

> As to the prospects of the company I can only say that from enquiries and, indeed, promises that Mr Ward and myself are constantly receiving, I infer that there is every possibility of a large increase of the trade of the harbour if this work be carried out.

Additional directors were appointed, including C. R. Collins, possibly because he was a leading Conservative who would give an impression of political balance, and C. R. Stooke who, as a gentleman of independent means, might be expected (correctly as it turned out) to lend money to the company. The harsh facts of the situation are apparent from the early minute books of the Teignmouth Quay Company; by the time the record begins in January 1892 the directors were clearly in trouble.

Under the Provisional Order of 1887, a time limit was set for the completion of the new quays and, when the Board of Trade refused an extension, the secretary of the Quay Company was 'instructed to proceed to London and explain the circumstances'.[22] Eventually, the Board of Trade agreed that rates could be charged although the work was incomplete and in 1893 granted a second Provisional Order which confirmed the very extensive powers conferred in the first one to

> construct and maintain all such walls, piles, piers, wharves, tramways, landing stages and places, roads, approaches, waiting rooms, buildings, sheds, toll houses and gates, cranes, lifts, mooring posts and appliances as may be necessary or convenient in connection with the works authorised by this Order.[23]

The Quay Company needed an income and an extension of time because it was desperately short of cash. The directors changed their bank, borrowed from C. R. Stooke who had become managing director, and found themselves unable to pay their secretary, W. S. Wills, despite 'the great services he had rendered in developing the business of the company':

> Resolved that the secretary having received no remuneration ... during the last five years, the sum of £175 ... be granted to him out of the Capital Account.

On 11 February 1895 the secretary of the Quay Company reported the bankruptcy of E. T. Scammell, who had been absent from recent meetings. Scammell had gone to Australia from where he wrote a very lengthy letter, referred to as his public examination, explaining that he had made the journey, not to evade his creditors, but for the sake of his health and to take part in 'the gold enterprise' which would enable him to repay his debts. For the second time since the port of Teignmouth had won independence, the chief initiator of a new development had himself been obliged to withdraw because of financial failure. In this instance, unlike with George Hennet, failure was a result of local, rather than national, circumstances. It is likely that Scammell's business as a builders' merchant suffered from the lack of development in Teignmouth and its immediate neighbourhood after the short-lived building boom of the 1870s. Census returns show that the population of the parishes of East and West Teignmouth declined from 7,120 in 1881 to 7,006 in 1891. The opening up of the tunnels on both sides of the railway station from 1879 onwards destroyed some housing, especially on the Newton Abbot side, but this was not replaced at the time. Part of the wreckage of Scammell's personal business survived as the Devon Trading Company which retained a close association with the Quay Company. Scammell himself restored his solvency and his reputation by work for the Government of Western Australia, and subsequently for the Canadian Pacific Railway, where his energy and talents had more scope than in his home town of Teignmouth. He died in Toronto at the age of ninety.[24] His name is engraved at the base of the Baptist chapel, within a stone's throw of the Company's quays which were the object of his more material concern.

Scammell's bankruptcy must have seemed a hard blow to the struggling Quay Company. Fortunately, most other members of the original sponsoring group remained. Collins and Seale Hayne were among those appointed trustees for the debenture holders and Anson Cartwright continued as chairman. Cartwright, unlike some other leaders of opinion, was fully aware of current needs in both trade and tourism. He argued in favour of facilities for larger ships as well as additional amenities for visitors, such as a pure and adequate water supply.

In 1894 an Urban District Council replaced the Local Board, which had itself taken over from the Improvement Commissioners in 1850, and Cartwright resigned all his public offices in Teignmouth. This third stage in the evolution of democratic local government was a watershed in the affairs of the town and the port. Parry, in his modestly-entitled *Notes on Old Teignmouth*, remarks:

> In 1894 the Urban District Council assumed control of the affairs of the town, and Old Teignmouth may be said to have come to an end.

The close connection between these two facts only became clear after the First World War, and more patently after the Second, when councillors sought to create a new town at the cost of the old and, while sometimes neglecting the interests of the port, concentrated resources on the kind of alien entertainment which drew easy money in Blackpool and Skegness. For the time being, this lack of respect for what Parry called 'Old Teignmouth' was not apparent and, by unanimously electing the Harbour Master, T. W. Hutchings, as their first chairman, the new councillors recognised the continuing value of the port to the local community. The Quay Company was helped in a more direct way when Whiteway Wilkinson, a partner in one of the largest clay exporting firms, and George Player, coal merchant and shipowner, joined the board and brought new business.

Meanwhile, a cut-back in expenditure was clearly necessary to stop the directors' habit of borrowing among themselves, and the minutes of proceedings illustrate economies with a depressing intimacy:

> Resolved that the smaller bay horse be sold and that the boy Charlie have a week's notice to leave on Saturday ...[25]

All the workmen, except one, were dismissed when the fendering of the quays was complete. Strenuous efforts were made to collect outstanding debts and the steam crane was offered for sale at £40 and disposed of for £12 10s. References to loose cement and weak piling suggest parsimony in completing the construction work which had to be paid for later. These economies, some reasonable and some unwise, helped to put the company on an even keel and in November 1903, for the first time, the secretary was paid a salary in addition to a commission on net revenue.

The Quay Company enjoyed some luck because the construction of the Teign Valley Railway, although it destroyed the chance of a revival of mineral ore coastwise exports, gave a useful temporary boost to imports: Messrs. Dickson of Dunsford, for example, imported 720 loads of sleepers from Riga in 1896. Gradually too, the more positive side of the company's policy began to bear fruit. Considerable success was achieved in letting sites to individuals and firms who usually, though not always, were likely to contribute to the trade of the harbour. A few of those who were granted sites, for themselves or for companies they represented, were members of the board like George Player and Whiteway Wilkinson, who appear to have been scrupulous in withdrawing from discussion concerning the financial arrangements. Others who were granted sites included the Liverpool North Shore Flour and Rice Mill Company, the Devon Trading Company, which dealt in timber and building materials, and the Acetylene Illuminating Company, which imported calcium carbide. One of the tenants engaged in foreign trade was the Jadoo Company which was started with a flourish of trumpets but soon stopped trading. The company imported 'moss fibre' from the continent and then exported 'jadoo'; what process, if any, was carried out in the quayside warehouse was not made known. Colonel Halford Thompson, the proprietor, explained at a dinner in the *Railway Hotel* that 'jadoo' was the Hindu word for 'magic', an appropriate description for the miraculous fertiliser which he had discovered. The dinner celebrated, the Colonel said, the despatch of the first consignment in the schooner *Aim Well* for London where it would be transhipped to the West Indies and used to produce huge crops of 'cocoa, nutmegs and rubber'; great things were expected of it. But only one repeat cargo, to Guernsey, was sent from Teignmouth and the Jadoo Company disappeared along with its colourful proprietor. Only the name remained on the warehouse, to mystify a later generation of visitors and to encourage local people to weave a tale.

A more modest enterprise, which had begun a little earlier, lasted very much longer. Every spring a small fleet of French schooners arrived in Teignmouth from the tiny port of Perros with cargoes of early potatoes for Sercombe and Company of Exeter; each vessel rarely carried more than 30 tons or so. Occasionally onions were brought in as a whole or part cargo, but most of the Breton peasant-sailors who cycled around the roads of the Westcountry with strings of onions perched precariously on their handlebars had landed their produce at Torquay, not Teignmouth. The revenue accruing to the port of Teignmouth from this trade was insignificant, but the picturesque ships with French religious and family names, gaily-coloured hulls and dark brown sails were an even greater attraction to early visitors than the fleet of Brixham trawlers in their heyday. The present official link between Perros-Guirec and Teignmouth has a much stronger historical justification than most such twinnings.

In order to attract further new trade the Quay Company proposed concessionary inclusive charges: for example, they offered Messrs. Reed and Smith, paper manufacturers of Cullompton, a rate of 10d. per ton, inclusive of harbour dues, on woodpulp provided the annual import exceeded 2,000 tons. Anxious to increase revenue in whatever way possible, the company resolved that 'half dues be charged on all goods landed from or discharged into barges by vessels lying within the Company's limits', but they accepted a compromise offer from Messrs. Watts, Blake, Bearne of 1d. a ton for coal sent upstream on their clay barges.[26]

These initiatives by the Quay Company were matched by a progressive policy on the part of the Harbour Commission. A permanent committee was appointed to review harbour dues in relation to charges at other ports and presumably also in line with concessions offered by the Quay Company. This committee recommended, and the Commission itself approved, reductions on the import of woodpulp, oats, soap and 'jadoo' fibre and on the export of granite chippings. It considered possible rebates on the import of petroleum and agreed to concessions on the export of earthenware for large quantities. More important, the Commission went ahead with harbour improvements by extending both the groyne at the Point and the retaining wall at the Ness; the Bench rocks at the foot of the Ness were partially removed by blasting. The bar was still troublesome and, as an alternative to the steam dredger, the Commissioners experimented with a mechanical blower from Messrs. Merryweather which, they were given to understand, had been successfully used at Harwich and Littlehampton. They were sufficiently impressed to purchase one second-hand for £300 and the Harbour Master reported that it was immediately effective. The Harbour Commissioners explained in a note to the local press how the blower worked: that water was 'forced under a high pressure from the nozzle in a powerful downward jet, which, impinging upon the sand, at once disperses it and it is carried away by the tide'.

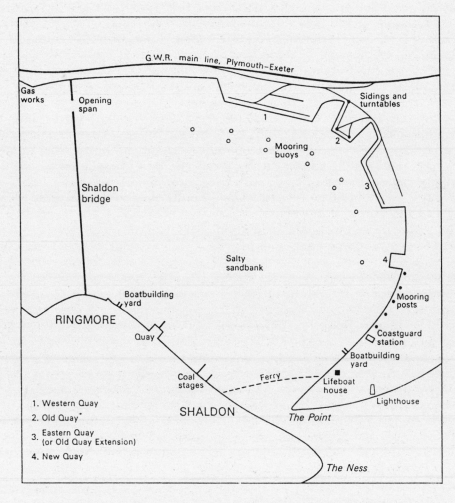

Fig. 7 Teignmouth Harbour, c. 1900. The pattern of the quays has not changed since 1900, but the jetties at Shaldon, the mooring buoys and the railway sidings have disappeared or are obscured. A fish quay has been built between Eastern and New Quays.

Dredging in the harbour itself was less successful. The Quay Company had borrowed the Commissioners' dredger on favourable terms to dredge their new berths, but the work does not appear to have been adequately done; when in 1901 the owners of the S.S. *Millgate*, which had loaded clay at the Old Quay, brought an action for damages to their vessel caused by lying in a bad berth, the Company felt obliged to settle for £192. Further dredging caused a ridge to develop near the deep water channel which was dangerous to navigation and provoked a quarrel with the Harbour Commission about responsibility and cost of removal. The relations between the two bodies had already become strained, despite some overlapping membership, as a result of the financial difficulties of the company; the Commissioners complained, for example, that the Quay Company borrowed their barge for dredging and then used it for carrying coal and mixing cement. After some acrimonious correspondence, harmony was restored and the ridge removed to the satisfaction of the Harbour Commission.

The eight berths, five of them new, were thought to be satisfactory and in November 1904 Captain Finch, a surveyor, and Mr. Bartlett, the company's diver, reported that they were all 'fit for any vessels to lie in'. These developments, and the controversy surrounding them, stimulated considerable public interest and one of the Commissioners, Whiteway Wilkinson, suggested that the press should be admitted to their meetings. This was too radical a proposal for the time and he had only one supporter; but, apparently as a consequence of agitation by the Urban District Council, the Board of Trade appointed 'two carefully selected persons' to the Commission, Preston Cooke, J.P., and Alfred Findeisen, both local people who came to play an important part in discussions.

Although progress since the inauguration of the harbour improvement scheme in 1888 had been erratic, it seemed that by 1904 most of the initial problems had been overcome and rewards were about to be reaped. Trade figures justified this confidence: in 1904 foreign imports were 15,529 tons compared with 6,870 tons 10 years earlier and only 1,170 tons in 1884. It was foreign imports particularly which the originators of the scheme hoped to attract and the detailed returns indicate their success. The Import Book for 1904 shows that most traditional foreign imports revived: hides and oak extract for Messrs. Vicary's tannery, flints for the Bovey Pottery Company, timber and slates for the building industry. 'General goods' were imported from Antwerp, traffic which presaged a possible regular service. By far the most important new trade was the import of woodpulp for Messrs. Reed and Smith of Cullompton and the Hele Paper Company of Silverton for which a concessionary rate had been granted on an annual import in excess of 2,000 tons: in fact, the total for 1904 was over 10,000 tons in large cargoes which averaged 600 tons. Woodpulp replaced rags in the Devonshire paper industry from the 1880s onwards and Teignmouth was able to establish a large new import trade in substitution for a much smaller, older one.

The majority of vessels which brought in cargoes of woodpulp were Norwegian and Swedish steamships and one of these, the Norwegian steamer *Bembro*, brought from Christiania (Oslo) the largest cargo so far imported into Teignmouth, 1,126 tons. Occasionally these vessels discharged small consignments of other Scandinavian products, such as calcium carbide. The consular records show that in 1904 26 Norwegian and Swedish vessels arrived in Teignmouth compared with 15 in 1894 and four in 1884. Of these, 19 brought woodpulp and one timber; the others arrived in ballast to load clay. Apparently the steamers which were chartered for woodpulp were of too large a capacity to meet the requirements of the clay companies for their Scandinavian customers and they usually sailed light to English, Welsh or Scottish coal ports. A Vice-Consulate for Sweden and Norway had been set up as soon as the port became independent and Arthur Owen was Vice-Consul for some 40 years; his duties were largely nominal, but by the time Pike Ward took over in 1895 the work was appreciable. Entries in the consular records show that he was concerned with such details as the collection of 'Church dues' from Swedish vessels, as well as with more general matters affecting the welfare of crews and the interests of owners.[27] And not only did the consular office itself become more important: the fact that the steamer *Elsa*, to take one example, paid dues on a register tonnage of 843, had a crew of 17 and stayed in port for six days suggests the very important contribution which this new business made both to the revenue of the harbour and to the local economy. One particular consequence of the frequent arrival of large ships was the provision of a powerful steam tug, the *Regia*, newly built at Liverpool, to replace the old and unseaworthy *Pioneer* which was broken up in 1893. The *Regia* was owned by the Regia Steam Tug Company whose office was in Regia House, now the *Regia Hotel*, and gave satisfactory service until she was sold in 1915. She worked with, and sometimes competed with, the tug *Teign* which was owned and managed by local people and provided what services were needed, either by large steamers or by sailing vessels without auxiliary engines, until 1924.

The basic trades in coal and clay were doing well and benefited from increased quayside accommodation. Despite competition from other ports, the tonnage of coal imported rose from 29,052 in 1894 to 36,892 in 1904. Since sailing vessels were increasingly being replaced by steamers, discharging methods were speeded up and distribution became more efficient, although one proposal, for the erection of an overhead tramway from the Old Quay to the Gas Works just above Shaldon Bridge, was not pursued. Up to the 1880s, some coal cargoes were still quite small, but the harbour records for 1904 show that by this time there were no cargoes of less than 100 tons and only 12 under 200 tons. Some local merchants probably did not wish to deal with very large consignments and the average size of imports was still modest at 330 tons; on the other hand there were nine cargoes of over 600 tons. George Player apparently reached an agreement with the Broomhill Colliery Company of Newcastle whom he had earlier regarded as a rival. At first, the company imported in their own vessels and the S.S. *Broomhill* made regular voyages with cargoes of around 570 tons. Later in the year the *G. Player*, one of two steamers owned by George Player, brought in a cargo of 709 tons for which the consignees were recorded as the Broomhill Colliery Company; this was one of the biggest coal cargoes imported into Teignmouth so far. Apart from the increasing size of cargoes, the coal trade was also healthy in that the range of markets was widening and importers during 1904 included merchants as far away as Yeovil; on the other hand, the growing commercial activity of Torquay harbour was reflected in the loss of the Brixham market.

A similar trend towards larger cargoes was evident in the clay trade. Exports to British and Irish ports increased between 1894 and 1904 from 56,002 tons to 76,720 tons and the average size of cargoes from 186 tons to 214 tons. Foreign imports nearly doubled in the same period from 13,588 tons to 23,758 tons; the average size of foreign cargoes remained constant at 260 tons, but this overall figure obscured the fact that a widening range of demand for small consignments was balanced by an expanding market in Italy and Spain which was supplied in very large cargoes. Exports to Genoa, for example, included one cargo of 650 tons and one, the largest for the year, of 770 tons. The method of loading overside from barges continued and owners of sailing vessels and some steamers appear to have been reluctant to incur additional dues by using the Quay Company's wharves, or preferred their vessels to load always afloat, despite the opportunity for quicker loading at the quayside. The increasing size of vessels caused complications because the Harbour Commission imposed a limit on the length of vessels using the buoys of 120 feet, later raised to 130 feet. The Harbour Master reported that he had great difficulty in enforcing this restriction. Early in 1901, for example, he said that the captain of the *Princess of Wales*, 144 feet long, threatened that he would hold the Commissioners responsible if his vessel was damaged by taking the ground at the quay; later he reported that the master of the *Cuttica* refused to move at his orders and had to be warned by the Clerk.

One incident, just beyond the period under review, described at length by the Harbour Master, emphasises the problems of a small port unable to adapt its facilities easily to the changing pattern of maritime commerce:

> On the 23rd. inst. [June 1905] the s.s. *Harold* arrived in the Harbour and, as I saw that she was moving to No. 1 Salty Tier, I got a boat and went off. I found that she was attached to the Harbour Buoy at the stern and riding flood to her own anchor at the bow. I had an interview with the Captain and told him he must move his vessel as she was over the limit. He replied 'I have instructions from my owner to moor her in this way'. I said 'You are aware I am the Harbour Master ... I have to tell you that if you disobey me you are liable to a penalty not exceeding £20'. He said 'If I obey you I shall get the sack: if I obey the owner you tell me I shall be fined £20'.[28]

The S.S. *Harold* stayed at the buoys and loaded; the Justices imposed a nominal penalty of £1. It was perhaps as a result of this incident that the restriction on length was removed a year or so later. Meanwhile, the Quay Company benefited from the unsuitability of the moorings for large vessels and sought to drive home their advantage by arranging for the erection of clay stores on the Western Quay. The company was also able to provide facilities when clay-carrying vessels loaded extra cargo, as when the *Charlotte* took on 50 tons of earthenware pipes for Seville in addition to 230 tons of clay. Such 'topping-up' cargo was rare despite advertisements from time to time in *Lloyd's List* for vessels fixed to load clay in Teignmouth for foreign parts.

The general coasting trade, too, showed signs of recovery after the depression of the 1880s, although it was not as buoyant as the coal and clay trades. The import of fertilisers, for long an important trade, recovered to the level of the 1870s and cement imports increased from a few very small cargoes to 22 full and part cargoes, totalling approximately 2,400 tons, in 1904. Coastwise exports, apart from clay, were not as large as the mineral exports of earlier years but included substantial quantities of bricks sent to the Isle of Wight and the Channel Islands by Candy & Co. of Chudleigh and Hexter Humpherson of Newton Abbot. For a short time, petroleum in barrels was imported from Cardiff and Plymouth but this trade was lost when petroleum was carried direct from the U.S.A. to the Exe estuary.

On the other hand, one major success was the establishment, after many attempts, of a steamship service on a regular and scheduled basis, this time from Liverpool, not London. The Powell Line of Liverpool, which had its beginnings in the 1830s and introduced steamers from 1850, sent one of its vessels, the *South Coast*, to Teignmouth experimentally in 1898. A regular service was built up which, beginning with consignments of flour and oilcake, attracted cargoes of increasing size and variety.[29] In 1904, 12 steamers arrived at approximately monthly intervals, including the *British*

Monarch which brought 353 tons of general cargo from Liverpool and returned with 420 tons of clay; frequently, however, steamers arrived with part-cargoes which meant that it was not feasible to load bulk clay outwards. The increasing proportion of steamships, in both coastal and foreign trade, was significant for local employment. On 23 December the *Teignmouth Post* commented that the last week had been one of the most remunerative to the lumpers of Teignmouth 'than any' for the year: during this period six steamers had discharged at the Quay Extension, 'a thing unprecedented in the annals of the Port'. The writer pointed out that, although steamers did not provide as much business for shopkeepers as sailing vessels since they were in dock for a shorter time, they gave more work to lumpers because the crews of steamers did not work cargo.

This general expansion around 1900 did not include the Newfoundland trade. The Mediterranean market for codfish was lost and the home market was weak. A feature of this traditional trade in its last days was the contrast between very fast passages and slow discharge. In the autumn of 1877 the schooner *Cicerone*, with a cargo for G. P. Ward, reached Teignmouth from St John's in 13 days, land to land in 11 days which was said to be a record. But in the same year the *Star of Peace* took 49 days to unload her cargo; according to a Customs Officer, who may have been suspicious of smuggling, 'there were frequent intervals in which she was silent, no doubt awaiting a market'. Dried cod was not a very palatable food and the year after the slow discharge by the *Star of Peace* two Teignmouth shopkeepers were fined for selling codfish 'unfit for human food'. One of the defendants said that he had purchased it from Mr. Ward and he and his family had eaten it for breakfast for three weeks without coming to any harm.[30] Bankruptcies in Newfoundland added to the problems of Westcountry traders and the last cargo of codfish came from St John's to Teignmouth in 1893. For a little longer small cargoes of fish and other products were imported from Iceland, carried by the locally-owned schooner which has been referred to earlier, the *S.R. and H.*. Newfoundland merchants who had moved to Liverpool, like the Bowrings, began to introduce steamships from the 1870s onwards, but those who still traded to Westcountry ports remained faithful to sailing ships to the end. The *Blodwen*, one of the fleet of 'Immortal Sail' from Portmadoc, brought fish to Exeter in the 1900s and a small Salcombe schooner, the *Lady St Johns*, maintained a Devon trading link with Newfoundland until 1930.[31] For Teignmouth in the 20th century only personal associations and memories remained. E. J. Tozer, a member of a Teignmouth partnership of solicitors and sometime secretary to the Harbour Commission, was described in *Kelly's Directory* as late as 1914 as 'commissioner for Supreme Court of Newfoundland'. Older residents remember the whalebone arches on the seafront, 'presented by Pike Ward Esquire', which probably came from whaling expeditions based on St John's. Today the gaunt storehouse, with its thick walls and narrow windows, near the Custom House and overlooking the bustle of the harbour, stands as a memorial to three centuries of distant endeavour.

These romantic survivals need to be balanced by the harsh facts, for example, concerning William Revell of Ipplepen. William Revell served as a seaman in the Newfoundland trade in the schooner *Mayflower* and the brigs *Susan* and *Hope*; after 26 years at sea he was discharged because of 'frequent attacks of rheumatism'. His first request to Trinity House for a pension was made in 1842 and then his employer, Richard Weeks of Ipplepen in whose house Revell lived as a lodger, wrote: 'Any assistance you may be able to extend to him will be given where it is much wanted'.

Finally, in 1849, Revell sent a doctor's report: 'I find him very infirm suffering from rheumatic affliction of the limbs, almost incapable of earning anything, at times quite a cripple'. These requests were countersigned by the Vicar of Ipplepen and Robert Boden of Ringmore who had personal experience of what the Newfoundland trade was like.[32]

Despite the final loss of the dwindling Newfoundland trade, total traffic increased appreciably between 1898 and 1904. The measure of success which had been achieved by the Quay Company was reflected in its own financial recovery and in the accounts of the Harbour Commission. From 1895 onwards an annual statement of accounts is attached to the Commission minute book: for the first three years income declined, but from the financial year 1898-9 onwards it increased consistently for the next six years, which suggests that a policy of lowering rates had, as the Commissioners hoped, increased total revenue. Altogether, it seemed that the initiatives which had been taken at the depth of the depression in 1886 and the policies pursued since then had fully justified themselves. Altogether, despite the fact that a policy of modernisation was not adopted until 1886 and then suffered a number of setbacks, it seemed that by 1904 the affairs of the harbour and the port were in good shape. The next year, in a not over-generous gesture, the Harbour Commissioners increased the Harbour Master's salary to £100 a year.[33]

Chapter Eight

Struggle for Survival: 1904-1939

At this time, when the port seemed to be growing busier almost every day, a new problem raised its head: the conflict between the shipping interest and the tourist interest, with the residents who belonged to neither group themselves divided. It was said that 'to satisfy the shipping interest' the outlet pipe between the Old and New Quays was too small and that consequently what should have gone out to sea on the ebb tide was, in heavy rainstorms, coming back into the streets and houses (as it still occasionally does). It is more likely that the pipe was too small for reasons of economy rather than to satisfy the Harbour Authorities. In most matters there was still harmony because Teignmouth was a tightly-knit community where each person respected the other's interest and complications had not arisen through the influx of large numbers of retired people. Directories around the turn of the century illustrate how people of different occupations lived cheek by jowl. In Teign Street those who were listed included 'sea captain', 'ship's chandler', 'sailor's outfitter'and 'marine engineer' as well as 'brewer', 'baker', 'shoemaker' and, rather surprisingly, 'cowkeeper'. In the larger houses on the Strand some occupations were dual and a 'master mariner', for example, put himself down as 'lodgings', also.

The editorial and correspondence columns of the *Teignmouth Post* make it clear that public opinion considered the comings and goings of ships as much an attraction to visitors in the early 20th century as 'the bustle and importance of commerce' had been in the late 18th. On 5 July 1901, a correspondent drew attention to 'the very fine craft' which had come into the harbour in addition to steamships:

> the French schooner *Louise* from Bordeaux with tan extract, the German dandy *Bremerhaven* from Bremen with oilcake, the Irish brigantine *Gartsherrie* from Newcastle with coal, the Italian barquentine *Papa Giovanni* from Rotterdam in ballast.

Teignmouth people apparently thought that the varied attractions of a busy commercial harbour would bring dollars from America. A poster which, by a remarkable piece of local initiative, circulated in cities of the eastern seaboard of the United States showed, not Edwardian bathing belles disporting themselves on the beach or yachts sailing in the Regatta, but merchant ships loading from barges in midstream and a large steamer discharging into railway trucks.

This range of activity also brought to Teignmouth those with a professional interest in shipping. A correspondent of *The Syren and Shipping* commented on a vessel 'which attracted a good deal of attention while she recently lay at Teignmouth, Devon':

> The vessel was iron built throughout, with a straight stem and three short masts, hinged to allow of their being lowered when required in passing up rivers or canals ... A petroleum motor of about 60 h.p. was right aft, and when once started could be controlled by the captain on the poop deck ... The motor ... was always used to go in and out of port, thus saving all towage fees ... This little vessel carried 335 tons on a draught of about 11ft. (and) ... has the advantage of being able to serve most of the small ports around the coast.

Apart from the romantic and technical interest which the harbour generated, local people appreciated that the port was valuable for economic reasons because it gave employment, even if somewhat erratically, throughout the year. By this time not many crews were working cargo, except those serving in Russian ships, and what was on offer was eagerly sought after. When a steamer was due with a large consignment of wood pulp three lumpers (Messrs. Broom, Butcher and Whitlock) rowed out to meet her; they were unlucky because their boat capsized in a squall under the Ness.

Older customs continued in the port of Teignmouth alongside the new. Nothing makes the mixed character of the port in the early 20th century clearer than the careers of the last two Teignmouth ship-owners, James Finch and George Player; both followed the modern pattern of ownership by an individual or a limited company rather than a partnership in sixty-fourths but, whereas Finch stayed in sail, Player invested in steam as early as 1899, one of the first Westcountry owners in a small port to do so.

Finch, unlike most of his predecessors, did not enter ship-owning through a seagoing career. From an apparently humble origin, he started a coal merchant's business and began to purchase sailing vessels at a time when prices were low because of competition from steamships and growing foreign participation in traditionally British trades. Between 1896 and 1903 he purchased six vessels:

Vessel	built	purchased
Millie Bain (brigantine)	1872	1896
Eliza Bain (schooner)	1864	1898
Netherton (brigantine)	1872	1901
Eldra (barquentine)	1873	1901
William (barquentine)	1872	1903
Countess of Devon	1873	1903[1]

These vessels were not old by contemporary standards but most of them had been engaged in hard foreign trade and some had been damaged. The *Countess of Devon*, for example, had carried coal from Wales to South America and chrome ore from the Sea of Marmara to Glasgow. The *Netherton* encountered a hurricane on a voyage from Leith to Martinique and had subsequently been damaged by collision in the English Channel and abandoned at Weymouth.

The fate of some of Finch's vessels suggests that, like those of John Temple, they were not always adequately repaired or maintained. The *Millie Bain* sprang a leak off Holland and the crew spent 30 hours at the pumps; two steamers, including one bound for Teignmouth, were unable to render assistance, but the crew and the Teignmouth master, Sam Lockyer, were eventually rescued by a German tug. The crews of two other vessels were less fortunate. In 1907 the *Countess of Devon* sank in a storm off the Mersey and no one was saved. In 1910 the *William* was reported floating derelict in the North Sea by another ship and her loss remained a mystery. At the official enquiry, the Teignmouth shipwright who worked for Finch said he had seen vessels 'a lot worse' and there was no suggestion of criminal negligence. The facts brought out at the enquiry suggested three possible causes of the disaster: neither the master nor the mate held a certificate, the *William*'s copper bottom had been removed when she was last under repair, and she left Blyth with a slight list. £745 was collected in Teignmouth for the dependents of the local members of the crew. The *Eliza Bain* had been wrecked earlier, within a few years of purchase, but a local report does not give any hint of unseaworthiness. She sailed for Sunderland with clay on 27 November 1902 and was lost with all hands when she struck one of the piers at the harbour entrance in bad visibility; it was said that the lights had been altered very recently and that the captain, who knew the coast well, was not aware of the change. James Finch named his house after the *Eldra*, a vessel for which he seems to have had a particular affection; but in November 1903, two years after Finch bought her, three of the crew claimed that she was unseaworthy and, given the choice of going to prison for six months or going to sea, chose prison. The magistrate accepted Finch's argument that the men planned to miss the tide at Teignmouth so that the ship would be neaped for at least a week.[2]

Whatever the rights and wrongs of this particular case, and whether or not Finch evaded the protective legislation inspired by Samuel Plimsoll, it is clear from crew agreements that he managed his fleet in an extremely economical way. The crew of the *Eldra* signed on on terms which strike a present-day reader as harsh:

> The crew shall work all cargo and ballast where and when required, no member of the crew to leave when the vessel is discharging, loading or loaded, any member of the crew wanting to leave shall give the master 24 hours notice before the cargo is discharged at final port of discharge in the U.K.

The *Eldra* traded to coastal and near continental ports, including frequent visits to Teignmouth and fairly regular voyages to the east and west coasts of Scotland. When in dock in the Firth of Forth one of the crew was injured and the entry in the log illustrates the harsh realities of life at sea for the ordinary seaman:

> sending is wages to the infirmary witch is £1. 11s. 9d. Paying for the ambulance from Bridgness to Idenburgh £1. 10s. ... due to seaman 1s. 9d.[3]

This entry was signed by W. H. Brokenshire, the *Eldra*'s master. Brokenshire's seamanship may have been better than his spelling but it seems clear that he, or more probably his ship, failed to win the confidence of the crew. From Bridgness, the *Eldra* went to Dysart and Paimpol and then did a round trip from Glasgow to Teignmouth. At the end of this voyage, in December 1913, the crew consisted of a seaman from Newfoundland, a Norwegian, a Spaniard and a German aged 65, plus the cook who came from Shaldon; the only other local man had deserted at Falmouth. The *Eldra*, like the *Netherton*, was lost at the height of the U-boat campaign in 1917 when she was captured by a German submarine and sunk by bombs; a cynic might remark that the bombs need not have been very powerful.

It was not only seamen who suffered from Finch's economical management. One of the Teignmouth pilots brought an action for assault in September 1900 when 'he (Finch) called me a chucklehead and tried to throw me into the harbour'. Apparently the pilot said that his ship needed two tugs when Finch thought that one was enough; on this occasion the magistrates found against Finch, but showed where their sympathies lay by fining him one shilling. In other respects also Finch asserted what he regarded as his rights. In 1893 he purchased the New Quay from the Earl of Devon into whose hands it had passed after having been sold by George Templer to the Duke of Somerset. The New Quay appeared redundant after the building of the Western Quay and the extensions to the Old Quay, especially as it had no rail connection and poor road access; on the other hand, it may have appealed to Finch because it had space for storage and office accommodation and offered three possible working berths. The berths were not entirely satisfactory, even though the depth of water was much greater than it is now, and Finch sought to improve matters by ordering ballast to be discharged, presumably to make the berths more nearly level. He did this without the approval of the Harbour Commission and a motion was moved in the Harbour Committee, of which he was chairman, that he should be ordered to remove it. Finch refused to accept the resolution, but eventually appears to have recognised the authority of the Harbour Commission, although whether he took away the ballast is not clear. After Finch had become a Commissioner, he continually pressed for improvements to the harbour entrance; in 1903 the British Dredging Company wrote to the Clerk that they 'had been informed' (possibly by Finch) that the Commission proposed dredging the bar and they wished to tender, but the Clerk was instructed to reply that they had no such intention.

Finch's concern was understandable because his vessels were frequently delayed or inconvenienced: the *Eldra*, for example, on one occasion had to take on the last 20 tons of her cargo from a barge outside the bar and shortly afterwards the *Countess of Devon*, coming in fully laden on a draught of 13 feet, grounded and had to jettison 50 tons of her coal cargo before she was towed off by two tugs, one a more powerful tug from Plymouth. Despite these accidents to his ships, Finch appears to have done well financially and when he died in 1929 the will of 'James William Finch, gentleman', showed that he left a fortune of some £18,000. Wealth and status had come the hard way, for himself and others. Finch's memorial stands in the windswept cemetery high above the town, next to that of George Player, but remote from the simple headstones of generations of small ship-owners who lived and died in the waterside parishes of St Nicholas and West Teignmouth.

George Player pursued a different policy from Finch and was perhaps more typical of Westcountry ship-owners at this time. He also was both coal merchant and ship-owner but his business was much larger. An advertisement in the *Teignmouth Post* in 1904 announced:

> Player's West of England Coal Depot
> Cargoes now discharging and on passage per *Staperayder*, *Lisette*,
> *Tarragona*, *Alma*, *Frau Minna Petersen*, *Falke*, *Anna* and
> *Sweiks* ...

Some of the vessels with foreign-sounding names were British-owned but the list shows the extent and range of Player's chartering. He also owned vessels himself and had the capital resources to purchase new ones. The first vessel to appear on the Teignmouth Register as owned by George Player was the schooner *Natalla* in 1896; three years after purchase she was replaced by the steamship *Player*, built to order at Irvine. By this time George Player had turned himself into the Player Steamship Company Limited with a nominal capital of £10,000.

In 1904 a much larger vessel, the *G. Player*, was launched by the Ailsa Shipbuilding Company of Troon, the naming ceremony by Miss Player being reported in the local press. The *G. Player* was of 267 tons register and had a speed of 10½ knots. The official papers of the *Player* and the *G. Player* show that these steamers gave new opportunities for employment but that the better-paid jobs went to outsiders. Henry George, who hailed from South Wales, was appointed mate of the *Player*, then took over as master of the new *G. Player* and stayed with her until she was sold. He had a very high reputation and earned salvage money for himself and his employer when he carried out a remarkable feat of seamanship in towing to Plymouth the disabled German tug *Unterweser No. 15*, broken down off Portland in bad weather. For a short time, the mate of the *G. Player* was a Teignmouth man, Henry Sharland , but the first and second engineers were almost invariably Scots and local seamen seem not to have won advancement beyond firemen; as such, under the terms of agreement, they were required to interchange with seamen at the master's discretion. But wages were rather higher than in sail, the crew supplied their own food, which was probably an advantage, and they were not normally expected to work cargo.

The *G. Player* was primarily a collier although she occasionally carried other cargo: in April 1911, for example, she brought to Teignmouth some 300 tons of pig iron for Messrs. Willey of Exeter. But, like the Scandinavian steamers which brought woodpulp, Player's owned and chartered vessels were of too large a capacity to meet the normal needs of the clay companies. Moreover, the companies' insistence on clean holds was a practical drawback to loading a direct cargo after discharging coal. Up to 1910, the *G. Player* traded fairly regularly to Teignmouth from Scotland and the north-east coast: five voyages in 1906 and nine in 1908, in which year the Player Steamship Company did well and paid a dividend of six per cent as well as putting a small sum to reserves. The *G. Player* was an infrequent visitor to Teignmouth after 1910 and during the first six months of 1913 did not come at all, making most of her voyages from South Wales to France with coal and from North Wales to south coast ports with stone.[4] In June 1914 she was sold to John Kelly and Company of Belfast, her sister ship, the *Player*, having been sold abroad two years earlier. Under her new name of *Clew Bay*, the *G. Player* continued to be smartly kept and admonitory notices, like 'Wipe your feet', displayed in highly polished brass, had to be strictly observed.[5] The coal store and turntables on the Old Quay where Player's steamers discharged their cargoes fell into disuse and ruin until they were demolished to make an open quay for cranes and conveyors, a process of modernisation in line with Player's own attempts to adapt a small port to a large-scale model.

Player's steamships, like Finch's sailing vessels, were handicapped by the shortcomings of the port which both owners tried unsuccessfully to overcome. In September 1907 the directors of the Quay Company resolved that

> Mr Player be informed that if he berths the s.s. *G. Player* alongside the Old Quay it must be done at his own risk as he is aware of the siltage.[6]

At a subsequent meeting of the Harbour Commission, George Player asked the depth of water on the bar at high water neap tides; he probably asked this question because, a few weeks before, the *G. Player*, with a full cargo of 700 tons, waited off the bar for three tides and then stranded when trying to come in, remaining aground for a further two days.

The full story of Player's steamers, a sad tale of enterprise ill-rewarded, can be gleaned from the records or, in a more intimate way, from the diary of a local tradesman, Mr. Albert Best, who commented on the happenings in the harbour. Almost as soon as the *Player* arrived, on 19 March 1899, Mr. Best appreciated the problems:

> ss Player arrived to Bar. Neap tides and much sea with E. wind. She did not venture to run in.

Mr Best also remarked that as soon as Player's ships were in dock they were discharged quickly. The *G. Player*, he wrote, unloaded her full cargo of 700 tons of coal in 14 hours, 40 men working from 6 a.m. to 8 p.m. for which they received 16 shillings. Unfortunately speed of discharge did not make up for delays in entering and leaving the harbour. The master and the pilots did all they could, as is clear from a news item in the *Teignmouth Post*:

> The *G. Player* approached Teignmouth in a tremendous sea and the pilots were unable to cross the bar. The tug *Regia* steamed out as far as the Ness and the pilot on board [J. Matthews] showed the steamer the proper channel by waving a flag on a pole. The *G. Player* came in safely while hundreds of people watched from the shore in torrential rain.[7]

The impression given by the high trade and revenue figures for 1904 had been misleadingly favourable. The experience of the last two Teignmouth ship-owners, one depending on old ships and one introducing new, proved that the basic problems of the difficult entrance and silting in the harbour itself had not been solved. Nor did other harbour activities suggest a more encouraging future for the port. After Mansfield's death in 1879 the Strand Shipyard experienced varied fortunes under the management of local people, first Flemmick and Schank (who called themselves the Teignmouth Ship and Yacht Company) and then Gann and Palmer who operated the yard until shortly before the First World War. No merchant vessel was built after 1879 although repair jobs were carried out much later, including survey and major repair on the Chester schooner *Elizabeth Jane* in 1909 which may have been the last work done on a merchant vessel. The records of the Strand Shipyard have been lost apart from a little miscellaneous correspondence; this includes a letter to Captain Schank from the Governor of H.M. Prison, Reading – would he make an offer for two tons of oakum? The reply if any, was not filed.

Casualties, delays and legal actions emphasised the problems of the Quay Company and the Harbour Commission. Even in the prosperous year of 1904 there was one serious mishap which attracted a good deal of attention. The large Russian schooner *Krauss* was chartered to bring a cargo of coal from Newcastle and then load outwards with clay for Genoa; arriving at neap tides, she waited at Dartmouth and was then towed to Teignmouth by the tug *Teign*, but grounded on the bar and reached the Old Quay with a foot of water in her holds. The owners of the *Teign* claimed salvage, as did the pilot and the owners of the *Regia* which had assisted in the rescue operation. In the Admiralty Court Mr. Justice Barnes granted the *Regia*'s claim but ordered that it should be paid, as well as other costs, by the owners of the *Teign* because her captain had been negligent. A few years later another Russian schooner, the *Settie*, was in the news for a different reason. Outward bound for Lisbon, she ran aground on a sandbank and one of her crew jumped overboard; despite his protests, he was forcibly returned. The *Emerald*, which ran aground on Shaldon beach in the autumn of 1906, was another casualty which attracted a good deal of interest because she had been converted back to sail from steam, an apparently retrograde step taken by a few owners at this time because steam engines for ships were very extravagant of fuel, a point which must have worried George Player when his ships were delayed.

The Salcombe schooner *Grace*, 87 tons, was lost on Teignmouth bar on 16 October 1907; she was a regular Newfoundland trader, and was wrecked when coming in to load clay coastwise after having discharged her codfish at Exeter. Her captain, George Wyatt, owned 12 shares[8] and may have over-persuaded the master of the Exmouth tug *Queen of the Exe* to press on with the short voyage. It was extremely rough and on the same day the barge *Glencoe*, on passage from Rochester to Teignmouth with cement, lost her topmast and suffered other damage although she eventually arrived safely. When the *Grace* bumped heavily on the bar the tow-rope parted and she drove ashore under the Ness: 'the hurried departure (of the *Queen of the Exe*) was the cause of some comment', but Captain Wyatt, his wife and the two crew members were rescued by the combined efforts of the captain of the *Regia* and coastguards and pilots, while the lifeboat *Alfred Staniforth* stood by. The *Teignmouth Post* reported that the *Grace*'s keel and planks were as good as new and that 'few who saw her could believe she was 38 years old and had made so many voyages to Newfoundland and back'. Her bowsprit was reputedly incorporated in a skiff, the *Solitaire*, which was used for many years by a member of the Morgan Giles family and is now in Exeter Maritime Museum. Her figurehead has also survived.[9] It was not only sailing vessels which suffered from the poor state of Teignmouth bar and harbour. A few months after the loss of the *Grace*, the Norwegian steamer *Rap*, entering with a full cargo of woodpulp in tow of the *Regia*, grounded on Salty sandbank and had to be lightened by barges. Long delays were experienced by clay-laden vessels waiting for spring tides and in three days in November 1908 an accumulation of 28 vessels proceeded to sea.

In the same year a minor casualty brought the Harbour Commission to the verge of bankruptcy. The Brixham schooner *Via*, 126 tons, touched the ground when loading clay at one of the inner tiers of buoys. She sprang a leak, the cargo had to be discharged and she went to Plymouth for repairs. Her owner brought an action against the Harbour Commissioners, who were advised to offer up to £300. After long discussion they decided instead to fight the case in the Admiralty Court. The *Via* had been built in 1864 for the Azores fruit trade but had long been reduced to coasting and had recently stranded off Cromer; counsel for the Harbour Commission argued that she was an old, weak and damaged vessel not fit to take the ground when laden in any berth. On the other side, it was claimed that the *Via* had not fallen out of class and that she was subjected to undue strain because there was a deep pit where she grounded at low tide. Mr Justice Deane pointed out that no evidence had been offered to show that the *Via* was unfit to be moored in a level berth and severely criticised the Harbour Master, T. W. Hutchings, who said he was not aware of her arrival for four or five days; in that case, remarked the judge, 'I don't see the good of your being Harbour Master'.[10] The owner of the *Via* was awarded damages of £400, plus costs, and the total bill came to £1628 8s. 8d., slightly more than the Commission's revenue from harbour dues for that year.

This financial disaster had important results affecting both the officers concerned and the policy of the Commission. In the first place, it led to the resignation of the Harbour Master when one of the Board of Trade representatives on the Harbour Commission, Mr Findeisen, tactfully moved that 'in view of his age the Harbour Master be given an opportunity to retire'. Hutchings took the hint but, perhaps because he and his relatives had served the harbour well over a long period, he was allowed to keep his other office of Collector of Dues for a further two years. When he died on 22 October 1915 at the age of 82 he was mourned as Teignmouth's 'most esteemed townsman', having compensated for his apparent neglect of his official duties by a great deal of voluntary work for local government and education and the Wesleyan Methodist Church. His character as an employer is suggested by the fact that his schooner *Jehu* always recruited a local crew and, unlike the *Eldra*, retained them. The second personal consequence of the *Via* judgment affected the Commission's Clerk, E. J. Tozer:

> The clerk read a letter from Messrs Tozer and Dell (which meant a letter from himself) stating that a considerable number of Harbour mortgages were held by clients of theirs and that they did not feel justified in advising their clients to allow their money to remain.

This threat upset the Commisssioners and, after some unpleasantness, Tozer also resigned:

> Resolved that Mr Tozer, having on so many occasions expressed his intention of giving up the Clerkship, the Commissioners accept his resignation...[11]

E. J. Tozer's resignation severed a family link with the Harbour Commission which dated from 1859 and which was restored later.

The personal consequences of the *Via* judgment were less significant than the effects on policy. The Commissioners felt unable to pursue their programme of improvements and reluctantly declined an offer from the Urban District Council to undertake jointly an extension of the seawall to give further protection to the harbour entrance. Even normal maintenance work had to be curtailed. The mechanical blower, which had seemed effective at first, failed to do all that was hoped for and caused complaints from visitors about the noise, not the first or last time that the interests of the commercial harbour and of tourism seemed to conflict. The Commissioners were asked by the Council to operate the machine in northerly and westerly winds only, which they were reluctant to do, but the problem was solved when the blower broke down through lack of maintenance. In March 1912 the dredger was laid up 'on account of the present price of coal'.

In the hope of avoiding further disastrous losses, the Commissioners sought advice on how to protect themselves against actions for damages. They eventually decided that pilots and coastguards should be paid 6d. for serving a warning notice on the masters of all vessels entering the harbour. These indemnity notes appear to have worked for a time and the Clerks of the Harbour Authorities at Bridport, Wisbech and Glasson Dock, harbours with somewhat similar problems to those of Teignmouth, wrote to ask for information about them. But actions were still brought. In September 1910 the Harbour Master reported with regard to a claim by the owner of the schooner *Brockenholm* that the captain had refused to accept the warning and that 'in consequence of the Captain's abusive language the Pilot left the vessel without serving the notice'. The final blow came when James Finch put his own interests before those of the Commission of which he was a member: the Commissioners paid him £100 for alleged damages to one of his vessels because they 'were at the moment holding back cheques, having no assets at the Bank', and could not defend an action.[12]

The Quay Company was faced with similar problems to those of the Harbour Commission but tackled them in a different way. The Company normally settled claims by negotiation and tried at the same time to remove any cause for claims by careful berthing arrangements. In 1909, after a payment to the owner of the Thames barge *Lord Tennyson* for damage and demurrage, the directors resolved that:

> all captains of vessels coming alongside the quays shall make known to the berthing master the shape of the vessel's bottoms and any peculiarity in their construction.[13]

In January 1906 Captain Piller was appointed berthing master at a salary of 21s. per week of seven days and given 'a Cap bearing a proper badge, Teignmouth Quay Company Limited Berthing Master'. Despite his cap, Mr Piller apparently found it difficult to enforce his authority and, after the company had unsuccessfully defended an action brought by the owners of the brigantine *Adela*, he was peremptorily dismissed.[14] Shortly before the action was brought, the young master of the *Adela*, Captain Benjamin Robinson, committed suicide as a result, it was said, of worry over the damage caused by a bad berth.

The Company and the Commissioners were partners in trouble but they sometimes tried to pass blame from one to the other and the earlier quarrel about responsibility for dredging was re-opened. After protracted argument, the solicitors to the Quay Company wrote a statesmanlike letter to the Commissioners' Clerk which finally ended the dispute:

> Our clients (the Teignmouth Quay Company) feel that litigation between your Commissioners and them, both parties being interested in the trade of the Port of Teignmouth, is greatly to be deplored as, whatever its result, it can only tend to prevent two local bodies, having similar interests, from working in harmony.[15]

Harmony was in fact restored as a result of this letter. By an agreement made in March 1914, the Harbour Commissioners supplied their dredger to the Quay Company free of charge and the Company paid for the coal and labour. The agreement unfortunately came too late. Numerous actions for damages lowered the harbour's reputation and trade was affected, not only in this indirect way, but also as a result of the increase in dues which the Commissioners felt obliged to impose at the beginning of the financial year 1911-12. Import and export figures for 1913 show the extent of the decline from the relatively prosperous year of 1904.

At a time when British foreign trade was generally flourishing, Teignmouth's foreign imports declined from 15,529 tons in 1904 to 13,137 tons in 1913. Clay exports overseas increased slightly from 23,808 tons to 24,496 tons, mainly because of the growth of the Baltic market, but there were no topping-up cargoes and no other foreign exports. Exports of iron ore to the continent by the Ilsington Mining Company were only a short-lived revival of the declining traffic in mineral ores which finally ceased in 1908. Coastwise trade suffered an even more serious setback. Coastal exports of clay dropped from 76,720 tons to 60,105 tons and imports of coal even more sharply from 37,107 tons to 16,693 tons. These figures suggest that the increase in rates had less effect on foreign than on coastal trade, which suffered from intense competition: coal from the facilities offered by neighbouring ports and clay from the more economical and reliable service provided by the railways for short hauls to such destinations as the Bristol area and South Wales. Although the income of the Harbour Commission rose from £1,743 in the financial year 1910-11 to £2,100 in 1911-12 as a result of the increased charges, it fell in each of the next three years. After 1910 the number of officially licensed pilots, which had averaged five since 1856, dropped to three.[16] In 1911 the coal trade to Shaldon, which had been declining since about 1870, stopped altogether as a result of a dramatic incident described in the *Teignmouth Post* of 25 August. The ketch *Aquilla*, unloading cargo for a local merchant, heeled over in a strong tide, her mainmast snapped and the jetty 'crumbled like matchwood'. Mr Elliff, the merchant concerned, was confined to a wheelchair after a serious illness but wheeled himself to the jetty, struggled to his feet trying to direct operations, collapsed and was carried dying to his house nearby. Apart from one or two salvaged cargoes, this was the last shipment in a trade which had existed from time immemorial.

During the decade from 1904 virtually no new traffic was attracted and other south Devon ports were doing better than Teignmouth. Exmouth imported 11 cargoes of timber in 1913 whereas Teignmouth only received five, all for one importer, and an enquiry from an Exmouth timber firm addressed to the Teignmouth Quay Company was not pursued. Six cargoes of basic slag were imported into Exmouth, none to Teignmouth.[17] At Torquay newly-built and locally-owned colliers traded regularly without the interruptions suffered by steam vessels at Teignmouth and in the years immediately before the War the S.S. *Webburn* and the S.S. *Cherrybrook* arrived every few days, joined on one occasion by the S.S. *G. Player*, apparently diverted from Teignmouth. In July 1914, the month after the *G. Player* was sold, a highly mechanised collier, the S.S. *Torquay*, was launched for Messrs. Renwick Wilton and Company whose activities at this time were based on Torquay and Dartmouth. The south coast service from London with vessels frequently calling at Torquay in both directions was prospering and in 1913 the steamers *Cornish Coast*, *Devon Coast*, *Dorset Coast* and *Suffolk Coast* made calls from Liverpool and landed cargo which presumably would otherwise have gone to Teignmouth. The Torquay Borough Treasurer's accounts show a regular, if modest, expenditure on dredging and quay maintenance.[18]

The stagnation of maritime trade at Teignmouth contrasted, not only with developments at Torquay and Exmouth, but also with national trends. 1911 and 1912 were record years for British shipbuilding, British overseas trade and British ship-owners' profits. A leading firm of shipbrokers reported in 1912 that 'the results of the year have been – for steamship owners in particular – beyond the dreams of avarice'. For the boom year of 1913 Board of Trade returns showed that both imports and exports were a record and the editor of *Lloyd's List* wrote, 'never before have such figures been presented'.[19] Sporadic troubles in the docks and shipyards, decreasing demand for coal and falling freight rates warned of an approaching slump, but British maritime trade generally in the years immediately preceding the First World War enjoyed outstanding prosperity, a prosperity which Teignmouth did not share.

Previous setbacks in the trade of the port in the 1830s, 1850s and 1880s had been partly or largely a result of the general economic situation; this one, perhaps the most serious of all, was caused by problems peculiar to Teignmouth.

The outbreak of war in August 1914 caused an immediate decline in trade and that meticulous recorder of events, Albert Best, commented in his diary on 31 December 1914, in a mood of apparent regret rather than relief, that 'there were no steamships in the harbour to sound their hooters'. There was a hint of panic in a resolution passed by the Harbour Commissioners in December when, after a meeting with senior military officers,

> it was decided that the Harbour Master should be instructed by the Clerk to arrange for a tug to take the first vessel available and sink her across the channel of the bar on receipt of instructions by telegram from the Brigadier General.[20]

The harbour entrance suffered from neglect and in October 1914, when the steamer *Torquay* (exceptionally diverted to Teignmouth) ran aground, she had to discharge or jettison 300 tons of cargo. It was an ill wind that blew nobody any good and this was probably the biggest bonus for beachcombers in the long history of bar strandings; it was said that 30 fishing boats picked up three or four tons apiece of 'best house coal'.

Soon the enforcement of restrictions by the Admiralty took effect. Messrs. Powell, for example, complained of the delay caused to their steamers by these restrictions and discontinued their service from Liverpool in September 1915; imports of woodpulp had stopped a few months earlier. By the financial year 1915-16, dues from imports had shrunk to £237 and the efforts of the Commissioners to recover from the effects of the *Via* judgment were nullified. On 1 March 1916 it was resolved that 'owing to the financial position of the Commission all expenditure on the river shall at once cease'. At a special meeting in April the River Surveyor and the Engineer were given notice, the Inland Revenue solicitor threatened proceedings for arrears of tax, and the Harbour Master reported that the rudder of the dredger had fallen off because the bolts were eaten away by rust.[21]

In this renewed crisis the Commissioners again tried to economise and to attract new trade. When their Clerk died in May 1917 his assistant applied for the job and was appointed when he agreed to serve, 'under the circumstances', at a reduced salary. He was instructed to get in touch with the naval and military authorities to present to them the advantages and accommodation of the port. Some military traffic had already used the harbour but without much financial reward to the Commissioners. The Harbour Master, for instance, reported that the steamship *Howden* arrived on 29 July 1916 to load hay for the Army Department:

> He asked the Captain who would pay the harbour dues – the Captain replied that Captain Phillips of Devonport would pay – when Captain Phillips arrived he said apply to the Naval Transport Department.[22]

It was poetic justice that on a subsequent visit the *Howden* grounded on the bar: two tugs and the lifeboat tried to tow her off but she eventually freed herself and then ran aground under the Ness. It seems surprising that she moored at the quay 'with no apparent damage'.

Perhaps partly as a result of this casualty, very little military freight was dealt with. One slight bonus arising from the war was the landing of cargo from the Pacific Steam Navigation Company's liner *Galicia* which was mined three miles east of Teignmouth pier on 12 May 1917, when bound to Valparaiso with passengers, mails and miscellaneous exports. All the passengers and crew were saved, 53 of them by the Teignmouth lifeboat, *Alfred Staniforth*.[23] 1,698 tons of salvaged goods were brought into the harbour by small steamers and there is a tradition that they included three motor-cars, one of which was driven around the streets by George Player. But this exceptional traffic only lasted a short time and in July 1918 the Harbour Master reported that in the previous month just one vessel had arrived, the yacht *Moira*.

The virtual cessation of trade consequent upon the war was as harmful to the finances of the Quay Company as it was to those of the Harbour Commission. As early as 1 March 1915, 'the financial position was considered and an offer was made by the secretary to accept a reduction of his salary of £50 a year'. This offer was welcomed on the understanding that the full salary would be paid as soon as the company was in a better position; the chairman, somewhat ungraciously, proposed a reduction of £150 but found no seconder. At the next meeting the directors agreed to forego their fees. The death of the secretary, W. S. Wills, in July 1916, was given as a reason for delay in the payment of interest on the debenture stock of the company. A month or so later a special committee consisting of the chairman and three directors was appointed to deal with finance and the Minute Book for the next few years records only purely formal business.[24] When the end of the war was in sight, the Harbour Commissioners showed themselves much more determined and optimistic than the directors of the Quay Company. They made a request to the Board of Trade for Treasury assistance and were granted a loan of £500, interest-free for six months from the Armistice. They gave careful consideration to schemes, however unrealistic, which might bring back commercial shipping to the harbour: one proposal, for example, to transport Welsh coal by rail to Teignmouth and thence by sea to northern France, and another, 'a scheme of considerable magnitude', to export refined copper which would be produced in the Teign valley. Neither of these schemes materialised and, after the Peace, trade only haltingly returned.

The *Teignmouth Post* reflected local interest in the harbour by commenting on signs of revival, however slight, for example, the export of two coke cargoes from the Gas Works in the French ketch *Corbiere* and the import of 200 tons of cement from Cowes in the auxiliary schooner *Gaspe*, 'the first American vessel to enter Teignmouth harbour'. Shortly before the second anniversary of Peace, the editor remarked that 'Teignmouth harbour presents a busy appearance' and 'the number of craft lying at the buoys reminds one of pre-war days'.[25] New developments gave hope for a return of prosperity. The Channel Shipbreaking Company was granted a lease of the Western Quay and, shortly after taking over, caused a local sensation by bringing in the ex-German cruiser *Stuttgart*. The *Stuttgart*, nearly 400 feet long, was the largest vessel to enter the harbour since the *Caroline* in 1860. She successfully rounded the Point in charge of four tugs and three pilots, watched by 'a crowd of several thousand persons'; when she berthed it was remarked that she was 'the exact length of Alexandra Terrace'. Shipbreaking provided employment in difficult times and raised hopes for an expanding industry to which Teignmouth was well suited. Merchant, as well as naval, vessels came in for demolition, and scrap iron and brass were exported to Rotterdam and Antwerp.

1. View from the parapet of the Public Rooms, Teignmouth. This steel engraving, number 2889 in the catalogue by Somers Cocks, was engraved by J. Eke after an original by T. H. Williams and was published by R. Jennings in 1830. In front of the bridge, which was opened in 1827, the masts of sailing vessels project above the roof tops. The Public Assembly Rooms were completed in 1826.

2. Perspective view of Ringmore and Shaldon from Teignmouth, *c.* 1830.

3. New Quay, built 1820-1: granite ready for export, a harbour scene portrayed with artistic licence.

4. View from the Dawlish road looking towards Shaldon. A lithograph by George Rowe, published in Teignmouth by G. Collins in 1835. The print is number 2905 in Somers Cocks' catalogue.

5. A perspective view of Teignmouth from Shaldon, *c.* 1850.

6. The main line railway and the quay connection, *c*. 1850: transport could now be by truck as well as by barge.

7. Quay extensions and improvements, 1888-93: the newly-piled Western Quay and transit sheds under construction.

8. *Gauntlet* at the seaward Shaldon jetty, August 1896.

9. Teignmouth harbour beach: the rowing ferry, as well as the power-driven one, still in use *c.* 1900.

10. Captain A. Johnson (right), Harbour Master, and Captain C. Johnson, master of the *Jehu*.

11. Whalebone arches, 'presented by Pike Ward, Esquire'.

12. Russian vessel, carrying paper pulp, aground on Bench Rocks, 1906.

13. Lifeboat Day: *Alfred Staniforth* returns from exercise under the admiring eyes of visitors.

14. (*above*) The wooden Shaldon bridge before major reconstruction.
15. (*below*) Edwardian Teignmouth: the sands.

16. The Regency Centre: the Royal Library, now W. H. Smith.

17. S.S. *Maria Amalia* at Teignmouth, loading clay from lorries at the Eastern Quay, *c.* 1937. This photograph was taken before the 'big ramp' was installed.

18. S.S. *Suffolk Coast* at Teignmouth cement berth and sailing vessel *Gustaf* at Teignmouth No. 1 dock. The photograph was taken about 1930. Note the railway lines and wagon, long since gone.

19. *Result* approaching the partially-reconstructed Western Quay.

20. S.S. *Warrenfield* arriving at Teignmouth with a cargo of coal, probably for the Newton Abbot power station, *c*. 1950.

21. (*above*) Discharging slates, *c*. 1960.
22. (*below*) *Kingsnorth Fisher* passing small boats on one of her first visits.

23.   M.V. *Flevo* aground on Bench Rocks, October 1977.

24. Chipboard from Finland being discharged at the 'big ramp', March 1981.

25. (*above*) Timber being stored on the Quays at Teignmouth, 1981.

26. (*below*) Discharging paper reels at the port of Teignmouth, 1984.

27. Aerial view of the Quays at Teignmouth, 1984.

Other developments and revivals were equally encouraging. Instone and Company established a bunkering service for their regular steamers between London and the continent, presumably to save higher costs at Brixham or Dartmouth, and in one month, March 1920, five vessels loaded between 30 and 50 tons of bunkers each. Powell and Company, which had become part of the Coast Lines Group, resumed their service from Liverpool in 1921 and a service from Hull was started by the Rix Line, a family business which had been founded in 1902. A traditional foreign trade revived with the import of flints from Dieppe for the Bovey Pottery Company and in October 1922 the motor vessel *Ina* brought in the first post-war cargo of woodpulp for Messrs. Reed and Smith. The *Teignmouth Post* commented on the return to normal conditions with the arrival of the first German vessel in September 1923 and, in the same month, the first timber carrier from Archangel. Clay traffic also picked up, although coastwise trade recovered more slowly than foreign.[26] The revenue of the Harbour Commission exaggerated this revival because some dues were increased by 100 per cent in March 1921, but the figures seemed very satisfactory and income rose by an even higher proportion from less than £500 in 1920-1 to more than £2,000 in 1923-4. In the light of their improved finances, the Harbour Commissioners increased the salaries of their Harbour Master and Clerk and, in order to win wider support and understanding, began discussions which led in 1924 to the broadening of membership by the addition of representatives from Teignmouth and neighbouring Local Authorities.[27]

The peak year of post-war revival was 1924. By this time the export of clay to foreign destinations at 24,771 tons was almost as high as it had ever been. Foreign imports, on the other hand, at 9,125 tons had not yet recovered to the earlier figure of 15,529 tons. Coal imports in 1924 were negligible, three cargoes totalling 745 tons, and clay exports to coastwise ports were only 11,740 tons compared with 76,720 tons. But general coastwise trade had picked up well: imports of oilcake, for example, reached 7,741 tons compared with 1,382 tons in 1904 and cement imports had recovered to earlier levels although imports of flour and fertiliser were smaller. These figures in themselves give only a very rough indication of the extent and character of the post-war recovery. The fact that Teignmouth was beginning to re-establish itself as a distribution centre for South Devon and further afield is shown by the destination of foreign and coastwise imports.

Imports of basic slag in 1924 were not large, only slightly more than one-third of the total trade in fertilisers, but the range of delivery was evidence of Teignmouth's favourable geographical situation: importing firms at Plymouth, Exeter, Taunton, Barnstaple, Paignton, Chudleigh and Ashburton shared the four cargoes. Another foreign import was much larger and illustrated the same point. During the autumn of 1924, 4,939 tons of cider apples came from Normandy as well as two small consignments of French cider; distribution was to Henley and Son of Newton Abbot and the Taunton Cider Company of Norton Fitzwarren besides smaller firms at Staverton, Uffculme and Bradninch. The long-standing connection with Perros and nearby ports in Brittany was revived with the import of 678 tons of potatoes, in 21 cargoes. Teignmouth's function as a distribution centre was shown equally clearly by imports coastwise, especially by the service from Liverpool. Coast Lines advertised sailings every 10 days and their steamers brought in regular consignments of oilcake and flour for small-scale distribution as well as a wide variety of other goods: tanning extract for Tremlett and Company of Exeter and Vicary and Sons of

Newton Abbot; paint, glass and wood shavings, mainly for Exeter firms; iron-work for the local Council; tinned fruit for Deller's Cafe at Paignton, and individual items, like a washing machine for 'Mr Sandford, Teignmouth'.

Such miscellaneous cargoes came to Teignmouth, as they came to other Westcountry ports, because coastal shipping was competitive with rail and had not yet been challenged and defeated by the long distance lorry. Teignmouth was more favourably placed than better-equipped Westcountry ports such as Plymouth in relation to main centres of population. Moreover, the population of Teignmouth's immediate hinterland was increasing more rapidly than that of the country as a whole: between 1921 and 1931 census figures show that the population of neighbouring urban centres, Paignton, Torquay, Newton Abbot and Exeter, increased from 127,301 to 145,618. Whatever influence these favourable circumstances exercised on imports, traffic did not extend to exports; general export trade, coastwise and foreign, remained insignificant, although the occasional practice of topping-up clay cargoes revived with the despatch of four small consignments of tallow from Thomas and Company of Exeter.[28]

This summary of Teignmouth's trade in 1924 suggests that the battle for survival had been won. But within a year or so, local problems destroyed the mood of confidence which improving trade had encouraged: the nature of these problems, primarily financial, is clear from the records of proceedings of the Quay Company and the Harbour Commissioners. The Channel Shipbreaking Company was in trouble in the early 1920s, asked for a reduction in rent and, when it was refused, called in a receiver. The Quay Company's refusal arose from its own predicament. In 1925 one director resigned when his colleagues decided to pay a dividend on the preference shares and a year later it was resolved that 'Preference share dividend be paid as and when the funds are available'; this kind of Micawber resolution was repeated in subsequent years.[29] One has some sympathy with the Quay Company because their customers were also in financial straits with the onset of the post-war slump. The Whitehall Asphalt Company, for example, which imported six cargoes in 1923, went bankrupt and was only able to meet part of its debts.

The Harbour Commission was little better off. The Ministry of Transport asked for repayment of the Treasury loan which had been granted at the end of the war and the Commissioners felt obliged to sell their dredger. They declined an offer of £300 from Philip and Son of Dartmouth and tried instead to sell it to the Sutton Harbour Improvement Company; eventually they accepted £35 10s., apparently from a local scrap merchant. The Commissioners were pressed to reduce harbour charges in order to attract new trade or ward off competition, but their concessions seem to have been self-defeating: kainit fertiliser, for example, as an 'enumerated article' was listed at 1s. 8d. per ton and the Commissioners reduced the rate successively to 10d., 7½d., and finally 6d., but very little was imported.

Teignmouth was not alone in its financial problems. The second report of the Port Facilities Committee of the United Kingdom Chamber of Shipping, published in 1930, and referring to a somewhat earlier period, drew attention to the difficulties of many other small Westcountry ports. Of Bridgwater the Committee wrote:

> Of recent years the tonnage handled has much diminished due, it is stated, to the severe competition from road and rail transport, which has resulted in a considerable loss of revenue and consequent lack of funds to prevent silting up of the channel and approaches, and to maintain or improve the facilities at the port.

On Par the Committee was more specific:

> Reconstruction of two berths is urgently needed. The owner of the harbour [Colonel Treffry], although anxious to proceed with the work, ... is unable to do so owing to financial difficulties in connection with recently incurred death duties.

At Padstow 'the Harbour Commissioners are stated to have no funds' and at Penzance 'the debt on the harbour still approximates £36,000'. Exmouth, like Teignmouth one of the small ports not included in the survey, had similar problems: when the lock-gate needed repair in the 1920s it was removed and Exmouth Dock became, as it has remained, a tidal harbour. For the Teignmouth Harbour Commissioners, income began to fall steadily and alarmingly, with only one hint of recovery, from the peak of nearly £2,300 in 1924 to £1,141 in 1930.

An old threat showed itself when the Commissioners were confronted with a large claim for damages. On 7 September 1925 the S.S. *Coombe Dingle*, proceeding to sea, damaged her propeller on an obstruction and the Commissioner's diver found a large stone projecting upwards from the river bed and broken pieces of blade beside it. After taking counsel's opinion, the Commissioners settled for £307 5s. 1d., a reduction of £100 on the claim originally made by Charles Hill and Sons of Bristol. It was reported that 'the serving of notices (of indemnity) had been stopped some time since' and the Commissioners took out an additional premium to cover themselves against damage to vessels whether or not caused by negligence.[30]

In this situation the Commissioners were again obliged to seek economies, however harsh or petty: the Harbour Master, Captain C. Johnson, was in poor health and for a time a deputy was paid a small honorarium, but then Captain Johnson was told that if on any future occasion he found himself unable to do his outdoor duties he would be immediately dismissed. When the lease of the tide gauge at the New Quay came up for review it was not renewed. Despite this apparently urgent need for economy, the Commissioners agreed at about the same time, in March 1928, to give a temporary subsidy to the tug *Bonchurch* whose owners threatened withdrawal in the light of falling demand which was partly an inevitable result of dwindling trade and partly a consequence of the installation in most sailing vessels of auxiliary engines. When the matter came up again six months later, the Commissioners tried unsuccessfully to persuade the Quay Company to contribute and then reluctantly stopped their subsidy. The *Bonchurch* was kept in commission a little longer but was transferred to the port of Hull on 19 March 1931. The *Bonchurch* was the last in a succession of sea-going tugs which began with George Hennet's *Industry* in 1852: the *Great Extended*, re-named the *Pioneer*, which served the port from 1866 until she sank at her moorings in 1893; the *Sensation* and the *Louisa* which both operated for much of the same period; and the *Regia* and the *Teign* which worked side by side, and sometimes in competition, until the *Regia* was sold in 1915 and the *Teign* in 1924, when the *Bonchurch* herself arrived.

The fortunes of the steam tugs which served the port of Teignmouth for nearly a century is a story of evolving social habits and important changes in the maritime economy. When in June 1852, the *Industry* made an inaugural trip to Babbacombe Bay 'the party consisted of the most influential gentlemen of the town'. By the summer of 1868 the *Great Extended* ran special trips for shop assistants who had been released by their employers at four o'clock on Thursday afternoons in response to the Half

Holiday movement and skipper Hallett was said to be 'exceedingly obliging' to his new-found customers. By 1876 both the *Great Extended* and the *Sensation* were running excursions twice weekly to Torquay and Dartmouth with 'very desirable accommodation' for all classes of passengers. Then the Board of Trade stepped in and it was no longer feasible for tugs to carry fare-paying passengers. Some enterprising owners, in the Kingsbridge estuary for example, worked the other way round and purchased properly-equipped passenger steamers which could also be used on occasion as tugs; but this custom was never followed at Teignmouth where the paddle steamers *Duke of Devonshire* and *Duchess of Devonshire*, while popular with passengers, were completely unsuitable for towing duties.

The tugs also earned extra revenue for their owners by taking what opportunities they could for salvage, and these opportunities were frequent as long as most ships were dependent on sail. The *Great Extended* towed the Dutch brigantine *Cito*, bound for Par in ballast, into harbour when she flew distress signals because her crew was exhausted and a few years later, under her new name of *Pioneer*, brought in the American brigantine *Marie* when (like the *Caroline*) she had become embayed and touched ground near Maidencombe. Even steamers needed help occasionally; the *St Albans*, for example, was towed to Plymouth by the *Great Extended* and the *Sensation* working together after she lost her propeller off Start Point. But as power became more common and as ships became more easily manoeuvrable there was less need for tugs and they gradually disappeared from virtually all the small South Devon ports. Some 50 years after the *Bonchurch* was sold Teignmouth Harbour Commissioners provided themselves with a purpose-built vessel, appropriately christened *Teign*, which was a small workboat, all that was necessary when technology made accidents at sea less frequent and difficulties in entering or leaving harbour more easily overcome.

At a time when these developments could not have been foreseen the Harbour Master tried to dispel despondency by reporting that two large vessels, the *Gloucester Coast*, 212 feet long, and the German steamer *Falke*, 240 feet, which came in to load 700 tons of clay for Seville, had entered and left the harbour without a tug and without mishap. What the Harbour Master did not say was that many sailing vessels, some without auxiliary engines, were still coming to Teignmouth and would have to order tugs from elsewhere or make do with local motor-boats. The reason why sailing vessels still used the port was much the same as that which led to the so-called 'grain race' from the smaller estuary ports of Australia: owners of sailing vessels could tolerate delays because their running costs were much lower than they were for the owners of steamers. The contrast is shown by the experience of the port during the coal strike of 1926.

Renwick Wilton and Whiteway and Ball, two leading coal merchants of Torquay, needed coal quickly and imported from the continent to Teignmouth by steamers such as the *Runnelstone* which brought in the largest post-war cargo, 1,000 tons. Similarly, Candy and Company of Heathfield and Whiteways of Whimple brought their fuel by steamer and so did Watts, Blake, Bearne and Company who needed coke rather than coal. While the steamers were given a quick turn-round, the shipping correspondent of the *Teignmouth Post* noted that 'the three-masted schooner *Raymond* which has been lying in the river idle for some months has loaded clay and sailed'. There was very little clay moving coastwise owing to the scarcity of coal in the potteries and the *Raymond*, unlike a steamer, was prepared to wait. Sailing ship owners knew that, even if their ships received quick despatch, the elements might delay them: the schooner *Als* took 29 days to reach Leith from Teignmouth and when in sight of the Firth of Forth she was driven nearly 200 miles off course.

Teignmouth was one of the very few ports where sailing ships were still able to scrape a living in the late 1920s and through the depth of the economic depression from 1929 to 1931. The port, though far from prosperous, presented a maritime scene of great interest and traditional charm. The anonymous author of one of the most popular holiday guides, 'Through the window from London to Penzance', drew passenger's attention to the view as their train passed out of the cutting just beyond Teignmouth Station: the thumbnail sketches which illustrate this section of the journey show the harbour with a cluster of tall-masted ships, the Ness in the background, and the riverside scenes animated by barges and small boats.

Those who lived in Teignmouth and those who came to stay as visitors for a period had a better opportunity to appreciate the picturesque than the passing tourist on his way elsewhere. Old seamen recall wistfully the scene some 60 years ago when the brigantine *Francis and Jane*, the brigantine *Waterwitch* and the barge *Sepoy* sailed from Teignmouth in company. They recall also the feat of seamanship a few years later when the two-masted schooner *Pacific*, light from Exmouth, sailed into the harbour unaided with all sails set except topsails and rounded the Point to tie up at the Old Quay. These romantic memories do not alter the fact that not too many seamen's sons took up a career at sea. Most were like the younger John Whitear who inherited a love for the sea but had no wish to experience his father's tribulations. Seamen's sons were probably dissuaded from following a family tradition, not only by their awareness of hardship at sea, but also because there was little public sympathy with the seaman's lot. One of the stories current in the Lockyer family, for instance, is that of Sam Lockyer who, after being shipwrecked off Land's End was rescued by a trawler and then found that a shopkeeper refused the only coin he had because it was discoloured by seawater.

In those last days of sail the variety of ships in harbour was perhaps greater than at any other time. During 1931 the *Alert* came to Teignmouth three times to load clay, once for Westonpoint and twice for Glasgow. She was a handsome wooden schooner, A1 at Lloyd's and 'a real aristocrat of the coasting trade'. Her fine lines persuaded the Marquis of Anglesey to purchase her as a yacht but the conversion never took place and she was eventually broken up at Port Dinorwic. A year or so earlier the brigantine *Hilda* of Faversham, another 'aristocrat', ran herself aground on the harbour beach so that her owner could save the expense of drydocking while the crew followed the injunction of Captain Fox 'to make her look well' and seaworthy.

Many of these ships had earned the title, 'Westcountry schooner', by adoption rather than by birth and some had come to Devon and Cornwall because they had lost their local export trade. The *Jane Banks*, for example, first came to Teignmouth with coal for George Player under her original name of *Frau Minna Petersen* and she stayed on in the trade between Teignmouth and the north-east coast; the name when she was launched in Porthmadog was a compliment to one of the largest importers of Welsh slate. The *Happy Harry*, which spent some time in the Teignmouth-Glasgow trade, had been launched at Millom by the Hodbarrow Mining Company and named after one of the directors who was presumably happy because profits were high. While some export trades declined, clay, both china clay from Cornwall and ball clay from Devon, enjoyed a relatively stable and steadily expanding home and overseas market as new uses were developed. Clay was not a popular cargo because it was liable to set solid in a ship's hold, as in a railway truck, but it became more acceptable to shipmasters as the clay companies reduced moisture content in response to their customers' requirements. So sailing ship owners were ready to take a cargo even though it was still sometimes loaded very slowly from barges.

The ships which tied up to the buoys in the Teign estuary were examples of the worst and the best which had survived. A few still boasted the imitation painted gunports which were an elegant survival from a more warlike age; the masts of others had been drastically cut down and their decks cluttered with obsolescent machinery. Two of the very last British merchant schooners in commission represented the worst and the best. The schooner *Result* had become a powered ketch and ferried slag from the Channel Islands to the Western Quay. When she motored up the Exeter Ship Canal on her last voyage she wore a blue band around her hull in mourning for her owner-master, probably the last British vessel to follow this ancient custom. She seemed destined for restoration at the Exeter Maritime Museum, near the place of her birth. The schooner *Kathleen and May*, on the other hand, was lovingly maintained in virtually her full rig; she carried clay from Teignmouth direct to a pottery in Cobh harbour and then, in her last working days, moved to North Devon. She was restored and displayed in Plymouth and then moved to the Thames where it was thought she would be appreciated by more people. Now none of these historic vessels can be seen in Teignmouth or any other Westcountry port which gave them sustenance to the end of their working lives.

One 'old timer' may still be trading in distant waters though her whereabouts is unknown. The Barnstaple-registered schooner *Eilian* is not strictly an 'old timer' because she was built as recently as 1908 in Almwich, the last vessel launched in that ancient port. She had an easily-managed rig on pole masts and a paraffin engine. The official papers of the *Eilian* show the problems which were faced by the owners of sailing ships, even relatively modern ones, when freights were low. In 1925 the crew agreement and log of the *Eilian* show that she was doing reasonably well. Her master and crew all came from villages in North Devon, Appledore, Braunton and Heaton, and were paid on percentage. Her voyages appear to have been co-operative and friendly affairs and for a short time the crew included two 'stewardesses', one of whom was a relative of the master. Seventeen coastal and continental voyages were completed in six months and the *Eilian* always carried cargoes, apart from four short ballast passages to Teignmouth. By 1931 things were very different. The master was still G. P. Hartnoll of Braunton and he was engaged 'on shares', but all the crew were paid monthly wages which varied from £7 for the mate to £3 10s. for the cook; the complement had been reduced by one. Only the master, mate and cook came from North Devon villages. The others joined the *Eilian* in Teignmouth, where Hartnoll himself eventually settled down to become Senior Pilot. The *Eilian* was driven hard, completed 22 voyages in six months and was at sea over Christmas, but the very difficult trading conditions were shown by the fact that eight voyages were in ballast and on three other trips the *Eilian* carried less than a full cargo. From Teignmouth to Queenborough, for example, she loaded only 140 tons of clay instead of her full capacity of 215 tons.

One particular incident illustrates the problems of sailing ship owners more vividly than the experience of the *Eilian* does over several years. The schooner *C and F Nurse* was owned by a Nurse family consortium based first on Gloucester and then

Bridgwater. They were conscientious owners and kept their ship well but were obliged to accept cargo for small and difficult harbours such as Ballinacura, Lydney, Gweek, South Alloa and Lyme Regis. In July 1927 the *C and F Nurse* loaded 195 tons of clay at Teignmouth for Antwerp and was apparently below her marks; there was a lengthy correspondence between the master, the Marine Superintendent and the London Office of the Registrar General of Shipping. The owners, clearly anxious to obey the law, replaced the master and no prosecution followed. The incident shows the pressure under which owners and masters of sailing ships operated at this time.[31]

As maritime trade slowly built up again after 1931 much of it passed to experimental composite vessels, to foreign motor coasters or to those British steamers which were efficiently managed. Examples of all three came to Teignmouth. The *Advance* was a Norwegian schooner which loaded clay in Teignmouth for Scandinavian ports after discharging her timber cargo elsewhere; like the Belgian vessel which had so impressed the correspondent of *The Syren and Shipping* in 1907, she combined the best of both worlds. When she first appeared on the horizon she looked on fire because the exhaust fumes from her powerful engine were funnelled through one of her steel masts. Teignmouth also attracted a large number of the small and efficient Dutch motor coasters which were mostly family-owned and family-crewed. They were specially designed for small ports and could carry a substantial cargo on a very shallow draught. One resentful British owner is said to have remarked that they could sail into the heart of Devon on the morning dew.

It was the steam-powered vessels which kept a good share of trade for British ships. These too, were well represented in the port of Teignmouth during the 1930s. Many of them carried coal for the Newton Abbot power station and discharged it by grab at the Western Quay, to the dismay of nearby residents. Despite the nature of their cargo, some of these were as well-kept as the best of the sailing ships. The 'Force' line steamers, owned by the West Coast Shipping Company and registered in Whitehaven, in particular, were an adornment to the harbour with their yacht-like appearance and fresh paint. Two of the most modern of the Company's vessels, the *Dalegarth Force* and the *Greta Force* each carried more than 900 tons. Not all the colliers which came into Teignmouth were up to this standard. The *Galacum*, for example, which appears to have been on time charter, was probably the ugliest and dirtiest vessel ever to visit the port; her design was not unlike the 'flat-iron' colliers which passed under the Thames bridges.

This very busy coal traffic was one sign that the port was recovering as the country got over the worst of the economic depression. What caused Teignmouth to pick up trade more quickly than most Devon ports was a board room revolution in the Quay Company in 1932 which brought in new directors and a new secretary. The change in fortunes of the Quay Company and of the port was largely the work of two of these new men, T. M. Swain as chairman and R. W. Sing as secretary. Swain played a leading part on the boards of both the Quay Company and the Devon Trading Company and in his dual role made sure that the Devon Trading Company did not exercise its controlling interest to the detriment of its smaller partner. Although he worked from Exeter, Swain had a long and close association with Teignmouth and, despite his quarrels with the Urban District Council over road access to the quays, regarded himself as a strong local patriot. Sing was appointed secretary to the Quay Company after relevant experience in managing the successful coastal service from

Bristol and Newport to Bideford and Ilfracombe. He set himself the task of bringing the port back to prosperity and did so with determination and skill. At the outbreak of war he drove hard bargains with the Ministries for the storage of essential supplies in the Company's warehouses and throughout his long period of office, during which he became a director as well as secretary, he sought new trade wherever it might be found. Occasionally Sing followed a will o' the wisp, like the possible export of sugar beet, but often he won, kept and adapted facilities to new traffic. Cider, for example (imported, not exported, strangely enough) came first in barrels, then in containers which had been used in the North African Campaigns, and finally in chartered French wine tankers which discharged by pipeline. Sing was often to be seen around the quays following the rules of all good dock management: close supervision and inspiration by example. Neither Swain nor Sing took a very active part in public affairs as Mansfield and Scammell had done but, like these two men, they illustrated the crucial role played by individuals, as distinct from market forces, in the history of the port of Teignmouth.

The new management began by putting its own house in order. It was found that repairs to buildings had been charged to the company instead of to tenants and debts were collected under threat of legal proceedings. The affair of Monsieur Bourgeot's cider barrels showed the new broom at work. Monsieur Bourgeot was told in July 1934 that, unless rent was paid for storage of his barrels, which had apparently been left lying on the quay, they would be sold. They were in fact sold for £26 and, when Monsieur Bougeot complained, it was resolved 'that the company is not prepared to enter into further correspondence'. As a result of measures of this kind, a profit of £1609 4s. 11d. was made for the year ending 25 March 1934. In June 1935 preference dividends were paid for the years 1929, 1930, 1931 and 1932 and they were brought up to date in June 1936; the first dividend on ordinary shares was paid in 1937.

Increased profit meant that work could be done on the Old Quay, two sides of which had collapsed; it was brought into use by an expenditure of some £3,000. The Western Quay was strengthened and rail access improved to deal with the increasingly large coal cargoes. Mechanical equipment was purchased to expedite loading and discharging, a ramp was built for the export of roadstone and negotiations were opened for the erection of a sugar-beet factory on the quayside.[32] Shortly after taking over, the new management hired the services of a diver to inspect some of the berths and it was reported that 'on the higher part of the quay' he picked up 'several large pieces of stone, a bag of cement, a six-cylinder engine and the chassis of a motor-car'.[33] Restoration work was long overdue: it was fortunate for the port that a more rigorous administration and better financial prospects made such restoration and improvement possible before it was too late.

The Harbour Commission followed in the wake of the Quay Company but its finances recovered much more slowly. The Commissioners were still faced with the recurrent problem of the harbour bar to which the Harbour Master from time to time drew their attention. He reported in December 1933 for example:

> Three vessels had been off the bar, two loaded with timber and one with coal, but owing to the rough sea on the bar and neap tides they had gone to Dartmouth to await fine weather; the *Suffolk Coast* and the *Magrix* were delayed for several days after discharging. The *Magrix* loaded with coal unfortunately grounded on the bar coming in on the night of 7 December but got off on the morning tide.[34]

Between 1918 and 1939 there was no appreciable change in the size of ships engaged in the clay trade and cargoes increased only marginally: an average of 273 tons in 1924, 292 tons in 1931 and, when international trade had begun to revive, 333 tons in 1933. It was the colliers, usually bringing in between 600 and 900 tons, which suffered most from the continuing shortcomings of the harbour entrance. When Mr. Dobson of Messrs. Renwick Wilton and Company complained, after the Harbour Master's report, that great difficulty had been experienced in getting into the harbour for the last two or three months, the chairman replied that they were doing the best they could: 12 men in 12 boats had been sent to scrape the bar with cockle rakes. This was a far cry from Messrs. Merryweather's mechanical blower or Priestman's steam dredger, 'complete including all recent improvements'. But the Commissioners had enough confidence in the future to negotiate, in collaboration with the Quay Company, concessionary dues for Unilever which attracted valuable regular traffic to the Coast Lines service from Liverpool and, after 1935, customers in Devon and east Cornwall were supplied from Lancashire factories, via Teignmouth. The port became a major distribution centre for soap products as it had been for specialised cargoes in 1924. Reduced dues did not adversely affect the Commissioners' total revenue which increased from £1,160 in the financial year 1930-1 to £1,782 in 1934-5; it remained steady at around this figure for the next few years.

The revitalised Quay Company, working closely with the Harbour Commission and taking advantage of the improving national economic situation, transformed the fortunes of the port in much the same way as George Hennet had done nearly a century before, though in a less dramatic fashion. Similarly, Morgan Giles, who came to Teignmouth shortly after the First World War, followed the example of James Mansfield and, over a narrower range of craft, built up an equally high reputation. Morgan Giles, who had been in business in Hamble as a yacht broker and naval architect, bought the Strand Shipyard when it was derelict and had been unoccupied since the failure of Gann and Palmer some six years before. He had taken on a daunting task at a difficult time. He wrote to a complaining client in Amsterdam in July 1920:

... the industry is in a terrible state of confusion as the result of the War and constant strikes which make it impossible to progress with anything.[35]

Morgan Giles achieved success by the same methods that James Mansfield had used, the employment of highly skilled reliable craftsmen backed up by strict and economical management. In the early days the Yard built racing dinghies, including those of the International 14-ft. Class, and motor launches, among them the *White Heather* and the *Lady Cable* which became very popular in the Teignmouth passenger trade. Later Morgan Giles specialised in building yachts where price was not the most important factor and in equally high-quality work for the Royal National Lifeboat Institution. Yachts which came from the Yard in the 1930s included the *Hispania VI* for King Alfonso of Spain and six for use on the River Nile which were so successful that many more were built in the Sudan to the same design. Work done for the Lifeboat Institution included new boats for Aberdeen, Beaumaris and Buckie as well as regular maintenance on local boats from Weymouth, Exmouth, Torbay and Plymouth. One of the outstanding achievements of the Yard in its earlier days was the conversion of the French pilot cutter *Jolie Brise* to a yacht, done with such care and skill that she won the first Fastnet Race. This victory was a unique Teignmouth triumph because the professional skipper of the *Jolie Brise* was Sidney Briggs, a Teignmouthian by adoption. Sidney Briggs sailed on Thames barges from the age of 12 and first came to Teignmouth in the schooner *Betty Russell* in 1911; on a subsequent visit he married the daughter of the landlord of the *Ship Inn* and made his home close by Western Quay where he lived for the next 60 years.

Teignmouth was a demanding harbour which built up a demanding trade across the Atlantic. Survival came to depend on skill in handling boats and ships which was quickly learnt by those who were born in Teignmouth or, like Briggs, came to live there. A Victorian commentator wrote that 'the worst sort of sailors' come from Teignmouth, but this was a moral, rather than a practical, judgment. A fairer assessment was made by the Reverend John Sweete who visited Devon towards the end of the 18th century in search of the picturesque and found his attention rivetted on two small vessels entering the Teign estuary. 'I was a good deal amused', he wrote (using the word in its contemporary sense) 'by the dexterity of the Seamen'. While waiting for the ferry, Sweete watched a sloop and fishing vessel entering the harbour:

> The wind was blowing strong from the West, and full in their teeth, and the tide about half flow, they had no little difficulty in entering ... (but I admired) ... the beautiful appearance of the vessels as they scudded along gunnel to when they caught a side breeze.[36]

The activities of the Strand Shipyard, as well as the interest of the Morgan Giles family in yachting, brought so many pleasure craft to Teignmouth that there was often a greater variety of small boats in the harbour than of merchant ships. Not many of these pleasure craft ventured beyond Shaldon Bridge because navigation was difficult. Between the wars the deep water channel up to the Stover Canal was regularly dredged and dredging was viable because the sand, although not of good quality, had some commercial value and members of the Vallance family had a useful sideline in towing one or two loaded sand boats up to Newton Jetty on their return journey with empty clay barges; one of the Teign dredgers, from which the crane had been removed, is beached at Archbrook. But, while the dredged channel was marked in a way understood by lightermen and other local people, it was awkward for strangers because the River Teign, unlike the Exe, does not appear to have been subject to Trinity House inspection. After the First World War no seagoing vessel passed beyond Shaldon Bridge and a passage by a masted pleasure craft was rare; the last time the drawbridge was opened, except for maintenance work, is said to have been in the early 1920s when the steam yacht *Firefly*, owned by the squire of Netherton, used to anchor in deep water off Netherton Point.

By this time steam yachts were going out of fashion, but Teignmouth became a centre for small steamboat activities and the warning sirens of these unusual vessels surprised the crews of merchant ships entering the harbour. The use of steamboats for pleasure continued in Teignmouth long after almost anywhere else, just as commercial sail had done. The *Minette*, which had a hull as shapely as the famous Windermere launches, came to the estuary in 1978 from an owner in Torquay and was overhauled at Matthews Boatyard.[37] Boats specially designed to take steam engines were built around this time by James Belton on the New Quay and a small group of enthusiasts, inspired by Kenneth Sclater of Shaldon and Commander

Parsons of the Morgan Giles Yard, indulged their hobby during the summer months to the delight and interest of visitors.

So these steamboat activities, which had originally been stimulated by the Strand Shipyard, continued well after its demise. It was the success of the rehabilitated Shipyard in the 1930s, as well as the growing trade to and from the quays, which meant that the Harbour Authorities were in a much more confident frame of mind to meet the wartime problems in September 1939 than they had been in August 1914.

Chapter Nine

Rehabilitation and Development: 1939-1984

Less than a year after the outbreak of war Teignmouth found itself in the front line, as it had been in Napoleonic times. Most foreign markets were already closed to Teignmouth's chief export when the German occupation of the Channel ports meant that coastwise trade was strangled as well. Shortly after the fall of France in spring 1940 Convoy C.W.9 suffered severe losses despite its protective screen of miscellaneous vessels, including two Belgian pilot cutters towing barrage balloons. One of the cutters, re-named H.M.S. *Borealis*, was sunk and 10 merchant ships were lost or severely damaged, including the *Polly M*, a Metcalf vessel which traded regularly to Teignmouth.[1] The town, as well as local shipping, suffered from aerial attack. In the course of 21 air raids between July 1940 and February 1944, 228 houses were demolished and more than 2,000 damaged. Of the 79 people who were killed 14 were serving in the Royal Navy or Royal Naval Reserve and apparently home on leave, a fact which suggests that Teignmouth's traditional links with the sea were being maintained.[2]

In the summer of 1940 the Harbour Commissioners were called upon to take immediate action to repel invasion. A deputation led by the chairman told Admiral French and Captain Rée that 'the Harbour Commissioners would be only too willing to do all they could (to obstruct seaplanes) but they had no staff and no official who could do the work'. Captain Rée brought naval ingenuity to bear and reassured them:

> ... two craft were coming up from Dartmouth with buoys and wire for obstruction purposes and what with what we had in the shape of a piece of the Pier and other things they could manage.[3]

At this time of emergency the Authorities took other measures of an equally drastic kind. The Admiralty acquired use of the harbour in return for a lump sum of £200 and requisitioned small boats. One of the boats commandeered, to the great concern of the Harbour Master, was Mr. Heath's water boat which serviced vessels moored in midstream. The water boat, moored off the Strand Shipyard when not in use, was a familiar sight to Teignmouth residents, the more knowledgeable of whom looked for the bucket hoisted mast-high which was the traditional sign that the ship needed water. Another cause for local concern was the extinction, on orders from the Ministry of War Transport, of the public right of way along the harbour beach. The secretary of the Harbour Commission informed the Ministry that the Commissioners were

> of opinion that all rights of way which the public had enjoyed for all time be restored on the conclusion of hostilities.[4]

A much more serious matter in a national, rather than a local, context was the evacuation of British troops from Dunkirk. What boats set out from Teignmouth on this occasion is a matter of dispute. It seems certain that no Teignmouth boat manned by its own crew directly participated in the rescue work, presumably because the distance was too great to be covered in the time available or perhaps because the Teignmouth seamen not already on active service were reluctant to volunteer since they were not told at the time what they were volunteering for. The *Lady Cable* joined the Dunkirk expedition but she is said to have set out from Torquay, not Teignmouth. The tug *Heron* was the only vessel which sailed direct from Teignmouth and she did not reach her destination. Few Devon seamen from Teignmouth or anywhere else took part in this reverse Armada.[5]

The exigencies of war broke one of the longest Teignmouth maritime traditions when the Lifeboat Station was closed in 1940. Before the establishment of a Lifeboat Service rescue work was normally directed by Coastguard and Customs Officers. On 10 December 1840, for example, the *Exeter Flying Post* reported that the brig *Howard*, with a cargo of timber from Miramichi, came to anchor off Teignmouth intending to run in with the evening tide. A strong wind prevented the pilot from boarding and when the wind rose to gale force the *Howard* was driven ashore. Twelve of the 13 crew were saved by

> the exertions of Lieutenant O'Reilly with the men of the coastguard, Mr Maxton with his men belonging to the customs ... and a great number of inhabitants.

Teignmouth's high reputation for saving life at sea was built up partly because the early Regattas, unusually for Devon, combined utility with pleasure by demonstrating rescue equipment such as 'Captain Manby's apparatus' and 'Mr Offord's expanding fluke grapnel'.[6] Probably for this reason Teignmouth was given one of the first lifeboats provided by the Shipwrecked Fishermen and Mariners Benevolent Society which was passed over to the Royal National Lifeboat Institution in 1854; a new Station was built in 1862 on a site given by the Earl of Devon, the previous one having been on the harbour beach.[7] An experimental iron lifeboat, the *China*, largely paid for by donations from English residents in China, was sent to this new Station a year later. It was this lifeboat which in the great storm of 10-11 January 1866 started an argument which is not dead yet. The reproof administered by the Official Inquiry, that 'the crew did not show a readiness to volunteer their services on an occasion when it might have been expected of them', was much gentler than the reception meted out by local people when the crew came back; some of them were ashamed to walk through the town. The Inquiry elicited the evidence that 'one of the crew refused to go because he should get wet and take a chill' while another said 'I am not going to be killed'. The boat was ready for launching soon after the news was received that scores of ships had been driven ashore in Torbay when the wind suddenly changed after they had taken shelter, but Lieutenant Burney, the Coastguard Officer, refused to let his men go because he considered the risk too great and then the rest of the crew demurred. Instead, the lifeboat was taken over the hills to Torquay and this delay meant that it was able to save only 11 men from two ships.[8] Things were even worse a few years later when the brig *John* got into difficulties immediately on leaving Teignmouth harbour; the launching place for the lifeboat was obstructed, 'almost everybody was giving orders' and the lifeboat was only got afloat 'amidst much execration and blasphemy'. By the time it finally got alongside the *John* her crew had already been taken off by another vessel.[9]

The reputation of Teignmouth's lifeboat was restored when the crew made an outstanding rescue on 10 October 1907 and at the same time scored a point over their old rivals, Exmouth. When the schooner *Tehwija* was driven ashore on Pole Sand the Exmouth lifeboat was unable to reach her, but the Teignmouth boat did so after half-an-hour's pulling through the rough water of the bar and the *Tehwija*'s crew were saved when they jumped from the rigging just before their ship broke up. It was said that the captain's dog was rescued later, put on the train to Hull and travelled back to Finland with his master. For this exploit the Teignmouth lifeboat crew were formally thanked and Mr. Burden, the Lifeboat Secretary who had accompanied the boat, was awarded a gold medal by the Institution. These extreme examples of heroism and apparent cowardice and indiscipline are no different from elsewhere. The record as a whole suggests that Teignmouth lifeboatmen had done enough to earn official support for their Station even when manpower was scarce, but it was closed in 1940. The Lifeboat House, close to the Point, is still clearly recognisable although the Record Board has gone. The last Teignmouth lifeboat, the *Henry Finlay*, became the *Teignmouth Belle* and was good for another 40 years.

In 1940 urgent matters attracted attention away from the loss of the Lifeboat Station which might have been resisted. Some wartime rescue work was done without the help of a lifeboat. One of the pilots reported, for example, that he took charge when the *Restorer*, a salvage vessel which had herself been damaged, was towed on 'stern first down by the head'.[10] As the tide of war turned Teignmouth's contribution changed in character. From early in 1944 invasion barges began to arrive alongside the quays or made fast to buoys. A big petroleum carrier which anchored near Shaldon Bridge was moved at the urgent request of the Commissioners.

Throughout the whole period of the war Morgan Giles' Yard was extremely busy and vessels which were launched for the Admiralty and the R.A.F. included some 50 pinnaces of various kinds, four 72-ft. harbour defence launches and eight motor-torpedo boats. These M.T.B.s were probably the most valuable work done at the Yard; powered by three Packard 500 h.p. engines, they reached a speed of 40 knots on trials. Morgan Giles' Yard also carried out many repairs and refits. Among the vessels which came in for repair was the Belgian lifeboat *Minister Lippins*; having arrived with refugees she then served the R.A.F. from a base at Lyme Regis. This remarkable wartime stimulus to production, which was an unstinted co-operative effort, spread over to other estuary yards including Bulley's on the Old Quay which, like Morgan Giles', had a reputation for high-quality craftsmanship. For a time Morgan Giles' Yard continued with civilian orders and in 1942 the *Carissima*, one of the largest yachts built at Teignmouth since the turn of the century, was registered for a local owner. At the peak of wartime activity, up to 150 men (as well as women) were employed and work was never seriously interrupted although in one aerial attack several houses were destroyed near the Yard entrance.

Once the war was over and normal conditions in the harbour restored, trade gradually returned. In 1946 coastwise exports of clay resumed and there were small foreign imports of apples and slates; coal imports were over 20,000 tons and foreign exports of clay, benefiting from pent-up demand, were above their highest pre-war level at 39,312 tons. The clay trade, which had replaced the Newfoundland connection as a major source of livelihood in the region and kept the port going during difficult times, was the basis of post-war rehabilitation. The barge traffic lasted, surprisingly, until 1938 and for the last 10 years or so some of the towing had been done more economically by a purpose-built motor launch, the *Heron*, which replaced the steam tug *Kestrel*. When river transport finally stopped, there was increased pressure on other means of taking clay to the ships. Railway policy discouraged freight on main-line sidings and shunting operations interfered with the free flow of other traffic on the Teignmouth quays. Largely for these reasons, it was decided to concentrate on conveyance by road.

Road access to the quays was a matter of concern to the clay companies, the harbour authorities and nearby residents. A proposal to build a direct road from Shaldon Bridge to Western Quay was sponsored by commercial interests and supported by the Ministry of Transport, the River Board and Devon County Council, but at first opposed by Teignmouth Urban District Council, which on this occasion, as on others, showed an ambivalent attitude towards the expansion of a seaborne trade. The local Council accepted the highway engineers' panacea for traffic in towns, an inner ring road, which promised some relief from holiday congestion and took dock-bound lorries away from the narrow streets of the town, but at very high environmental cost. The parish of West Teignmouth, for long the home of those seafarers who lived on the Teignmouth side of the river, was bisected in a more damaging way than by the railway a century earlier. Mackworth Praed, the poet and politician whose family memorial stands in St James's churchyard, wrote nostalgically of vacations spent at Bitton House when he was a schoolboy and undergraduate. His *Fragment of a Descriptive Poem*, written in 1836, describes the unplanned charm which has now been planned away:

> No architect of classic school
> Had pondered there with line and rule ...
> The buildings in strange order lay,
> As if the streets had lost their way,
> Fantastic, puzzling, narrow, muddy,
> Excess of toil from lack of study

and the character of a maritime community which has been lost:

> 'Twas sweet to see the sports and labours
> And morning greetings of good neighbours,
> The seamen mending sails and oars,
> The matrons knitting at the doors ...

The section of the ring-road which destroyed many older houses and shops in West Teignmouth opened up an attractive vista of the harbour and the historic buildings around the Old Quay, but the motorist was not allowed to stop and the pedestrian was banned.

In the immediate post-war period the export of clay, carried to the ships entirely by road, increased more rapidly than at any other time in the port's history. By 1954 exports, at 122,960 tons, were above the peak before the First World War. They rose very steeply in the early 1960s to 300,000 tons and then levelled off at around 350,000 tons; in 1974 they were a record 365,598 tons. Traditional markets were retained and new ones developed. By 1967, Teignmouth, as one of the five leading United Kingdom ports for the export of crude minerals, was in the 'First Division' of the

table prepared by the Dock and Harbour Authorities Association.[11] In collaboration
with clay exporters, the Quay Company installed modern equipment: baskets and
shutes were replaced by ramps and conveyors while mobile cranes loaded refined
clay which was shipped in bags stacked on pallets. Watts, Blake, Bearne and
Company had by far the largest share of Teignmouth's export trade and sent some
eighty per cent of their total exports through the port, but English China Clays,
which had taken over three small companies around Kingsteignton between 1932
and 1957, also made a significant contribution.[12] Occasionally 'topping-up' cargoes
were carried: cement to Denmark, for example, and Monaco cruisers, built in the
Strand Shipyard, shipped as deck cargo by vessels taking clay to ports in the
Mediterranean.

Not everything proceeded smoothly in the post-war period of generally increasing
port prosperity. Coastwise coal imports, which reached a peak of 80,000 tons in 1958,
declined sharply and stopped altogether as a result of the closure of the Newton
Abbot power station. A very serious loss, even more for the town than for the port,
was the decline and ultimate demise of the Morgan Giles' family boatbuilding
business.

When F. C. Morgan Giles died in 1964 at the age of 81 his son, Michael Morgan
Giles who had served as Manager since his return from the war, took over
completely. Michael Morgan Giles helped to maintain the very high standards and
was closely associated with the design and construction of the successful Monaco
motor cruisers. But the firm ran into financial difficulties largely because prospective
owners were unable or unwilling to pay the cost of high-quality work. After it was
sold in 1969 much of the Yard was taken over by a Totnes firm which specialised in
glass fibre construction and there was no place for those who had acquired skills of
a more traditional kind; a few of them were employed by David Coysh who continued
wooden boat building in a shed on the Morgan Giles site for a little longer. Michael
Morgan Giles himself retired to the wild country of Dartmoor which was his second
love. In his remote farm he offered hospitality to those who shared his memories, but
he could not bear to visit Teignmouth again. The last occupant of the Yard, who
established a 'Teignmouth Boating Centre', stayed only a very short time and the site
became derelict.

The Strand Shipyard had slept for long periods before and had always revived
when prosperity returned; this time there could be no resurrection because the
Planning Authority approved an application for residential development. The site
immediately became too valuable ever to support productive work again. Bulldozers
demolished the building berths, the Patent Slip, the drawing office and the ancillary
workshops. They left the vandalised Regency Cottage next door which was a survival
from a quite different Teignmouth tradition. In its latter days the Shipyard seemed
to consist largely of rusty corrugated iron and may have appeared out of place in a
town which sought to attract retired elderly people and holiday visitors. From the
time the railway came there has been a conflict of interest and often the harm done
to Teignmouth by 'developers' has been more obvious than the benefits they
conferred. On the Teignmouth side of the estuary towards Shaldon Bridge a wooded
walkway to the town was destroyed to build terrace houses and the quays housed the
increasingly complex paraphernalia of a working port. At least these two
developments, environmentally harmful as they both were, had a clear economic
justification. The same can hardly be said for holiday flats approved for a site which

had recently given employment to 150 men. There was as yet no commemorative plaque on the Strand as there is on other historic sites in Teignmouth such as Templer's New Quay. Perhaps the most appropriate memorial to this ancient shipyard is the fleet of Morgan Giles boats scattered around the world, some of them long past their best but cared for with the same loving concern as went into their construction.

The Harbour Authorities, while not greatly concerned by the approaching disaster to the Strand Shipyard, were anxious to replace the lost coal imports and they were successful in attracting other imports in order to create a more balanced trade. Some were temporary and disappeared when factories closed or markets declined. Among these short-lived imports were thatching straw, lager, esparto grass, calcinated seaweed and fruit pulp. Other new or revived imports became well established: grain, animal feeding stuffs, fertiliser and building materials such as timber and slates made a significant contribution to an expanding import trade. The stimulation of exports was also important because the clay trade, which had grown rapidly immediately after the war, was showing signs of levelling off. Some of the new exports, such as lignite, coke and scrap iron fluctuated violently or disappeared altogether, but others, particularly agricultural products like barley and milk powder, showed more consistency.

The way in which the Quay Company tried to adapt the port's facilities to changing demand is shown by the history of the ramp on the Old Quay. In 1938, as a result of an agreement with the Stoneycombe Lime and Stone Company, the Quay Company built a low ramp which enabled stone chippings to be tipped directly into ship's holds. Considerable quantities were sent to London and south coast ports, mainly by Everard vessels and Dutch coasters on short-term charter, until the trade was stopped by road and rail competition; the ramp then became an additional loading point for some types of bulk clay and finally was used to load light scrap metal. When the ramp was demolished to allow more space for mobile equipment it had given good value for an original outlay of less than £500.[13]

The post-war growth in import and export trade was matched by a revival of the fishing industry. In 1902, the first year for which Teignmouth Fishing Boat Registers are extant, seven boats are shown as newly purchased by local owners. In the next 12 years, however, only eight were added to the Register, all 'second class' boats of less than 15 tons, and, according to *Kelly's Directory*, the number of men and boys engaged full-time in fishing declined from 202 in 1900 to 99 in 1912. Between 1919 and 1939 38 fishing boats were purchased by Teignmouth owners but, probably because of the collapse of the herring fishery in the early 1920s, 17 of these were recorded as 'no longer used for fishing'. Twelve others were sold or broken up before 1939 and six were requisitioned in 1942 and 1943.[14]

Recovery of the sea fishery was slow after the war, but by the 1960s five trawlers were regularly working from Teignmouth and in 1967 a fish landing jetty was constructed between the Eastern and New Quays with the help of a ministry grant. Among the first vessels to use the new jetty were two 43-foot trawlers, the *Thisldome* and the *Gerry Ann*, built for two local fishermen by the Morgan Giles yard after the firm had changed hands; the choice of name, *Thisldome*, is an example of the unsophisticated humour which is one strand of the maritime tradition. At the opening ceremony for the new jetty the District Fishery Inspector remarked that 7,000 lbs of fish had been landed at Teignmouth in 12 months compared with 400 lbs in 1936 and he hoped that the jetty, which he believed to be 'the first of its kind ... built in the south-west for twenty-five years', would lead to a further large increase.[14] Optimism was justified because the fleet of Teignmouth trawlers increased to 12 or so and, outgrowing the limited facilities of the jetty, brought extra trade to Brixham and, occasionally, to the commercial quays at Teignmouth.

Teignmouth was not the only Westcountry port which experienced a revival after the Second World War. Others, such as Watchet, Bideford and Exmouth, recaptured some of their older trade and attracted new. Even Padstow, which had been virtually derelict since the 1930s and was handicapped by probably the most dangerous bar of all the western ports, dealt with diverted cargoes at times of crisis. It seemed possible that the forecast of Captain John Coppack in 1895, although not taken seriously at the time, would come true. Captain Coppack had the *Kathleen and May* built to his order, under her original name of *Lizzie May*, and he knew the ships and small ports of the west coast extremely well. Speaking at the inauguration of a new rail link, Hawarden Bridge, he declared:

> ... that bridge sounds the death knell of this little port [Connah's Quay]. Within fifty years, or even less, grass will be growing where we are all standing. But, although probably none of us will be here to see it, within another fifty years Merseyside will have gorged itself, and become so unwieldy, these little ports will again come into their own.[15]

Since the very small ships of the 18th and 19th centuries have gone for good, the success of 'these little ports', whether in north-west or south-west England, is likely to depend (apart from political considerations) on their ability to give safe, economical, reliable and expeditious service in competition with the older giants like Liverpool and London and the newer ones such as Southampton and Felixstowe.

Two incidents in the 1950s showed that the port of Teignmouth was unable to guarantee such service. The steamer *Deneb*, which had a laden draught of almost 17 feet, was specially fixed to load at the peak of spring tides, but arrived an hour too late, waited off the bar for several days and then secured a fresh charter from Newport. The Spanish motor vessel *Virgin de Lluch*, also with a deeper draught than normally accepted, was delayed in loading and grounded on the bar. She remained there for nearly two weeks, an attraction to visitors at the height of the season but a bad advertisement for the port. Her crew rowed ashore to Mass, made friends in the town and seemed reluctant to leave when their ship eventually sailed safely away.

For the Harbour Commission incidents like these suggested that they were failing to meet the requirements laid down by Parliament, to provide the facilities for vessels 'to pass and re-pass to and from the sea ... with safety and facility'. Those Commissioners who were closely associated with the clay industry were anxious, not only to meet their legal obligations, but also to expand the export trade through Teignmouth. Much thought was therefore given to means of remedying the shortcomings of the harbour for large ships. One of the Commissioners' remedial measures was the resumption of small-scale dredging in the river. In addition to this regular contract dredging, the Commissioners spent more than £8,000 during 1955 and 1956 in an attempt to widen and deepen the fairway between the river beach and Salty sandbank; the work was fairly successful, although some of the sand scooped up was washed back into the deep water channel by exceptionally high tides.

Another improvement came about by a lucky chance. In June 1950 the Clerk reported to the Commissioners that Mrs. Lois Lucette of Staffordshire had offered a bequest of £1,500 to provide and maintain a lighted beacon in memory of her husband; she and her husband had spent many happy holidays in Teignmouth and she 'wanted to give Teignmouth something in return'.[16] After frustrating delays, mainly as a result of the bankruptcy of the firm which submitted the lowest tender, the Lucette memorial was formally unveiled on 23 April 1953. The work was done without cost to the Commissioners and the Shaldon beacon proved a useful complement to the lighthouse which their predecessors had erected a century before. But none of these improvements, whether paid for or provided free, solved the basic problem of the dangerous and unpredictable character of the bar which obstructed the harbour entrance. In 1967, after much discussion, agreement was reached that a working model of the harbour should be constructed by the Wallingford Hydraulics Research Station at a charge of some £30,000. A major share of the cost was borne by the Ball Clay Federation, but contributions were also made by other users, as well as by the Teignmouth and Newton Abbot Urban District Councils and Devon County Council, a rare example of unanimous encouragement to the port of Teignmouth in the interests of the regional economy.

While model tests were going on at Wallingford, there was a further increase in the size of ships using the harbour. A change in the balance of running costs between small and large ships emphasised an existing tendency for owners, both British and foreign, to dispose of older and smaller vessels which became increasingly uneconomic. The effects of the owners' calculations were clearly seen at Teignmouth. In four years from 1968 to 1972 the number of ships entering the port with a carrying capacity of more than 1,000 tons rose dramatically from four to 118.[17] For Teignmouth, the length of ships was always as critical as their draught. In 1972 the British motor vessel *Kingsnorth Fisher*, 284 feet long, came in to load a 200-ton transformer; she was the longest vessel ever to enter the port without a tug and, helped by her sophisticated navigational aids and favourable conditions, she arrived and sailed without delay. Other large ships were less fortunate. On 4 February 1973 the Dutch vessel *Carabeka III* sailed for Spezia with 1,490 tonnes of clay; she stranded on the bar and remained there for 24 hours. The next day another Dutch vessel, the *Agua*, coming in with a full cargo of grain from Bordeaux, also grounded. Neither ship was damaged but the Harbour Commissioners realised that the future of the port was under threat. Hitherto they had been reluctant to take action which would provide a long-term remedy, partly because of the cost and partly because the skill and resourcefulness of the pilots greatly reduced the problem.

The Teignmouth Pilotage service has a similar history to the Lifeboat service in which some of the pilots took a prominent part: the same combination merging into heroism and occasional argument leading to disorder or conflict. The casualties in the Pilotage service, though not fully recorded, were probably higher than in the Lifeboat service. A pilot boat overturned when coming over the bar on 23 March 1837 and five of the seven occupants, not all of them pilots, were drowned. On 20 August 1840 a pilot was drowned, together with his 12 year old son, when his boat was swamped, again on the bar. On 17 March 1866 the pilot who had gone, with lumpers, in search of an incoming vessel was drowned on his return.

There are many examples of pilots risking their lives to help or warn a ship in danger, and modern technology has not entirely eliminated the need for such risks to be taken. During an October gale in 1975 the Teignmouth pilots were unable to speak to the Cypriot vessel *Lidan* on radio when she was dragging her anchor off

Teignmouth at night. Her captain seemed unaware of the danger until the pilots boarded his vessel by ladder and steered her to safety under extremely difficult conditions. All three pilots, Alf Broom, Sid Hook and Ken Gribble, received a letter of commendation from the Board of Trinity House informing them that 'their actions were in keeping with the best traditions of the Pilotage Service'.[18] The pilots faced another demanding task in December 1980 when a timber-carrying vessel, the *Caro*, took a list under gale conditions, sheltered in Lyme Bay and, unable to enter Exmouth, made for Teignmouth. She was brought in safely, her cargo re-stowed and she resumed her voyage to the Isle of Man the next day.

It was a long time before pilots licensed by Trinity House were successful in asserting exclusive rights. In 1850 when

> Thomas Walls, captain and owner of the sloop *Speedy* was summoned on the complaint of William Gilpin and Thomas Clarke for employing William Hearn, a fisherman, to pilot a vessel into the harbour ... he not being a licensed pilot [19]

the case was dismissed. Soon after this the licensed pilots established their claim, but then quarrelled among themselves when work was scarce. In 1876, for example, William Matthews was summoned by William Gilpin (who seems to have been unduly anxious to resort to the law) for personal assault when they both tried to take a Russian vessel out of the harbour.[20] By 1900 or so the Teignmouth pilots appear to have built up a working partnership and, according to the memory of an older seaman, they shared out their takings on Saturday mornings once a fortnight in a back room of the *Jolly Sailor*. Eventually satisfactory arrangements were made by the Teignmouth subcommission of Pilotage which gave each pilot a reasonable living although, as in most maritime occupations, there was still a chance of large fluctuations in earnings. The resources available to pilots were brought up-to-date and four-oared gigs were replaced, first by motor boats and then by an ex-R.N.L.I. Lifeboat, the *Storm Siren*.

When the scheme for improving the harbour entrance was put forward in detail by the Harbour Commission not all the pilots were convinced of its value and public opinion was generally hostile. Individuals and societies who felt their interests threatened came together in 'The Harbour Preservation Fighting Fund Committee' which was effective in winning a Public Inquiry and raising money to brief counsel. The Inspector at the Inquiry, held in 1974, recommended that the Commissioners' proposals should be approved, subject to some amendments and to additional evidence on particular points. In the light of these further submissions the Secretary of State for the Environment ordered a second Public Enquiry.

This second Inquiry showed even more clearly than the first the wide divergence of views, despite the scientific backing for the Commissioners' proposal which was based on Captain Spratt's analysis in 1856, itself endorsed by the famous names of Rennie and Brunel. It was agreed on both sides that a training wall would possibly, though not certainly, stabilise the bar and maintain a 'duct' or channel through it in a position favourable to the passage of large ships. What was not agreed was the likely or possible side effects: the danger to small craft, the threat of wave turbulence within the harbour, and the possible or likely erosion of beaches on both sides of the estuary. On these three points the 'experts' appeared to be evenly divided but a clear majority of those with local knowledge and experience considered that the potential risks from a training wall outweighed the likely benefits. Spokesmen who represented professional fishermen and holiday anglers emphasised the danger of small boats being wrecked on a rubble wall which would be submerged at high tide. The views of other boatmen were forcibly put by Sidney Hook and Frank Hook. Sidney Hook spoke as 'the seventh generation of his family' to live close by the river beach; he considered that the proposed wall would train the swell into the estuary and 'the waves would bounce round the harbour'. Frank Hook was a boatman on Shaldon Beach; since 'Shaldon was built on sand' he thought that its flimsy defence would soon be breached and he was certain that the harbour wall would do more harm than good.[21]

The Inspector agreed with his Assessor that 'there is unquestioned need, if possible, to stabilise the bar or, even better, to remove the bar altogether'. But he thought that the present proposal presented serious and unpredictable dangers and that alternative ways of dealing with the navigational problem had not been adequately explored or costed. He therefore advised that the Order requested by the Harbour Commissioners should not be made; the Secretary of State accepted his Inspector's Report. It was clear from the debate at the Inquiry that, while the 'wall' proposal had aroused much worry and protest, there was general agreement that the difficulties facing large ships ought to be eased. A number of witnesses were worried about the traffic and other likely consequences of expansion but only one witness (who apparently had not been born in Teignmouth) suggested that trade should be diverted to a deep-water port. Most witnesses at the Inquiry apparently wanted the port to prosper; what was at issue was not the desirability of improvement to the harbour entrance but the method. This point was succinctly put by counsel for the objectors in his opening address to the Inspector:

> The difficulties in navigating the estuary were recognised and his clients welcomed reasonable measures to mitigate them. They considered that insufficient research had been conducted into the alternatives. The training wall would only improve matters temporarily and would create serious hazards and other disadvantages ... [22]

The Harbour Commissioners followed the implied advice of the Inspector to try alternative ways of making the harbour more easily accessible to large ships. A policy of continuous dredging was adopted and a small dredger was replaced by a larger one. A new permanent and automatically-operated navigation light, said to be the brainchild of the chairman of the Harbour Commission and the Harbour Master, was installed in 1979 to replace the antiquated system under which the pilots fixed temporary lights to buoys marking the deep water channel. Since the rejection of the Harbour Commissioners' plan there have been occasional strandings on the bar for a tide or two and some delays to large ships at neap tides, but the only serious casualty was to a vessel which struck, not on the the bar, but on the rocks at the foot of the Ness; the Dutch vessel *Flevo* had to be lightened before she could be refloated and then went away for drydocking and repair. So Teignmouth's reputation as a reasonably safe port did not suffer as a result of the decision not to build a training wall. Trading figures proved the point. During the year of the first Public Inquiry trade passing through the port totalled just over 400,000 tonnes; by 1981 it had grown to 586,000 tonnes and then levelled off at around 600,000 tonnes.

Teignmouth benefited, not only from measures which were adopted as an alternative to a training wall, but also from good fortune as a result of circumstances outside the Harbour Authorities' control. In September 1977 the German vessel *Jupiter* discharged 610 tons of wheat from Amsterdam and immediately re-loaded the same cargo for Rotterdam. This must have been one of the oddest port operations since the heyday of smuggling. The apparent abuse of Common Market regulations was not repeated but Teignmouth benefited in more legitimate ways from Britain's entry into the European Economic Community. Trade with fellow members substantially increased and Teignmouth was well placed geographically for this growth of cross-Channel traffic. Oceanic trade, which employed ships much too large for Teignmouth, became a less important part of Britain's total maritime trade than the short and middle sea routes where smaller ships were economically viable. Moreover, from the 1970s onwards, some of the overseas imports which were still growing, such as animal feed, were transhipped from the continent in small vessels rather than sent direct to a major (and expensive) British port.

The other element of good fortune was partly a result of this stimulus to European trade. The design of vessels had begun to change with the Dutch coasters of the 1930s which were built, as has already been pointed out, to carry large cargoes on a relatively shallow draught. This purpose of ship design was still more evident in the 1950s and 1960s. The German vessel *Cargo Liner I*, despite her rather ugly name, was a beautifully-designed ship which gave a maximum capacity for bulk cargo and very comfortable accommodation to officers and crew. When she came to Teignmouth the *Cargo Liner I* was carrying 1,100 tonnes of grain on a draught of nine feet; compared with the traditional deep-keeled sailing vessel this was roughly double the cargo on half the draught. Such ultra-modern vessels were designed to serve, not only 'bar ports' like Teignmouth, but also up-river ports on the continent. In order to pass under low bridges they had no fixed masts or derricks and were entirely dependent on quayside equipment. At Teignmouth this point was appreciated and cargo handling machinery was kept up-to-date.

Some examples of a quick turn-round show that ships could be discharged or loaded speedily without using any gear of their own. A record discharge rate was achieved by the German vessel *Maas* which started unloading a cargo of 1,020 tonnes of coal from Ghent at 0715 and completed the same evening. A Dutch vessel, the *Carabeka VI*, broke the loading record by shipping 1,800 tons of clay for Tarragona in 13 hours of continuous operation. The Spanish vessel *Illa de Ons* broke a record of a different kind when she arrived on 22 October 1981 with 1,167 tonnes of chipboard from Corunna and sailed the next day with 1,400 tonnes of clay for Santander.[23] Efficient cargo handling equipment was matched by an economical labour force because, since Teignmouth was outside the National Dock Labour Scheme, the number of dock workers engaged could be closely related to demand and they could be casually employed. Teignmouth's continued exclusion from the scheme also meant that the port was not automatically drawn into disputes originating elsewhere. After one of the most damaging strikes the Teignmouth Quay Company displayed a banner, 'We never closed'.

From 1979 to 1982 some £700,000 was spent by the Teignmouth Quay Company on modernisation; work included re-surfacing the quays, demolishing the big ramp and erecting enlarged transit sheds. New facilities meant new methods. Forklift trucks operating in a large area of open space at one level replaced men with wheelbarrows walking across planks to the upper floors of warehouses designed for the small consignments of the 19th century. Some imports, such as chipboard, slates and timber which arrived in pre-packaged form, were well adapted to these modern methods of discharge: others, like animal feed, came in bulk and, since they were unloaded by grab, presented problems of dust pollution which were not easily soluble.

The tonnage which passed through the port annually in the early 1980s rose to some 600,000 tonnes and exceeded even the optimistic forecast which George Hennet had made at the Independence celebrations in 1835. But Teignmouth had become a different sort of maritime community from the one Hennet knew, if indeed it was one at all. The last merchant vessel built and owned in Teignmouth, the schooner *S.R. and H.*, was launched in 1872; the last merchant vessel owned in Teignmouth, the brigantine *Eldra*, sank in 1917; the last merchant vessel registered in Teignmouth, the steamer *Alicia*, was sold in 1930. And after 1945 it is unlikely that any member of the crew of a merchant vessel visiting Teignmouth would have been born there. Only in one way was an older maritime tradition revived as a result of increasing prosperity: the control of harbour affairs passed more completely into local hands.

Teignmouth Harbour Commission, which had been welcomed in 1836 because 'there will not be any profit to accrue to any individual'[24] but had allowed itself to become less than fully representative, instigated a reform of its constitution so that all local interests, including environmental and recreational ones, would have a voice. Teignmouth Quay Company, which had been created in 1886 in an upsurge of local enthusiasm but had come under control from Bristol as a result of a take-over by United Builders Merchants, once again returned to Devonshire management in 1979. Even before these organisational changes came about, there were signs of growing interest and initiative in harbour affairs. In 1978 the Teignmouth Quay Company, when still under control from Bristol, commemorated the 125th Anniversary of Independence by sponsoring celebrations which gained a good deal of press publicity. A few years later the Harbour Commissioners invited the public to suggest a name for their new workboat and chose one of the suggestions, *Teign*, which perpetuated the name of a sea-going tug which had given service to the port in good times and bad. The Commissioners then invited guests to the launching, just as Teignmouth shipbuilders had done. The occasion may not have been as grand as when 300 guests were invited to the launch of the *Oscar* (and were thrown into the water when she capsized) but it was a significant revival of a very old custom.

The definition of a maritime community is not only a matter of the statistics of seaborne trade or the constitution of harbour authorities or the degree of public involvement in maritime affairs; it is also, much more vaguely, a question of maritime adventure. Two dramatic incidents showed that, for Teignmouth, the spirit of maritime adventure was not dead.

The first example is perhaps more accurately described as 'pseudo-adventure'. Donald Crowhurst was persuaded by the Publicity Officer for Teignmouth to take part in the *Sunday Times* Round the World Yacht Race in 1968 and to name his sponsored boat *Teignmouth Electron*. The boat was not as well equipped as her rivals and Crowhurst himself was inexperienced in ocean sailing. He did remarkably well, but falsified his log and, rather than face humiliating exposure, apparently drowned himself. *Teignmouth Electron* was found, fully seaworthy but abandoned, by the British liner *Picardy* and ended her days in the Cayman Islands where she was recognised by the Commissioner of Police, himself a Teignmouth man.[25]

The other adventure, a few years later, had a happier ending. It is recorded in the diary of Captain Neil Gamble who took charge of two trawlers, *Osvor* and *Oguname*, which were given to the government of Nigeria under a scheme of international aid. They had been built on the Humber and were fitted out by a marine engineer on the Old Quay. Captain Gamble's diary shows that the Nigerian crews were poor seamen. He had engine trouble which obliged him to put into a Portuguese port, he was attacked by pirates off Dakar, and when within a mile of their destination the trawlers were fired on as suspected gunrunners to Biafran rebels. Captain Gamble carried out his mission and returned safely to his home close to the Old Quay after an adventure which was parallel to many of those undertaken by Teignmouth seamen centuries before.[26]

Teignmouth shared in efforts to keep a spirit of adventure alive by giving sea experience to boys bereft of opportunity as a result of the decline in the British Merchant Navy. Two Morgan Giles' yachts, the *Ailanthus* and the *Rona*, one launched from the Yard and the other substantially rebuilt there, passed into the hands of a Maritime Trust founded by Lord Amory which was a model for many similar experiments.[27] Boys (and girls) from Teignmouth and other Devon communities were given a love and respect for the sea even if they did not see the visions which filled the boyhood of Raleigh.

The survival of Teignmouth, in contrast to the disappearance of many other small Westcountry ports, has been primarily the result of successful adaptation, sometimes very late, to the changing pattern of maritime commerce. By the 1970s there appeared to be need for further modernisation and in 1983 the Teignmouth Quay Company's plans for extension of the quays and extra warehouse accommodation were approved in principle by the Local Authority. The welcome given by the Royal Fine Art Commission to the warehouse design was not matched locally; instead, opposition was comparable to that which had been aroused by the proposals of the Harbour Commission for a breakwater and was reinforced by the concern expressed by some of those with a lifetime of local experience for the possible effect of projections and dredging on the flow of the river. Such tensions within a maritime community are not uncommon; prosperity depends on their successful resolution.

✕✕✕✕✕✕✕✕✕✕✕✕✕✕✕✕

With the approach of the 1980s the pendulum of fortune for the port swung yet again. The volume of clay exports which had played such a major role in the earlier revival steadily decreased. In 1970 the exports of clay were 370,000 tonnes per annum, by 1984 the figures were 210,000 tonnes. The imports however began to increase dramatically, and over the same period had risen from 43,000 tonnes in 1970 to 473,000 tonnes in 1984. In 1973 the total tonnage handled by the port was 396,000, by 1979 it was 482,000 and by 1984 it had increased to 720,000.

Thus the port had continued to flourish and had reached an all-time trading record. The success of the port brought with it further problems in the form of transportation. The railway sidings having disappeared some years before, all cargoes were now dispersed by road. As in the case of the ships, economies forced the use of larger and heavier lorries and in order to reach the motorway a B-class road had to be used. The B3192 leaves Teignmouth by the long steep Exeter road and crosses Haldon Moor approximately 800 feet above sea level before joining the dual carriageway and so on to the M5 motorway. Once again this led to some expressions of concern but there was a general acceptance that the benefit to the town from a successful port outweighed the inconvenience caused by this route.

Exports	Clay	General Cargo	Total Tonnage
1984	210,091	36,173	246,264
1983	209,823	4,293	214,116
1982	229,686	5,622	235,308
1981	274,816	15,828	290,644
1980	313,038	6,433	319,471
1979	305,559	1,520	307,079
1975	275,849		275,849
1970	368,069	3,456	371,525
1965	263,969	3,895	267,864
1960	190,303	1,770	192,073
1954	123,042		123,042

Imports	Animal Feed	Chipboard	Coal	Paper Reels	Slates	General Cargo	Total Tonnage
1984	197,080	81,465	111,789	31,734	22,136	28,522	472,726
1983	170,168	63,218	24,179	14,002	18,042	23,428	313,037
1982	267,121	67,509	9,830	10,224	12,810	21,417	388,911
1981	202,034	62,914	674	7,210	11,002	12,079	295,913
1980	82,849	62,816			7,744	29,420	182,829
1979	91,755	49,456			4,015	29,997	175,223
1975	92,378				1,483	9,910	103,771
1970	3,782		41,635		668	11,345	57,430
1965			57,848		940	6,160	64,948
1960	1,060		41,527		1,010	9,154	52,751
1954			73,169			11,842	85,011

The Harbour Commissioners had continued the constant dredging to keep a deep navigable channel but were experiencing a growing problem at the north-east corner of the Salty. Ships now using the port such as M.V. *Rubin* and M.V. *Miniforest*, which have a length of nearly 300 feet, had to negotiate two sharp turns. Firstly the pilots taking a ship out must negotiate a sharp turn to the starboard to evade the north-east tip of Salty and then bring the ship hard to port to round the point to evade the notorious bench rocks which claimed the Dutch vessel *Flere* as mentioned earlier. The dredger used in the harbour carried some 150 tonnes of sand when loaded and dumped at sea either in the area off Bundle Head or to the east of Teignmouth Pier, and although the dredger M.V. *Tarway* was doing an invaluable job of maintaining the status quo it was not large enough to make any appreciable gains. Plans were made in July 1984 to dredge by land-based machinery some 15,000 cubic metres of sand from the north-east corner of Salty and dump it in a position some 100 yards downstream east of the bridge, but local opposition on environmental grounds persuaded the Commissioners to abandon the scheme and return to the more conventional dredging methods.

Easterly gales had persisted through most of the month of February 1985 and the sea front beaches at Teignmouth particularly at the eastern end had almost been denuded of sand. The Commissioners decided to use a dredger M.V. *Thames* to dredge the 15,000 cubic metres of sand from the north-east corner of Salty and dump it at sea under licence. The district council which owns the beach was approached by the Harbour Commissioners and informed that if it was its wish the Harbour Commissioners would seek permission from the Board of Trade to dump the full 15,000 cubic metres at sea at the East Cliff end of the beach rather than dump at Bundle Head. The district council agreed and the necessary licence was obtained and for once the authorities were in unison.

In a reorganisation of management the Harbour Commissioners appointed a small finance subcommittee which produced a five-year capital programme, for improvement of the river above and below the bridge. The Commissioners would then consider a viable dredging programme and, after seeking hydrological advice, would consult the district council and crown estate before implementation. Such a programme would ensure that not only would the shipping requirements be met but that in the event of even larger ships using the port then the navigational channel would be capable of accommodating them.

The Quay Company will be celebrating 100 years of trading on 9 September 1986 and this says much for the courage and determination of all those involved in keeping the port alive and active over those often difficult years.

Another major reform was about to be implemented in the pilotage service. For many years the pilots had been governed through Trinity House by a pilotage subcommittee on their behalf. The intention of the government was to change this system largely because of the numbers of pilots over the country and the small amount of work for them. The port of Teignmouth did not have this problem but nevertheless was due for reform. The Harbour Commissioners stated that they were not in a position to undertake this service although they would be prepared to be represented on a future board if required. History repeats itself, for, on 17 February 1985, M.V. *Simbria* and M.V. *Elias Jr.* approached the port during strong easterly gales. The pilots were unable to cross the bar because of the rough seas. Exactly as pilot J. Matthews on the tug *Regia* did 86 years before, waving the flag to show the proper channel, so did pilots Wittaker and Swallow by talking the ship in by short wave radio on *Storm Siren*. In February 1985 the port's senior pilot, Sidney Hook, was awarded the B.E.M. by the Duke of Edinburgh in a ceremony at Trinity House, London, for his services to pilotage at Teignmouth.

Valuable data on sand movement and depth of channel was being tabulated through the efforts of the commissioner John Ellyat together with the harbour master, producing records to guide the Harbour Commissioners in providing a five-year dredging plan within the harbour when required. In a port like Teignmouth with its changing sand banks and navigable channels it seemed logical that the pilots and Quay Company act in unison especially as the Harbour Commissioners only use the services of the harbour master in a self-employed capacity and have no means of running a pilotage service. The Quay Company which is responsible for 100 per cent of the whole of the operation of exporting and importing through Teignmouth saw the future role of the pilots' function as part of their function and sought control from the government.

U.B.M. had decided in 1979 to sell their interest in the Teignmouth Quay Company and in June 1979 it was purchased by two young enthusiasts for over one million pounds. The new managing director, Mr. Jeff Boyne, had been with the Quay

Company as a junior under the 'Swain' management and his experience and drive soon made its mark. Extensive alterations were carried out in the eastern dock, old sheds being demolished and huge modern warehouses built. The Western Quay was given the same upgrading and plans were prepared for the extension towards the bridge mentioned in Chapter 7. A second weighbridge was installed and in January 1985 the once famous *Old Quay* public house was demolished to make way for another warehouse and new offices.

During 1984 the national coal strike had a beneficial effect on the port; the port landed 111,000 tonnes of coal, much of which came from Germany. At first the Welsh miners picketed the docks in an effort to persuade the workforce and lorry drivers to black the cargoes, but without success. After a few weeks of picketing, the miners and dockers were actually drinking together in the *Old Quay*. Indeed, although the pickets had returned home before the inn was demolished, the South Wales miners returned for the last night celebrations and miners and dockers raised their glasses together.

The Quays had undergone a major reorganisation and were ready to meet the challenge leading to the next decade.

☆☆☆☆☆☆☆☆☆☆☆☆☆☆☆☆☆

One of the early Victorian lithographs of Teignmouth portrays a romantic estuary scene with a steamer (perhaps a London packet) entering the harbour under a cloud of black smoke. This environmental impact of industrial progress is a background theme to the story of Teignmouth and the Teign estuary and it has become increasingly difficult, as shown by the evidence given at recent Public Inquiries, for those who manage the Docks to convince the local community that their activities are both economically valuable and socially acceptable.

The story of Teignmouth and the Teign estuary is also a narrative of occasional collective disappointments and the bankruptcy of those who deserved better; but primarily it is an account of significant achievements by local families, stimulated from time to time by the ideas of an incomer. Through all these vicissitudes the port of Teignmouth has shown remarkable resilience over two centuries of rapid social and economic change. Many ancient ports of the Westcountry, having lapsed into dereliction, are brought to life every summer by the brash accessories of tourism; a few, as a result of much effort and no little argument, have largely kept both their character and their prosperity. Teignmouth belongs to this more fortunate category.

Notes

Introduction

1. J. Britton and E. W. Brayley, *Devonshire Illustrated with Historical and Descriptive Accounts* (1832), p. 99. Other evidence contradicts Britton and Brayley and suggests that in the first Shaldon Bridge, as well as in subsequent ones, the opening span was on the Teignmouth side of the river.
2. W. G. Maton, 1794: quoted by R. Pearse Chope, ed., *Early Tours in Devon and Cornwall* (Newton Abbot, 1967), p. 237.
3. *The Gentleman's Magazine*, lxiii (63), pp. 785-6.

Chapter 1

1. Susanna Guy, Catalogue Notes for an Exhibition, *The Mapping of Southwest England* (Exeter University Library, Oct. 1973). Teignmouth is shown on an earlier coastal defence map, but this does not indicate its relative importance.
2. M. M. Oppenheim (ed. W. E. Minchinton), *The Maritime History of Devon* (Exeter 1968) p. 6 *et seq.* Oppenheim's article was originally written for *Victoria County History c.* 1907.
3. Dorothy M. Gardiner ed., 'A Calendar of Early Chancery Proceedings relating to West Country Shipping 1388-1493', *Devon and Cornwall Record Society*, New Series, Vol. 21 (1976). Trans. from French.
4. H. P. R. Finberg, 'The Stannary of Tavistock' in *Trans. Devonshire Assoc.*, Vol. 81 (1949) p. 169.
5. 23 Henry VIII c. 8 quoted by H. Parry *Notes on Old Teignmouth* (Exeter 1914) p. 27.
6. Heywood Townshend, Historical Collections: *An exact account of the Proceedings of the Four Last Parliaments of Queen Elizabeth* (1680) p. 309.
7. Oppenheim pp. 52-3.
8. Report of William Culliford 1682-3, P.R.O. T64/140.
9. Calendars of Treasury Books, 11 Aug. 1684, H.M. Customs Library.
10. Culliford, as above.
11. A description of early settlement and the conflict between settlers and Westcountry fishing interests is given in G. T. Cell, *English Enterprise in Newfoundland 1577-1660* (Toronto 1969).
12. Lewes Roberts, *The Merchants Mappe of Commerce* (1638), quoted by H. A. Innis, *The Cod Fisheries* (Toronto 1954) p. 54. For a summary of Devon's share in the Newfoundland Fishery *see* Neville C. Oswald, 'Devon and the Cod Fishery of Newfoundland' in *Trans. Devonshire Assoc.*, Vol. 115 (1983) pp. 19-36.
13. W. B. Stephens, 'The Westcountry Ports and the Struggle for the Newfoundland Fisheries in the 17th Century' in *Trans. Devonshire Assoc.*, Vol. 88 (1956) pp. 90-99.
14. P. W. Bamford, *Fighting Ships and Prisons* (Minnesota 1973) p. 41.
15. G. Burnet, *History of his own Time* (Oxford, 1823 edn.) Vol. 4, p. 96.
16. Parry, *Notes on Old Teignmouth*, p.33.
17. Ibid, p. 35.
18. Devon Record Office, 1543 Z/PO 5.
19. T. N. Brushfield, 'Devonshire Briefs' in *Trans. Devonshire Assoc.*, Vol. 28 (1896) p. 675. J. H. Rowe, *Devon Notes and Queires*, Vol. 2 (1903) p. 160.
20. Letter Book of Robert Jordan, 2 Jan. 1792-11 Aug. 1800, in custody of Tozers, Solicitors, Teignmouth.

Chapter 2

1. House of Lords Record Office Minutes of Evidence, H.C., 1853, Vol. 3, Teignmouth Harbour Bill.
2. T. S. Willan, *The English Coasting Trade 1600-1756* (Manchester 1938) pp. 66-8.
3. Lewis Lloyd, *The Unity of Barmouth*, Gwynedd Archives Service, 1977.
4. Petition for an Independent Port 1801, D.R.O. 1919/Z.
5. J. A. Bulley, 'The Beginnings of the Devonshire Ball Clay Trade' in *Trans. Devonshire Assoc.*, vol. 87 (1955).
6. R. Polwhele, *History of Devonshire*, Vol. 1 (1793), footnote pp. 60-1. The lignite was more of a nuisance than an advantage. When used in pottery manufacture at the Indio Pottery, Bovey Tracey, it caused problems which made Josiah Wedgwood declare that 'We can carry their clay and flints from Devonshire into Staffordshire, there manufacturing them into ware, and send it back to their own doors, better and cheaper than they can make it'. Wedgwood's opinion was probably jaundiced and the owner of Indio said that he had made a tea-cannister, a 'gossiping bowl' and a bouquet of flowers which was 'the most astonishing and delicate production ... to be found in any collection of ceramic arts throughout the world'. *See* Norman Stretton, *The Indio Pottery at Bovey Tracey*, paper read at the Wellcome Institute of the History of Medicine, 17 Oct. 1970.
7. Account Book for Pound Living Mine, Upton Pyne, 24 Mar. 1788-15 Dec. 1792, Devon Record Office 51/24/129.
8. 'Tingmouth: An Account of Town Duties Receiv'd 21 Oct. 1773-21 June 1779', D.R.O.
9. Exeter Port Books, E190 1008/13, P.R.O.
10. W. G. Hoskins, *Industry, Trade and People in Exeter 1688-1806* (Exeter 1968), pp. 107-8.
11. Devon Epiphany Sessions 1792 and Devon Easter Sessions 1795, D.R.O.
12. Letter Book of Robert Jordan.
13. Fanny Burney's Diary, 1773, quoted by Jack Simmons, *A Devon Anthology* (1971) pp. 132-3.
14. Hall Family Papers, Westcountry Studies Library, Exeter.
15. D.R.O. 2085Z/24.
16. A. C. Wardle, 'The Newfoundland Trade' in *The Trade Winds* ed. C. Northcote Parkinson (1948), pp. 228-9.
17. *Teignmouth Gazette*, 4 May 1857.
18. Account Book of Captain Robert Wren, in custody of Town Clerk, Bideford.
19. Account Books of Captain William Fox, D.R.O. The government subsidy was introduced by Palliser's Act, 15 Geo III *c.* xxxi; *see* D. W. Prowse, *A History of Newfoundland* (1896), pp. 344-5. The description of Newfoundland climate comes from Stephen Parmenius, quoted by G. T. Cell, *English Enterprise in Newfoundland* p. 43.
20. Reynell Collection, D.R.O.
21. Exeter Port Books, E 190 Lady Day Quarter, P.R.O. The Port Books do not give a complete record of all ships or all cargo.
22. Diary of Joseph Farington, Vol. 5, p. 259.
23. Jean M. Murray, ed,. *The Newfoundland Journal of Aaron Thomas* (1968), p. 33 and p. 173.
24. Settlement Examination, Bovey Tracey, D.R.O.
25. D.R.O. 48/13/5/57.
26. Hamlyn Correspondence, D.R.O.
27. *Exeter Flying Post* 26 Dec. 1793 and 2 Jan. 1794. Trinity House Petitions, Library of Society of Genealogists, Petition of Sarah Lang, 1 Oct. 1788.
28. Letter Book of Robert Jordan.
29. J. H. Bohstedt, *Riots in England 1790-1816 with special reference to Devonshire*, Harvard Ph.D. thesis (1972), p. 131 *et seq.*
30. *Exeter Flying Post*, 25 Dec. 1778; 12 Mar. and 10 Sept. 1779. A piece of wreck and 'a pistol encrusted with oysters', supposed to have come from the *Bellona*, was picked up by a Teignmouth trawler in September 1840.
31. Grant of Letters of Marque, P.R.O., show preponderance of Dartmouth, e.g. Adm. 7.318, 320 and 325.

Chapter 3

1. Register of British Ships, Exeter Custom House.
2. Marine (Casualty) List, Lloyd's List, 7 Feb., 21 Feb., 7 April, 17 Oct. 1797; 17 Jan., 17 Feb., 5 June

1804; 17 Feb., 24 April 1807; 31 Jan., 28 Feb. 1812.

3. Ibid. 13 Dec., 1799; 7 Jan., 27 May, 25 Feb., 25 Nov., 16 Dec., 1800; 25 Aug. 1812. E. S. Maclay, *A History of American Privateers* (New York 1924), pp. 265-74.

4. Register of British Ships, E.C.H.

5. Letter Book of Robert Jordan. Other correspondence of Robert Jordan, dealing with the Teignmouth snow *Ann*, is quoted by W. F. C. Jordan in *Trans. Devonshire Assoc.*, Vol. 33 (1901), pp. 332-5.

6. Register of British Ships, Exeter C.H. and Marine (Casualty) List, Lloyd's List, 16 Jan., 19 Jan., 20 Feb., 19 Nov. 1810; 'Report from Paris, 1 Mar. 1810' (quoted in Lloyd's List). There were at least four vessels named *Friends* trading at this time but all facts appear to refer to the same ship.

7. An Act to charge the settled estates of James Templer with a sum of money, D.R.O. 66Z/Z1.

8. J. A. Bulley, 'The Beginnings of the Devonshire Ball Clay Trade'.

9. Register of Barges under Act 35 George III, D.R.O.

10. M. Dunsford, *Miscellaneous Observations in the course of two tours through several parts of the west of England* (Tiverton 1800). Punctuation has been amended.

11. The importance of Schank's ideas and experiments are summarised in Alan McGowan: The Ship, Vol. 4 1700-1820 (H.M.S.O. 1980) p. 19.

12. J. Charnock, *A History of Marine Architecture*, Vol. 3 (1802), pp. 359-61.

13. Notes on the South Devon Ball Clay Industry prepared by Mr. R. C. F. Whiteway-Wilkinson on behalf of Watts, Blake, Bearne & Co. These notes have been used by L. T. C. Rolt in *The Potter's Field* (Newton Abbot, 1974) which gives a full account of early partnerships.

14. Surveyors' Reports for the Port of Teignmouth 1834-69, National Maritime Museum.

15. Letter Book of Robert Jordan.

16. J. J. Colledge, *Ships of the Royal Navy* (Newton Abbot, 1969), Vol. 1.

17. *Exeter Flying Post*, 7 Mar. 1793; 16 Apr., 6 May 1795.

18. E. A. G. Clark, *Estuary Ports of the Exe and Teign*, London Ph.D. thesis (1956), statistical tables.

19. Marine (Casualty) List, Lloyd's List, 31 Jan. 1809.

Chapter 4

1. Letter Book of Captain William Fox, D.R.O.

2. *Reminiscences of John Hele of Alphington* (privately pub., 1870), Devon and Exeter Inst. Library.

3. P.M.G. Report No. 36 (1822), Post Office Records.

4. N. T. Carrington and other, *The Teignmouth, Dawlish and Torquay Guide* (undated),Library of Devon Inst., Exeter.

5. Register of British Ships, E. C. H. St Nicholas (Shaldon with Ringmore) Parish Register, 1813-37, D.R.O.

6. Surveyors' Reports, National Maritime Museum. Overseers of the Poor Rate and Account Books, West Teignmouth 1797-1825, individual assessments, D.R.O.

7. Export Book, Teignmouth Harbour Commission.

8. Memorandum Book of John Rendell of Aller, consulted by courtesy of Mr. E. R. Bindloss.

9. *Exeter Flying Post*, 19 Jan. 1843.

10. References to 'the Newfoundland trade' normally include the coast of Labrador which was constitutionally part of Newfoundland after 1713.

11. *Exeter Flying Post*, 18 Apr. 1816 and 9 Jan. 1823.

12. Bristol Presentments, especially No. 425, 24 Mar. 1823, and No. 438, 8 May 1823, Bristol Public Reference Library.

13. D. Keir, *The Bowring Story* (1926), pp. 53-4.

14. Geoffrey Dodsworth, *The Templer Family and Stover House* (Stover School Magazine, Dec. 1969).

15. M. C. Ewans, *The Haytor Granite Tramway and the Stover Canal* (Newton Abbot 1966) pp. 19-28. Memorandum of Agreement between George Templer and John MacCarthy, 15 Mar. 1821, D.R.O. *Western Luminary*, 27 Mar. and 10 July 1827.

16. M. A. Havinden, 'Lime as a Means of Agricultural Improvement', *Essays in honour of W. G. Hoskins* (1974). T. Moore, *History of Devonshire*, Vol. 1, p. 539.

17. *Exeter Flying Post*, 8 Apr. 1824 (advertisement).

18. W. H. Thornton, *Reminiscences of an Old West-Country Clergyman*, (Torquay, 1899), pp. 106-7.

19. Papers of Captain Willy Chambers, National Maritime Museum.

20. M. B. Forman, ed., *The Letters of John Keats* (1947), Letters No. 53, 54, 58, 65.

21. Trinity House Petitions of the persons named. Monthly Poor Book of West Teignmouth, 6 Sept. 1825 to 1 Apr. 1831, D.R.O.
22. Proposals to obtain a Private Bill for Teign, Port and Navigation Improvement, D.R.O.
23. Marine (Casualty) list, Lloyd's List, 5 Feb. 1805; 4 Mar. 1808; 31 Mar. 1812. (*Three Williams, Elizabeth, Argo, Good Intent*).
24. *Western Luminary*, 17 Jan. 1826.
25. An Act for improving, maintaining and regulating the Harbour of Teignmouth and the Navigation of the River Teign, 6 William IV.
26. Book of Proceedings of T.H.C., 28 June 1836-11 June 1850; 8 and 15 Aug., 14 Sept., 1837; 5 Apr., 1838.
27. M. C. Ewans, *The Haytor Granite Tramways* pp. 25-9.
28. H.L.R.C., 1853, Vol. 3. J. V. Somers Cocks, 'The Haytor Quarries' in *Devon and Cornwall Notes and Queries*, Vol. 32 (1971), pp. 13-15.
29. Register of British Ships, E.C.H.
30. W. G. Hoskins, *Industry, Trade and People in Exeter*, 1688-1800 (Manchester, 1935), p. 49.
31. H.L.R.C., H.C., 1853, Vol. 3.

Chapter 5

1. Particulars of Sale of Hackney Canal, 1901, D.R.O.
2. Notes prepared in support of Plans for Torquay-Newton Abbot Railway, undated, D.R.O.
3. *Exeter Flying Post*, 1 Feb. 1844.
4. Brunel Correspondence, University of Bristol Library.
5. Letter Book of Robert Jordan.
6. Letters to the Board Aug. 1848-Sept. 1850, 64/45, H.M.C. Library.
7. Ibid., Sept. 1850-Aug. 1852, 64/46.
8. Minute Book T.H.C., 14 Oct. 1852. The boundaries of the independent port were drawn to include Torquay, but in all other respects Torquay remained separate from Teignmouth. References in the text to 'the port of Teignmouth' exclude Torquay.
9. Ibid.
10. H.L.R.O., H.C., Vol. 3.
11. R. Newton, *Victorian Exeter* (Leicester 1968), p. 32.
12. *Western Times*, 5 Mar. 1853.
13. Western Luminary, 25 May 1853. The *Crystal Palace* made fast passages but was dismasted in 1857 and wrecked in 1862. *See* David R. MacGregor, *The Tea Clippers* (rev. ed. 1982), pp. 90-91.
14. Evidence of Thomas Woolcomb to Select Committee on Teignmouth Harbour Bill. H.L.R.C., H.C., 1853, Vol. 3.
15. Import Book T.H.C.
16. *Western Times*, 28 Feb. 1852 and *Western Luminary*, 2 Mar. 1852.
17. Bristol Presentments, 1830-50.
18. Register of British Ships, Teignmouth.
19. *Woolmer's Exeter Gazette*, 30 July 1859.

Chapter 6

1. Correspondence attached to Lloyd's Surveyors' Reports for Teignmouth, 1834-69, National Maritime Museum.
2. T. S. Spratt, *An Investigation of the Movements of Teignmouth Bar* (1856), Devon Inst. Library, Exeter.
3. Minute Book T.H.C. 25 Jan. 1857 and 26 Apr. 1860.
4. Rosalie Mander, *The Story of Elizabeth Barrett Browning* (1980) p. 26.
5. *Western Luminary*, 6 Aug. 1859.
6. Agreement and Account of Voyages and Crew of a Foreign-going ship (s.v. *Rifleman*), D.R.O.
7. Agreement and Account of Voyages and Crew of a Foreign-going ship (s.v. *S.R. and H.*), D.R.O.
8. *Western Times*, 21 July 1865. For character of crews *see* A. Shewan, *The Great Days of Sail* (Greenwich, 1973) p. 95.
9. Agreement and Account of Voyages and Crew of a Ship engaged in the Home Trade (s.v. *Fiona*), D.R.O. The tonnages of all ships are 'register' tons as recorded in the Register of British Ships;

carrying capacity is appreciably greater. Register tonnage was sometimes changed by alterations in design in order to reduce port dues. Information on the use of gambia and myrobalan from Mr. V. S. Pritchett.

10. *Teignmouth Gazette*, 26 Mar. and 2 Apr. 1860.

11. *Western Luminary*, 24 Mar. and 31 Mar. 1860 (correspondence).

12. *Teignmouth Times*, 27 Sept. and 4 Oct. 1861.

13. *Western Luminary*, 5 Sept. 1836 and *Western Times*, 9 May 1873.

14. *Morning Chronicle*, 'Labour and the Poor', Letter XLVI, 'The Coasting Trade', 3 Apr. 1850.

15. Official Papers of the *Witch o' the Wave* (Dartmouth), D.R.O.

16. *Exeter Flying Post*, 1 Nov. 1855, and *Western Luminary*, 28 Nov. 1857.

17. This information comes from the Whitear family papers by courtesy of Mrs. Mary Freeman; it has been supplemented from reports in *Western Times*, 15 Jan. 1875, and *Devon Weekly News*, 21 Jan. 1881. Information on Kennedys from Mitchell Library, Glasgow and on Malings from R. C. Bell: *Tyneside Pottery* (1971).

18. This account comes from conversations with Fred Drew and correspondence with Mrs. Charlotte Shute. An appreciation of Fred Drew in *Teignmouth Post*, 4 Jan. 1980, gives details which he modestly glossed over.

19. E. J. Bath, *One Hundred Years of Education in a Village School* (unpub. mss.), D.R.O.

20. *Western Gazette*, 16 Apr. 1879, and 17 Mar. 1909.

21. *Western Times*, 27 Mar. 1868; Clifford Estate Papers (unclass). Consulted by courtesy of Lord Clifford of Chudleigh.

22. *Exeter Flying Post*, 27 Mar. 1856.

23. Information from G. Vallance. Also L. T. C. Rolt, *The Potters Field* (Newton Abbot, 1974).

24. *A History of the Benedictine Nuns of Dunkirk*, ed. The Community (1957), pp. 159-61.

25. For examples of behaviour objected to *see Western Times* 10 Mar. 1874 and 6 Feb. 1885. Miss Weston's remarks were at Opening (1878).

26. *War Cry*, 17 June 1885; *Exeter Flying Post*, 3 Mar. 1886.

27. Missions to Seamen Annual Reports 1877-1934, Missions to Seamen Headquarters, London. Also correspondence consulted by courtesy of Mr. R. G. Andrews.

28. *Exeter Flying Post*, 5 Nov. 1879.

29. *Western Times*, 12 Nov. and 31 Dec. 1867.

30. *Exeter Flying Post*, 11 Dec. 1872.

31. *Devon Weekly Times*, 21 July 1889.

32. Records of Watts, Blake, Bearne, consulted by courtesy of the Company.

Chapter 7

1. Archives of Bridgewater Canal Trust and information from Mr. A. Hayman.

2. Letter Books, Teignmouth, 13 Apr. 1860-11 Oct. 1877, 64/158, H.M.C. Library.

3. Clifford Estate Papers (unclass.).

4. W. G. Hoskins, *Two Thousand Years in Exeter* (Exeter 1960), pp. 113-15.

5. Christopher J. Schmitz, *The Teign Valley Silver-Lead Mines 1806-1880* (rev. edn. 1980, Northern Mine Reseach Soc., British Mining No. 15) p. 35.

6. Library, Royal Cornwall Instn., Truro.

7. Schmitz, p. 63.

8. T.H.C. Export Book.

9. D. M. Stirling, *A History of Newton Abbot and Newton Bushel* (Newton Abbot, 1830).

10. T.H.C. Import Book.

11. Correspondence attached to Lloyd's Surveyors' Reports for Teignmouth, 1834-69, National Maritime Museum.

12. *Western Times*, 2 June and 4 Aug. 1868, 6 June 1871, 9 May 1879.

13. Register of British Ships, T.C.H. Parliamentary (Sessional) Papers, 1876 (374), LXVI 691. Accounts and Papers, 1878-9, LXVI, 'Return of all Ships ordered by the Board of Trade to be provisionally detained as unsafe', Table 6. Accounts and Papers, 1884, LXXI, 'Ships ordered to be detained', Table 10.

14. *Western Times*, 30 Oct. 1876.

15. Minute Book T.H.C. 20 Mar. 1865-2 Apr. 1868.

16. Letters from Board to Collector and v.v., H.M.C. Library.

17. *Western Times*, 17 Mar. and 23 Mar. 1886.

18. *Teignmouth Journal*, 1875, p. 12.

19. *Exeter Evening Post*, 10 Sept, 1886.

20. *Devon Weekly Times*, 26 Feb. 1886 and 9 Jan. 1891.

21. Ibid. 27 Jan. and 18 May 1888; 1 Aug. 1889.

22. Minute Book T.Q.C., 21 May 1892.

23. 1893 Provisional Order, D.R.O.

24. C. H. C. Robbins, *A History of Baptist Church* (Dawlish, 1965). This history, together with company minutes, established beyond reasonable doubt the common identity of the Rev. E. T. Scammell, part-time Baptist Minister, and E. T. Scammell, director of T.Q.C.

25. Minute Book, T.Q.C., 26 Jan. 1899.

26. Ibid. 27 Apr. and 1 July 1899.

27. Swedish and Norwegian Vice-Consulate Records 1853-1906 in custody of Pike Ward Ltd., Teignmouth.

28. Minute Book T.H.C., 11 Aug. 1904 and 26 June 1905.

29. T.H.C. Import and Export Books.

30. *Western Times*, 30 Nov. 1877. *Teignmouth Post*, 24 Apr. 1878.

31. Basil Greenhill, *The Merchant Schooners* (Newton Abbot, rev. edn. 1968), Vol. 1, p. 63.

32. Petitions addressed to Corporation of Trinity House, Library of Society of Genealogists, London.

33. Minute Book T.H.C., 23 Nov. 1905.

Chapter 8

1. Register of British Ships, T.C.H.

2. *Teignmouth Post*, 13 Nov. 1903.

3. Agreement and Account of Voyages and Crew of a Ship engaged in the Home Trade (s.v. *Eldra*), D.R.O.

4. Agreement and Account of Voyages and Crew of a Ship engaged in the Home Trade (S.S. *G. Player*), D.R.O.

5. Information from Captain F. W. G. Grant.

6. Minute Book T.Q.C., 5 Sept. 1907.

7. *Teignmouth Post*, 11 Oct. 1907 edited.

8. Register of British Ships, C. H. Salcombe.

9. The figurehead of the *Grace* is in the possession of one of the owner's descendants, Mrs. Pamela Page.

10. *Teignmouth Post*, 25 Sept. 1908 and 26 Mar. 1909.

11. Minute Book T.H.C., 9 Mar. 1911.

12. Ibid., 3 and 7 Oct. 1910.

13. Minute Book T.Q.C., 9 Aug. 1905.

14. Ibid., 25 Aug. 1910. The damage done to wooden ships as a result of lying in a bad berth is explained by an experienced master in W. J. Slade and Basil Greenhill, *Westcountry Coasting Ketches* (1974).

15. Ibid., 5 Mar. 1914.

16. Information from Mr. G. S. Thomson (Trinity House).

17. Trade Returns, Devon Dock, Pier and Steamship Company, Exmouth.

18. Borough of Torquay Harbour Ledger 1907-9, Public Library, Torquay.

19. Report of Messrs. E. H. Moss, Liverpool (Shipbrokers), quoted in *Lloyd's List*, 1 Jan. 1913; also *Lloyd's List*, 9 Jan. 1914.

20. Minute Book T.H.C., 14 Dec. 1914.

21. Ibid., 11 May 1916.

22. Ibid., 3 Aug. 1916.

23. G. Garr, *Wreck and Rescue on the Coast of Devon* (Truro, 1968), p. 170.

24. Minute Book T.Q.C., 12 Mar. 1917.

25. *Teignmouth Post*, 24 Oct. 1919; 19 July, 25 Aug. 1920.

26. Import and Export Books, T.H.C.

27. Minute Book T.H.C., 4 Jan. 1923.

28. Import and Export Books T.H.C.

29. Minute Book T.Q.C., 31 Aug. 1926.
30. Minute Book T.H.C., 16 Sept. 1925.
31. Details in this and preceding paragraphs come from personal memory and individuals' recollections plus ships' papers and harbour records, as defined earlier. Also D. W. Morgan, *Brief Glory* (Liverpool, 1948); H. Hughes, *Immortal Sails* (Prescot, Lancs. 1948); Basil Greenhill, *The Life and Death of the Merchant Sailing Ship, 1815-1965* (1980); articles by Michael Bouquet, *Ships Monthly*, Jan.-Feb. 1979.
32. Minute Book T.Q.C., 22 Nov. 1938.
33. Minute Book T.H.C., 13 July 1933.
34. Ibid., 14 Dec. 1933.
35. Correspondence consulted by courtesy of Mr. G. A. Evans, proprietor Teignmouth Boating Centre.
36. John Sweete, *Picturesque Sketches of Devon*, D.R.O. Much of the information on Morgan Giles' yard at this time and subsequently comes from a series of articles by G. K. Collyer in *Teignmouth News*, 19 Jan.-16 Feb. 1984.

Chapter 9

1. Admiralty War Diaries, Adm. 199/269 and 370, P.R.O. Also information from Mr. A. Hague, in command of H.M.S. *Borealis* at the time.
2. Newspaper cuttings, Westcountry Studies Library, Exeter; record of those buried in war graves, D.R.O.
3. Minute Book of T.H.C., 8 July 1940.
4. Ibid. 17 Sept. 1941.
5. Nicholas Harman, *Dunkirk, the Necessary Myth* (1980). Also information from Mr. W. J. B. Watts.
6. *Western Luminary*, 1 Sept. 1857.
7. Grahame Farr, *Wreck and Rescue on the Coast of Devon* (Truro, 1968) p. 162.
8. *Western Times*, 19 Jan. 1866; Diary of Albert Best, generously made available by Mr. P. I. M. Best.
9. *Western Times*, 31 oct. 1871.
10. Minute Book of T.H.C. 15 Sept. 1944.
11. Dock and Harbour Authorities Assocn., *Port Statistics for the Foreign Trade of the United Kingdom* (1967), p. 63. The composition, recovery and marketing of ball clay are described in E. M. Durrance and D. J. C. Laming (ed.), *The Geology of Devon* (Exeter, 1982), pp. 296-7.
12. R. Harris, *King's Teignton, a Parish History* (Kingsteignton Parochial Church Council, undated).
13. Minute Book T.Q.C.
14. *Teignmouth Post*, 8 Dec. 1967.
15. T. Coppack, *A Lifetime with Ships* (Prescot, Lancs., 1973), p. 214.
16. Minute Book, T.H.C. 22 June 1950.
17. Information from Pike Ward, Ltd.
18. Information from Mr. K. Lucas, Trinity House Lighthouse Service.
19. *Exeter Flying Post*, 1 May 1850.
20. *Western Times*, 15 Dec. 1876.
21. Report of Public Inquiry, 7-22 Oct. 1975 (Ref. P89/3/0102), pp. 52-60.
22. Ibid. p. 34.
23. Figures from T.Q.C. and Pike Ward. From 1972 onwards tonnages are given in metric measurement (1 tonne = 0.984 ton). Tonnages of cargoes are a better guide to the size of ships than the 'net register' tons of the ships themselves which varied according to changes in regulations and methods of measurement.
24. *Western Luminary*, 13 June 1836.
25. M. Tomalin and R. Hall, *The Strange Voyage of Donald Crowhurst* (1970); *Teignmouth Post*, 12 Nov. 1981.
26. Diary of Captain Neil Gamble.
27. *Teignmouth News*, 26 Jan. and 9 Feb. 1984 (G. K. Collyer).

Index

Ships are classified as follows:
* = warship or privateer
m.v. = motor vessel
s. = steamship
t. = motor or steam tug
yt. = yacht
All others are merchant ships